Organizing
Relationships

To Rick, Val, and Rachel for all their love and support. And to my colleagues who make workplace relationships the best part of my job.

Organizing
Relationships

Traditional and Emerging
Perspectives on
Workplace Relationships

Patricia M. Sias
Washington State University

Los Angeles • London • New Delhi • Singapore • Washington DC

For information:

 SAGE Publications, Inc.
2455 Teller Road
Thousand Oaks, California 91320
E-mail: order@sagepub.com

SAGE Publications India Pvt. Ltd.
B 1/I 1 Mohan Cooperative
  Industrial Area
Mathura Road, New Delhi 110 044
India

SAGE Publications Ltd.
1 Oliver's Yard
55 City Road
London EC1Y 1SP
United Kingdom

SAGE Publications
  Asia-Pacific Pte. Ltd.
33 Pekin Street #02-01
Far East Square
Singapore 048763

Library of Congress Cataloging-in-Publication Data

Sias, Patricia M., 1959-
Organizing relationships : traditional and emerging perspectives on workplace relationships/Patricia M. Sias.
    p. cm.
Includes bibliographical references and index.
ISBN 978-1-4129-5796-0 (cloth)
ISBN 978-1-4129-5797-7 (pbk.)

  1. Interpersonal relations. 2. Organizational behavior. 3. Employees. 4. Work environment—Social aspects. I. Title.

HD58.7.S553 2009
302.3'5—dc22   2008026113

08 09 10 11 12 10 9 8 7 6 5 4 3 2 1

Acquisitions Editor:	Todd Armstrong
Editorial Assistant:	Aja Baker
Production Editor:	Carla Freeman
Copy Editor:	Teresa Wilson
Typesetter:	C&M Digitals (P) Ltd.
Proofreader:	Penny Sippel
Indexer:	William Ragsdale
Cover Designer:	Candice Harman
Marketing Manager:	Carmel Schrire

Contents

Preface

I have had many different types of jobs throughout my life. Prior to joining academia, I worked as a photocopy clerk, a pizza maker, a pear packer, a library assistant, a switchboard operator, a day camp counselor, a clerical assistant, a receptionist, a legal secretary, and a personnel manager. While all of these jobs differed with respect to tasks and responsibilities, all were similar in one fundamental way—the importance of the relationships I had with others at work.

In each job, including my current faculty position, I found my coworkers to be important sources of information and support. Whether the tasks were mundane or complex, my relationships with others made the jobs more interesting, more rewarding, and in some cases, at least more tolerable. My relationships with supervisors often transformed to mentoring relationships that I found helpful as I progressed through my career. As a personnel manager, I learned the importance and the difficulties of forming and maintaining trusting, high-quality relationships with employees. I also learned how challenging it can be to manage the tensions of blending friendship and supervision, of blending subjectivity and objectivity.

These were the experiences that turned my attention toward workplace relationships while studying for my doctoral degree at the University of Texas. With Fred Jablin as my advisor, I obtained a thorough understanding of supervisor–subordinate relationships. I was perplexed, however, by the lack of attention to other types of workplace relationships. In particular, I was troubled that scholars only rarely addressed peer relationships and workplace friendships, especially since I found those types of relationships to be particularly important to my working experience. As a result, my dissertation and program of research over the past 15 years has centered on workplace relationships.

In addition to studying workplace relationships, I also address them in my teaching. And a continual source of frustration for me in both my research and teaching is the lack of a comprehensive and interdisciplinary source of information. Rather, I have filled my office shelves with several different books about different aspects of different types of workplace relationships. My courses are generally based on one or more of these books and a usually cumbersome compilation of readings. One motivation for writing this book, therefore, was to create a useful and comprehensive resource for scholars from a variety of disciplines conducting research and teaching courses relevant to workplace relationships.

Another motivation stems from my dissatisfaction with the body of knowledge we have generated thus far regarding workplace relationships. Perhaps because of the interpersonal relationship foundation of workplace relationship scholarship, our research tends to be rooted firmly in the postpositivist tradition. The majority of researchers, myself included, tend to conceptualize and study workplace relationships of various types using social scientific or social-psychological approaches. While I acknowledge the value of this research, and the fact that my own research is largely grounded in postpositivism, I know that there is still much we do not know about workplace relationships. And much of this knowledge could be generated by scholars examining workplace relationships from other theoretical perspectives. Thus, this book is a call to scholars from a variety of disciplines to broaden our theoretical lens and, therefore, broaden and deepen our understanding of workplace relationships.

These two motivations provided two specific goals for this book. The first goal was to provide a comprehensive and organized discussion of the current body of knowledge of workplace relationships, including supervisor–subordinate relationships, peer coworker relationships, workplace friendships, romantic workplace relationships, and customer/client relationships, as well as links between workplace relationships and society. The term *organizing relationships* in the book's title, therefore, has dual meaning. It both acknowledges relationships as a mechanism for organizing, and acknowledges my attempts at literally organizing existing workplace relationship research.

The second goal of the book was to develop a research agenda for the future. Specifically, my intent was to articulate the unique contributions that alternative theoretical perspectives, such as social construction theory, critical theory, and structuration theory, can provide to our understanding of workplace relationships. My hope is that this book will inspire scholars to pursue innovative research programs grounded in multiple theoretical perspectives. My dream is that in the not-so-distant future I will see such research reported in academic journals in multiple disciplines.

Finally, my work experiences have provided a strong pragmatic aspect to both my teaching and research. I'm always concerned with how knowledge and learning can improve practice. A third goal of this book, therefore, was to highlight the practical aspects of theory. As Craig and Muller (2007) note, communication is "inherently problematic" (p. xi) and there is no single theory that can fully address all practical communication problems. Instead, *practical* theory enables us to consider and examine real-world problems from multiple theoretical perspectives. Thus, just as multiple theoretical perspectives direct scholars' attention to different aspects of a phenomenon and therefore direct multiple research agendas, these theoretical perspectives also enable practitioners to understand a problematic situation in multiple ways, enabling a fuller understanding of the situation and multiple methods for addressing the situation.

To achieve these three goals, each chapter is organized into three sections. In the first section, I summarize and organize existing research regarding the specific chapter topic. In the second section, I articulate how the relationship type or issue addressed in the specific chapter would be conceptualized and studied from different theoretical perspectives and offer several research questions representing each perspective. In other words, I first describe where we are in that area of research, and then describe where we can go. At the end of each chapter is a third section titled "Practicing Theory." This section provides a case for consideration and analysis. In particular, I ask readers to consider the case from the various theoretical perspectives in order to obtain a full and complex understanding of the relationship issues addressed in the case. These cases provide readers the opportunity for "practicing theory."

Specifically, the book is organized as follows:

In Chapter 1, I provide an overview of the metatheoretical spirit of the book. I then lay out some primary assumptions and conceptualizations of the postpositivist, social construction, critical, and structuration theoretical perspectives. Recognizing my own grounding in postpositivist and social construction approaches, I do not attempt fully drawn discussions of critical and structuration theory, and readers are directed to such discussions by authors more qualified than me (e.g., Deetz, 2005; Giddens, 1984; Mumby, 2001). I do, however, tease out concerns and concepts drawn from those perspectives that are particularly relevant to workplace relationships and have the most potential for contributing to this body of work.

Hierarchy is a defining characteristic of organizations. As Cheney (1995) noted, it is difficult, if not impossible, to find a single organization that is truly nonhierarchical. Consequently, hierarchy plays an important role in workplace relationships. Not surprisingly, then, supervisor–subordinate relationships (work relationships in which one partner has formal authority over the other) have received a large amount of research attention. Chapter 2 reviews this literature. In particular, I discuss research that addresses the functions, developmental processes, and outcomes associated with supervisor–subordinate relationships and suggest a number of areas for future research guided by different theoretical perspectives.

Chapter 3 discusses another important type of workplace relationship— the peer coworker relationship. While most employees have only one supervisor, they have several peer coworkers. Consequently, most workplace relationships are those among peers. In Chapter 3, I review research on peer relationships, again addressing research on the functions, developmental processes, and outcomes of peer relationships and suggestions for research guided by multiple perspectives.

Friendships among coworkers are unique types of relationships. They develop between both peers and between supervisors and subordinates. They have unique functions and developmental processes. They differ, for example, from other workplace relationships in that they are voluntary, rather than imposed—we do not typically choose our coworkers, but we do choose which of those coworkers to befriend. They also differ from nonwork friendships in a number of ways. For example, workplace friends must negotiate the very difficult boundaries between friendly supportiveness and organizational requirements of objectivity. Moreover, when an individual ends a nonwork friendship, that person typically has the option of never having to see the former friend again. Coworkers have no such luxury—unless one of the partners quits or is transferred, they must continue to interact with each other for several hours every day. Chapter 4 discusses the relatively recent scholarship on workplace friendship.

Chapter 5 discusses research examining romantic relationships in the workplace. This is a particularly complex type of workplace relationship, given its combination of workplace and personal intimacy. As with friendships, workplace romantic relationships share many similarities with nonwork romantic relationships (e.g., they are initiated and ended for many of the same reasons, including infatuation, love, and jealousy). Workplace romantic relationships, however, differ from nonwork romances in a number of ways, which are detailed in Chapter 5.

In organizations of all types, employees interact with customers or clients. Chapter 6 discusses research on customer and client relationships, addressing the concept of relationship marketing, customer/client relationship types, characteristics and development, and the role of technology in customer relationship maintenance.

Finally, while Chapters 2–6 address relationships in which individuals engage as they carry out their daily work activities, Chapter 7 addresses the embedded nature of workplace relationships in the larger society. In particular, I discuss research that examines current societal trends and systems as they impact, and are impacted by, workplace relationships. Toward this end, Chapter 7 discusses technological development, globalization, the "new social contract," spirituality in the workplace, and work–family conflict and balance issues, focusing specifically on links between these phenomena and workplace relationships.

Acknowledgments

Writing the book was a daunting process, but that process was helped greatly by a number of important people. Todd Armstrong of SAGE Publications was an incredible help guiding me through every step of the process. His advice and support were invaluable to me as a novice book author. Scholars from various disciplines around the country were kind enough to read the book in its draft form. I was impressed by the thorough and careful read each provided and the very helpful and constructive suggestions for improving each chapter. Their comments led to a much improved book. Specifically, I acknowledge the help of the following individuals:

Patrice M. Buzzanell
Department of Communication, Purdue University

Lisa M. Finkelstein
Department of Psychology, Northern Illinois University

Janie Harden Fritz
Department of Communication & Rhetorical Studies,
Duquesne University

Jaesub Lee
School of Communication, University of Houston

Caryn E. Medved
Department of Communication Studies, Baruch College/CUNY

Christopher C. Rosen
Department of Management, University of Arkansas

Anthony R. Wheeler
Schmidt Labor Research Center, University of Rhode Island

Charles D. White
Culverhouse College of Commerce &
Business Administration, The University of Alabama

I hope the experience of reading this book is as rewarding as the experience I had writing it. It is a pleasure and a privilege to organize such a broad and diverse literature. And if the book comes close to accomplishing my three goals, I will be satisfied.

1

Organizing Workplace Relationships

Mark arrived at the office at 8:00 a.m. and immediately went to the kitchen to get a cup of coffee. Janet was also getting a cup of coffee, so the two of them discussed the meeting scheduled for later that afternoon and how they felt about the proposal on the meeting's agenda regarding expense reimbursement procedures. Both agreed that the new process would be really time-consuming and planned to argue against it. Tim walked in the kitchen just as Mark and Janet were finishing their conversation. Mark quickly left the room—he and Tim had had a pretty big argument a few days earlier, and Mark felt uncomfortable around Tim ever since. Mark then went to his office and looked at his calendar for the day. First up was a meeting with two other sales-people, Jenny and Pete, to discuss ideas about how to pitch the company's latest product. He was looking forward to this meeting and hoping they could come up with some creative ideas. After that, Mark would meet with his supervisor for his semiannual performance evaluation. He was hoping for no surprises in that meeting. Then lunch with a new client, so he had to make sure he wasn't late. He wanted to make sure that relationship got off on the right foot. That was just the first half of a typically busy day of work for Mark.

Consider Mark's morning and the typical daily activities in a typical organization, including directing, collaborating, information gathering, information sharing, rewarding, punishing, conflict, resolution of conflict, controlling, feedback, persuasion, presenting, interviewing, reporting, gossiping, debating, supporting, selling, buying, ordering, managing, leading, and following. All of these activities occur in the context of interpersonal relationships. In fact, virtually all organizational activities occur in the context of relationships, even in "virtual" organizations among "virtual" coworkers who operate in different physical locales. Relationships are the essence of living systems and the basis of organization (Wheatley, 1994, 2001). It is through relationships that systems maintain balance (Katz & Kahn, 1978), chaos becomes order, and fragmentation is made whole (Wheatley, 2001). Accordingly, as Wheatley (2001) noted, scholars should focus attention on "how a workplace organizes its relationships; not its tasks, functions, and hierarchies, but the patterns of relationships and the capacities available to form them" (p. 39).

Relationships in the workplace are particularly important and consequential interpersonal relationships. An individual with a full-time job, for example, is likely to spend as much, if not more, of his or her time interacting with coworkers than with friends and family. Even when we're not at work, we spend much of our time talking and thinking about work. We are largely defined by what we do for a living and with whom we work. Not surprisingly then, in many ways, our workplace relationships define who we are (Sluss & Ashforth, 2007).

In contrast to "acquaintances" or people who have limited contact with one another, an interpersonal *relationship* is characterized by repeated, patterned interaction over time (Sias, Krone, & Jablin, 2002). Unlike acquaintanceships, relationships are enduring, although some endure longer than others. Interpersonal relationships are also characterized by a feeling of connection beyond that experienced in an acquaintanceship. Again, relationships vary in the extent of this connection, but generally speaking, the closer the relationship, the stronger and more emotional the connection.

The term *workplace relationship* generally refers to all interpersonal relationships in which individuals engage as they perform their jobs, including supervisor–subordinate relationships, peer coworker relationships, workplace friendships, romantic relationships, and customer relationships. These relationships have been studied by a variety of scholars in a variety of disciplines. As a result, we know a great deal about workplace relationships and their role in organizational processes and individuals' lives.

Our study of workplace relationships has been limited, however. As the following chapters will demonstrate, the bulk of research on workplace relationships has been guided by a postpositivist perspective that conceptualizes workplace relationships in a specific way and centers on identifying relationships among variables with the goal of predicting effectiveness in specific contexts. Certainly this work is of great value, providing an enormous amount of knowledge about workplace relationships and their roles in organizational processes.

Relying on a single theoretical lens and conceptualization of a subject narrows our vision, however, much like using only a zoom lens on a camera limits our view of a photographic subject by focusing on one aspect of that subject. Broadcasters at sporting events typically place cameras at several spots around the field of play, some shooting close-up shots, others from a distance, all filming the action from a variety of angles and perspectives. I was struck by this recently when watching a soccer game on television. Due to technical difficulties, only one of the dozen or so cameras was operational during a 5-minute portion of the game. During that time, the single camera simply followed the ball from one side of the field, up and down the field as the game continued. Consistent with the old saying "You don't know what you've got til it's gone," I was struck by the fact that many of the most interesting elements of the game were out of view—defensive positioning, reactions of various defensive and offensive players, their coaches and, of course, the spectators. Although I could watch what would be considered the main part of the game (i.e., where the ball went), ignoring the other elements made for a limited and much less interesting viewing experience. The contrast was striking when the other cameras came back in use. Filming the subject from a variety of angles and perspectives provided a much more complex, full, and informative view. Seeing the field from many different angles, watching the players who were not controlling the ball, seeing the expressions of the coaches and the spectators shed insights into various aspects of the event and, as a result, made for a more rich, interesting, and rewarding experience. This experience highlighted for me the value of multiple perspectives.

The usefulness of multiple *theoretical* perspectives and "metatheory" has been widely debated in recent years. The debate centers largely on the extent to which a scholar should "choose" or commit to a particular theoretical perspective, or develop an understanding of multiple theoretical perspectives and conduct research on a particular phenomenon, such as workplace relationships, from varying perspectives. In the field of communication, Sheperd, St. John, and Striphas (2006), for example, claim an "unapologetically stubborn suspicion that communication theorists have become a bit too open minded with regard to perspectives on communication" (p. xi). While recognizing various theoretical perspectives, these authors argue that scholars generally experience resonance and commit to a particular theoretical perspective, and rightly so. Craig (1999), on the other hand, highlights the practicality and usefulness of understanding and accepting multiple theoretical perspectives and the insights each perspective can provide on a single phenomenon, such as workplace relationships. While a scholar is not required, nor even strongly encouraged to study a particular phenomenon from multiple perspectives, understanding the assumptions and value of varying perspectives can lead to a group of scholars studying that phenomenon from multiple perspectives and together developing a rich, deep, and complex body of knowledge about that phenomenon.

This orientation toward complementary holism (Albert et al., 1986) acknowledges multiple and interconnected frameworks that together provide a rich and complex context for understanding social reality. It is this orientation that guides this book and my treatment of workplace relationships. While my own research is grounded primarily in postpositivist and social construction theory, I appreciate the insights provided by colleagues who address workplace relationships from other theoretical perspectives. My appreciation is enabled, however, by my ability to understand their work and recognize the fundamentally unique conceptualizations of organizations, communication, and relationships that ground their research. Moreover, I don't just appreciate work grounded in other perspectives; I actively seek it out as I try to develop rich and more nuanced understandings of workplace relationships. This book is an attempt to encourage other scholars from various disciplines and perspectives to enter into a community of scholars studying workplace relationships from multiple theoretical perspectives.

As mentioned in the preface, one goal of this book is to provide a comprehensive discussion of existing workplace relationship research. Another goal, and the primary purpose of this chapter, is to show how considering workplace relationships from multiple perspectives, each valuable in its own right, can greatly enrich our understanding of workplace relationships and their role in organizational processes. Each perspective provides unique conceptualizations of organizations, communication, and relationships. These conceptualizations drive different research foci, each of which provides important insights. Each perspective draws practitioners' attention to different elements of an organizational phenomenon or situation. Thus, broadening our theoretical lenses can provide a more thorough and complex understanding of workplace relationship issues and dynamics, and this broadened understanding can enrich both research and practice.

Communication scholars have organized theoretical perspectives and traditions using a variety of organizing systems. Craig (1999, 2007) focuses on seven primary theoretical traditions that subsume virtually all areas of communication. More specific to organizational communication, Deetz (2001) categorized research into four primary perspectives or approaches: postpositivist, interpretive, critical, and postmodern. May and Mumby (2005) broadened Deetz's system by adding rhetorical, social construction, globalization, and structuration theory. I rely on a synthesis of Deetz (2001) and May and Mumby (2005) for this book, organizing each chapter around postpositivist, social construction, critical, and structuration theories. I chose these theoretical perspectives for a variety of reasons. Space limitations preclude me from discussing all possible theoretical perspectives. I, therefore, chose what I believe are the most widely used and most influential for the organizational communication discipline and potentially most useful for studying workplace relationships.

More specifically, *postpositivism* is largely recognized as the "dominant theoretical frame for studying organizations" (Mumby & May, 2005, p. 4). As seen in the remaining chapters of this book, the postpositivist perspective guides the bulk of workplace relationship research. I include *social constructionism* because it was the foundational theoretical perspective for the "interpretive turn" taken in organizational research (Mumby & May, 2005). The interpretive turn represented a watershed moment for organizational scholars (Deetz, 2001) in that the move from studying "communication in organizations" to studying "communication as constituting organizations" radically changed how we study communication and organizations (Allen, 2005). Social constructionism also grounds the other two theoretical perspectives covered in this book—critical theory and structuration theory.

Scholars began using *critical theory* in organizational research primarily in the 1980s as a rejection of the field's "managerial bias." Instead, individuals are given primacy and issues of power, politics, control, and marginalization received attention. This was another important paradigmatic shift for the field that warrants inclusion in this volume. Although scholars disagree on whether feminist theory is a distinct theoretical perspective or a subset of critical theory (Ashcraft, 2005), I include it with critical theory because of its roots in that tradition. Finally, *structuration theory* (which in many ways is rooted in postpositivism, social constructionism, and critical theory) is included because of the theory's enormous influence on organizational research over the past three decades, and because it combines aspects of the other three perspectives in novel and important ways.

In the following sections, I discuss the primary assumptions of each perspective, how each perspective conceptualizes organizations, communication, and workplace relationships, and the research agendas that are guided by those conceptualizations. Table 1.1 summarizes this discussion.

Postpositivist Approaches to Workplace Relationships

Postpositivism is rooted in the scientific method. It derives from positivism and developed in response to a variety of criticisms leveled against positivism during the 20th century. Similar to positivism, postpositivism is primarily concerned with the search for causal relationships that enable us to predict and control our environments (K. I. Miller, 2000). Postpositivism departs from positivism in a variety of ways, however. Corman (2005) recently provided an excellent summary of these debates and of postpositivism, and delineated several basic principles of postpositivism that guide theory and research in organizational communication.

According to the postpositivist perspective, the social sciences and the natural sciences, although not isomorphic, are united. That is, social beings occupy and operate in physical space (Corman, 2005). Human beings are physical objects and can be physically observed, much like other aspects of nature such as flora and fauna. This *naturalism* principle has important implications for research. First, because humans are physical objects, human behavior is observable and, therefore, can be measured and evaluated. Thus, postpositivist research focuses attention on human behavior. Second, as physical objects, individuals' behaviors affect, and are affected by, the physical world. Consequently, postpositivists are drawn to studies that identify causal linkages between the social and natural world, such as how physical proximity impacts human

Table 1.1 Theoretical Perspectives on Workplace Relationships

	Postpositivism	Social Construction	Critical Theory	Structuration Theory
Conceptualization of organizations	Real entities that exist beyond human perception "Contain" individuals Indicated by attitudes, behavior	Socially constructed Constituted in social practices Dynamic	Socially constructed Constituted in social practices Dynamic Systems of power, domination, and control	Socially constructed Constituted in social practices Dynamic Patterned social practices of organizational members across social systems
Conceptualization of communication	Occurs "inside" the relationship Indicates nature and status of the relationship	Constitutes social reality Constitutes relationships; as communication changes, so does the relationship	Constitutes social reality Constitutes relationships Essentializes and reifies organizational "realities" and relationships	Constitutes society and social systems Enables, produces, and reproduces structure Enabled and constrained by structure
Conceptualization of relationships	Real entities that exist beyond human perception "Contain" individuals Indicated by attitudes, communication behavior Predictive of outcomes (e.g., satisfaction, productivity, commitment) Influenced by physical environment	Socially constructed Exist in interaction Observable in interaction	Socially constructed Sites of power, domination, marginalization Sites of hegemonic, unobtrusive control	Socially constructed Constrained and enabled by structure

	Postpositivism	Social Construction	Critical Theory	Structuration Theory
Research goals	Measuring indicators of relationship quality and status Predicting outcomes of relationships	Understanding social construction process Understanding relationship development dynamics	Understanding social construction of power, marginalization, reification, consent, domination, universalism of managerial interests and rationality	Understanding production, reproduction, and institutionalization of relationships
Sample research topics/questions	Association between relationship quality and outcomes (e.g., supervisor–subordinate relationships and employee productivity, turnover, and satisfaction; coworker relationship quality and information amount and quality) Association between communication behavior (e.g., frequency, content) and relationship quality	How do individuals construct workplace relationships? How do employees communicatively transform workplace relationships? How do individuals construct organizational realities through interaction with supervisors and coworkers (e.g., how are decision premises constructed in conversations between workplace friends?)	How do employees enact and abuse power in workplace relationships? How is participation in relationships and relationship networks associated with access to information, power, and dominance? How do individuals become marginalized from relationships and relationship networks?	What structures constrain and enable workplace relationships? How are workplace relationship structures institutionalized in U.S. culture? What workplace relationship structures transcend time and space? How do individuals develop structures for developing and negotiating various types of workplace relationships?

(Continued)

Table 1.1 (Continued)

	Postpositivism	Social Construction	Critical Theory	Structuration Theory
Sample research topics/questions (continued)	Association between workplace relationships and context (e.g., physical proximity, technology, tasks, etc.) Association between individual characteristics (e.g., gender, age, dispositions) and relationship quality		How do workplace relationships and relationship networks reinforce (or destabilize) organizational dominance and control? How are specific relational dynamics (e.g., hierarchy in the supervisor–subordinate relationship) reified? How does macrolevel (societal) discourse engender employee consent to relationship power dynamics?	How are workplace relationships constrained by the organization's governing ideology?

relationship development (Sias & Cahill, 1998). Third, conceptualizing human beings as physical objects who occupy space *in* the natural world leads to the conceptualization of organizations as "containers" in which individuals carry out their work (R. C. Smith & Turner, 1995). Thus, while the naturalist principle unites the social and physical world, it also bifurcates the two by placing people (the social world) *inside* physical locations such as organizations (the physical world).

Postpositivism takes a *realist* stance, assuming a social reality exists, although we as human beings cannot actually see it. This principle stands in contrast to the positivism's antirealist stance that perceptions are what matter. Moreover, despite the fact that reality exists outside our perceptions, we can, and should, study that reality. *Transcendental reasoning* allows us to believe in the reality of things we cannot directly observe based on observing conditions that indicate the existence of something else (Corman, 2005). For example, although we cannot actually see or directly perceive organizations, we believe they exist because they are indicated in other observable phenomena, specifically observable coordinated human behavior.

Together, the postpositivist principles of naturalism and realism imply that reality exists, but is not directly observable. However, human beings, as occupiers of the natural, real world, *are* observable. To understand "reality," we must examine indicators of that reality. Thus, to understand the reality of an organization, we must examine indicators of that reality by observing human behavior. So, for example, we cannot see and directly study an organization's culture; however, the culture is indicated by employee behaviors and attitudes, which we can observe and assess. Communication is conceptualized, then, as an indication of a reality that otherwise transcends our perceptions. Communication is an observable, measurable act that indicates reality. Accordingly, postpositivist studies of organizational communication typically assess communication to understand and predict something else (e.g., organizational culture).

A postpositivist approach to workplace relationships functions similarly. From this perspective, the workplace relationship is an entity that exists in a reality that transcends our perceptions, but is indicated by observable indicators. Such indicators include individual self-report assessments (e.g., a measure of supervisor–subordinate relationship quality). They also include assessments of communication, such as self-reports of the frequency with which individuals communicate with one another, topics about which they communicate, their satisfaction with their communication with a coworker, and the like. Postpositivist research also can include observations of actual communication that indicate relationship status.

In sum, postpositivist studies of workplace relationships conceptualize relationships as "real" entities that transcend our perception. These entities "contain" the relationship partners who behave in specific and patterned ways in those relationships.

Workplace relationship research guided by postpositivism addresses a number of interesting and important issues. Postpositivist research assesses the nature of workplace relationships by examining observable indicators of the relationship such as communication and attitudinal measures. Accordingly, postpositivist research on workplace relationships examines issues such as how certain communication practices indicate and predict relationship quality, and how relationship quality or quantity predicts observable organizational outcomes such as employee satisfaction, productivity, career advancement, and the like. Postpositivist research also examines links between workplace relationships and the context in which they exist. For example, scholars have studied the impact of workplace characteristics such as proximity, climate, and workload on friendship development (Sias & Cahill, 1998). In addition, following the naturalism principle, scholars have examined the ways employees' physical attributes, such as biological sex, are associated with their relationships with others in the workplace (e.g., Sias, Smith, & Avdeyeva, 2003).

Social Construction Approaches to Workplace Relationships

Rather than conceptualizing reality as existing outside our perceptions, social construction theory conceptualizes reality as socially constructed. P. L. Berger and Luckmann (1966) laid the foundation of social constructionism in their seminal work *The Social Construction of Reality: A Treatise in the Sociology of Knowledge*. Their argument rests on a few fundamental assumptions. First, human behavior is grounded in knowledge; that is, our behavior is informed by our knowledge and understanding of the world around us. Second, knowledge results from social processes (Allen, 2005). Thus, rather than being objective and real, knowledge is socially constructed and socially contested. Third, social constructionism rejects the notion of an objective reality and instead maintains that reality is socially constructed. As Berger and Luckmann (1966) stated, "The sociology of knowledge is concerned with the analysis of the social construction of reality" (p. 19). In contrast to postpositivism, human beings do not behave in and react to reality; they construct it via social practices.

Social constructionism has a number of important implications for organizational researchers. First, human behavior does not simply indicate reality; it creates reality. Thus, reality is not objective, it is subjective—subject to the moment-by-moment social behavior that constitutes it. Second, reality is not static, it is dynamic—reality changes as social behavior changes. Third, the primary goal of social construction theory is to understand how humans create knowledge and social reality. Accordingly, social construction research focuses primarily on process, rather than product.

Consistent with this, organizational research guided by the social construction perspective conceptualizes organizations as socially constructed realities that are constituted in member interaction. An organization does not exist in a physical location; it exists in the interaction of its members. When discussing social construction theory in class, I ask my students, "Where is Washington State University?" They invariably answer with the university's physical location—Pullman, Washington. I explain that, according to social constructionists, Washington State University isn't "in" Pullman, Washington. It exists, instead, in the interaction of its members. Certainly, much of this interaction happens to occur in Pullman, but the organization itself exists in member interaction and, therefore, WSU is wherever members are interacting to do the work of the organization. This dynamic view of organizations is distinct from the postpositivist approach in important ways. Rather than examining communication as an indicator of the *organization,* social construction research examines the process of *organizing:* the role of communicating in creating, maintaining, and transforming organizations. The organization does not transcend our perception. It is directly observable in the organizing (i.e., communication) process.

Researchers studying workplace relationships from a social construction perspective conceptualize such entities as constituted in interaction. Thus, relationships do not exist outside the interaction of the relationship partners. More specifically, relationships do not exist outside the patterned interaction of the partners. Much research in the area of interpersonal relationships is grounded in social construction theory (e.g., Duck & Pittman, 1997). Relatively few studies of *workplace* relationships, however, take such an approach.

Studying workplace relationships from a social construction perspective requires the basic assumptions outlined above. First, the relationship does not exist in a reality that transcends our perceptions. Rather, it is constituted in the interaction of its members. Second, relationships are not containers for human behavior; they are constituted in human behavior. Given these assumptions, social construction studies of workplace relationships focus on examining communication behavior between relationship partners. Studying supervisor–subordinate relationships, for example, requires analyzing supervisor–subordinate interaction. Such examination does not simply provide an indication of the nature of that relationship; it demonstrates the actual construction, maintenance, and/or transformation of that relationship.

Research on workplace relationships grounded in the social construction perspective addresses issues associated with relationship dynamics and processes. This includes studies of how members construct functional or dysfunctional relationships with their supervisors and coworkers (e.g., Fairhurst & Chandler, 1989) and how employees transform their relationships with others (e.g., Sias, Heath, Perry, Silva, & Fix, 2004). Social constructionist research could also examine how individuals construct "organizational realities" through interaction with supervisors and other coworkers. For example, a social construction study might ascertain the ways in which coworker conversation among friends impacts employee decision making.

Social constructionism has become a central perspective in organizational research, both in driving innovative research agendas and also by virtue of the fact that social constructionism provides the foundation for other innovative and important theoretical perspectives, including critical theory and structuration theory, which are discussed below.

Critical Approaches to Workplace Relationships

Power and politics have always been important issues of study by organizational communication, management, and sociology scholars. Early formal theories of organization, such as bureaucratic theory (Weber, 1947) and administrative management theory (Fayol, 1949), held hierarchy and control at the core of organizational processes, emphasizing chain of command, order, control, and discipline. Until the mid-1980s, studies of organizational power and politics had a distinctly managerial bias in which the goal of such research was to enable management to more effectively (read "productively") control employees (Putnam & Pacanowsky, 1983).

Critical theory and critical approaches to organizing took a very different, and important, turn. Critical theories assume a radical stance on society and organization, emphasizing the individual over the organization. Critical scholars are concerned not with managerial effectiveness, but with the institutional oppression and exploitation of individuals. Issues of injustice, asymmetrical power relations, marginalization, and abuse are the concerns of critical research (Deetz, 1992; Mumby, 1988). Moreover, critical theorists situate organizational power and politics in larger political and economic systems and problematic societal discursive formations that reproduce and reify inequitable power relations. A thorough discussion of critical theory is beyond the scope of this chapter, and readers are directed to recent treatments by Deetz (2001) and Mumby (2000, 2001) for additional reading. For purposes of this chapter, I discuss a few primary assumptions and concerns of critical theory as they relate to organizations and workplace relationships.

Like the social construction perspective, critical theory conceptualizes language and communication as core to any understanding of organizational processes. Organizations are not tangible entities that exist outside our perception. Organizations are socially constructed dynamic entities constituted in the interaction of the organization members. Critical theory, however, goes beyond social constructionism in conceptualizing organizations as not just socially constructed, but as socially constructed systems of power, control, and domination. Thus, as members construct the organization, they construct a system of domination that empowers some while marginalizing others. A primary goal of critical research, therefore, is to identify and reveal the various methods of power, control, and domination, particularly the hidden or unobtrusive forms to which individuals are most vulnerable.

At a broad level, critical scholars study organizational power by focusing on "the relationships among communication, power and meaning" (Mumby, 2001, p. 595). More specifically, in his recent discussion of critical theory and organizational research, Deetz (2005) outlined four recurrent themes in critical research that address this broad issue. First, critical work shows a concern with *reification*, which refers to ways in which social, and socially constructed, phenomena become naturalized and unquestioned. In such research, critical scholars examine the reification and resulting hegemonic power of bureaucratic principles such as hierarchy, authority, and rationality (Putnam & Mumby, 1993). This reification process makes such principles appear natural, indispensable, and, therefore, unquestionable and immutable. An illustration of the power of reification and hegemony is provided by considering an organization without any hierarchy. While such organizations do exist (e.g., collectives), they are very rare and often considered to be "alternative" or, put less charitably, "weird."

Second, critical scholars are concerned with "*the suppression of conflicting interests and universalization of managerial interests*" (Deetz, 2005, p. 95). Critical research problematizes the largely unquestioned primacy of managerial/ organizational performance goals over the interests of individuals, noting that powerful organizational members, as well as organizational researchers, often assume a singular universal organizational interest, assuming that the interests of the organization and management are the interests of the employees. One of critical theory's central tenets is the questioning of organizational practices with respect to whose interests are served by such practices. Thus, for example, when executives of a large banking institution decided to increase business, and therefore profits, by opening branches on Saturdays, they did not consider how weekend hours might disrupt the branch employees' personal lives (Pearce, 1995).

A third theme of critical research is the *dominance of technical rationality* as the primary and optimal form of reasoning. Such instrumental reasoning, characterized by efficiency and means-end control, has dominated organizational research and practice, and made alternative forms of reasoning appear irrational (Deetz, 2005, p. 97). As a result, emotion, intuition, understanding, empathic concern, and a variety of "alternative" forms of reasoning are marginalized (Mumby & Putnam, 1992).

A fourth theme found in critical writings has to do with the issue of *consent*. In particular, although bureaucratic and authoritarian forms of management are characterized by direct and explicit forms of control, critical scholars are concerned with hidden, unobtrusive, and arguably more potent forms of control (e.g., concertive control, identification) and the processes by which individuals consent to such control (e.g., Barker, 1993; Tompkins & Cheney, 1985). For example, an employee may not think to resist his supervisor's continual verbal abuse not because of fear of retaliation, but because of deeply rooted assumptions linking formal rank and power; in other words, the employee "consents" to the abuse because to resist formal authority is counter to his ideological assumptions and worldview.

Critical scholars address these issues at two primary levels. At the level of micropractices, scholars examine power and control in the context of social relations among individuals and groups (Mumby, 2000). Theory and research at this level address the discursive construction of meaning, power, and identity in everyday communication. At a broader macrolevel, critical scholars center on revealing the hegemonic processes by which "discourses" of meaning, identity, and knowledge are constructed, reproduced, and maintained and how such discourses function to support and reify dominant power and political structures in society (e.g., Deetz, 1992). Such work, for example, highlights the societal dominance of technical reasoning or technical rationality that frames knowledge and meaning in reference to efficiency, predictability, rationality, and control (Deetz, 2005; Habermas, 1984; Mumby, 2000). Such knowledge constrains our participation as active agents not only in the context of organizations, but also in how we organize everyday life (Deetz, 1992).

Communication is clearly central to critical theory. Similar to social constructionism, critical theory conceptualizes communication as dynamic and constitutive of organizations. Critical theorists emphasize the power and political nature of communication, revealing the ways communication essentializes and reifies organizational structures and processes, making them appear real and natural and, therefore, immutable. Communication is the process by which organizational structures and practices become reified, by which managerial interests are promoted and individual or conflicting interests marginalized, by which alternative forms of reasoning become devalued, and by which unobtrusive and hidden forms of control are wielded by management and consented to by individuals.

Critical approaches to workplace relationships are guided by the above set of assumptions and conceptualizations. From this perspective, workplace relationships are conceptualized as socially constructed entities constituted in human interaction. A relationship does not exist outside the interaction of the relationship partners, and the quality and nature of the relationship is dependent upon the quality and nature of the interaction of the relationship members. Similar to social constructionism then, workplace relationships from a critical perspective are dynamic entities constituted in interaction, and as partner interaction changes or remains stable, so does the relationship. Critical theory, however, conceptualizes relationships not just as socially constructed entities, but as socially constructed sites of power, domination, resistance, and struggle. In relationships, individual members construct their knowledge, identities, and understanding of organizational processes, goals, and values.

The conceptualizations described above inform a unique research agenda. Critical workplace relationship research addresses issues such as how individuals communicatively enact and abuse power and control in various workplace relationships (e.g., with supervisors, peer coworkers, etc.). Moreover, critical research would examine how participation in workplace relationships constructs and maintains organizational power and domination systems; how communication and discourse includes and excludes individuals from participation in relationship networks; how workplace relationships provide, or deny, access to "voice" and influence; and the hegemonic processes (e.g., broader societal discursive formations) that engender the consent of employees to such dynamics. In addition, critical studies would examine the processes by which certain workplace relationship dynamics, such as hierarchy in the supervisor–subordinate relationship or discrimination in a cross-sex coworker relationship, become reified and taken as natural.

Structuration Theory and Workplace Relationships

Sociologist Anthony Giddens introduced structuration theory in response to the "orthodox consensus" that dominated sociology in the postwar period rooted in positivism. Giddens (1984) believed the logical empiricism of the natural sciences was inapplicable to social theory, arguing that societal factors acting in the same manner as causal relationships of natural sciences cannot explain human conduct (Baert, 1998). Instead, he argued, people call upon structures for the initiation of their actions, and the production of social life is a skilled performance by agents. Agents are responsible for the production and reproduction of social systems that guide their action. Consequently, Giddens advocated the study of actors as agents of social life. Structuration theory, therefore, has roots in the social construction perspective.

Giddens, however, argued that while positivism gave primacy to structure (e.g., structure determines individual behavior), social constructionists often gave primacy to agency (e.g., human behavior determines structure). Structuration theory reconceptualized this dichotomous relationship between individual and society as a dualism, emphasizing the inseparability of agency and structure united through social practices (Berends, Boersma, & Weggeman, 2003). A thorough discussion of structuration theory is beyond the scope of this chapter (see Berends et al., 2003; Giddens, 1979, 1984; and Poole & McPhee, 2005, for excellent treatments of the theory). I focus instead on the primary concepts of structuration theory as they apply to the study of workplace relationships: structure, systems, social and system integration, and time–space distanciation.

According to structuration theory, a social system exists through the reproduced social practices, or *structures,* of actors or groups of actors

(Giddens, 1984). These practices (recurring, regular, and structured actions of individuals situated within a social system) create and recreate the system (Giddens, 1984). Thus, structure is both outcome and medium. It is outcome in the sense that structure is produced and reproduced in interaction; it is the medium for interaction in the sense that actors do not construct social reality from nothing, but draw upon preexisting structural elements in their actions. Specifically, structure is comprised of rules and resources. Rules are implicit guidelines for action. Resources are all personal traits, abilities, knowledge, and possessions people bring to interactions. Actors (agents) draw upon structure to take part in system practices. Thus, structures enable human behavior. For example, my understanding of appropriate teaching behaviors and resources such as knowledge of course material, a classroom, and teaching technologies comprise a structure that enables me to deliver an effective lecture. At the same time, human behavior produces and reproduces structure. Thus, each time I lecture, I (re)produce the "teaching" structure. Production happens when people use rules and resources in interaction. Reproduction occurs when actions reinforce features of the systems already in place. This reciprocal process is known as the *duality of structure.*

As people continually reproduce structures in their interaction, they create and maintain systems. *Systems* are patterns of social relations across stretches of time and space, constituted in reproduced agents' practices. Social systems vary widely in their degree of "systemness." Some structures, such as the U.S. public school system, develop into highly institutionalized systems, while others, such as a newly formed political party, are less entrenched, systematic, and, consequently, less powerful.

The concepts of *integration* and *time–space distanciation* explain how structures become systematic and institutionalized. These concepts address the ways microlevel practices, informed by, and reproduced as, structures, are transported and appropriated across time and space, constructing institutionalized systematic structures at the macro or societal level. Essentially, as structures are enacted and reproduced across time and spaces, "orders of institutional relationships are formed, codified, memorialized, and concretized as contextual features in the structuration of social life" (Banks & Riley, 1991, p. 176). As Banks and Riley (1991) explain, time–space distanciation theorizes "the relation between action in the here and now and the reproduction of institutional context, practices, and expectations that stretch out potentially (and increasingly) vast distances and time spans" (p. 175). While *social integration* refers to the reciprocity of practices by co-present actors (e.g., individuals enact and reproduce specific structures in face-to-face interaction with one another), *system integration* refers to the same process as it occurs across time and space and "outside conditions of co-presence" (Giddens, 1984, p. 377). Social systems stretch across time and space (time–space distanciation) via the mechanisms of social and system integration. As structures are continually reinforced and "regrooved" across time and space (contexts), those structures become integrated at the system level and institutionalized. At that point, these structures become systemic and "taken for granted." Thus, for example, one is likely to find more similarities than differences in how lectures are delivered in undergraduate classes by different teachers at different universities across the United States.

Toward this end, structuration theory posits that agents act at three levels of consciousness. The *discursive* level refers to social practices that we can express and explain at a conscious level (e.g., we are highly conscious of our spoken words when presenting a formal proposal to a new client). As structures are reproduced and become more habitual, we operate at the *practical* level. This level refers to knowledge and skills we cannot put into words but use in action. It represents what we know and believe about social conditions and their own actions, but cannot express discursively (e.g., we know we should not violate informal rules, but find it hard to explain why). Finally, the *unconscious* refers to experiences we cannot easily call into awareness (e.g., although we probably engage in "hello," "how are you," "I'm fine" exchanges several times a day, we cannot easily recall and account for each instance).

Structuration theory has a number of important implications for organizational research. First, as mentioned above, structuration theory rejects the structure–agent dichotomy and, consequently, rejects the notion of an objective reality separate from human action. Instead, the theory is grounded in social constructionism, conceptualizing social systems (e.g., organizations) and, therefore, social reality as constituted in social practices. As social systems, organizations are conceptualized as the patterned social practices of organizational members, or systems. In this manner, structuration theory provides a dynamic conceptualization of organizations. Structuration theory also explains the process by which social systems become institutionalized and "taken for granted." Similar to critical theory, structuration theory problematizes those institutionalized social structures that have become so entrenched across time and space that they appear real, natural, reified, and unquestioned.

Communication plays an important role in structuration theory. Agents' social practices, including communication, constitute social systems. Thus, similar to social constructionism, communication does not reflect or indicate reality; it creates reality. Structuration theory goes beyond social constructionism, however, with the concept of the duality of structure—communication creates structures that *simultaneously* enable and constrain communication. This added component broadens the theoretical, and research, lens.

Structuration theory conceptualizes workplace relationships as communicatively constituted entities. Again, similar to social constructionism, workplace relationships exist in member interaction, and as interaction changes, so does the relationship. Beyond this, however, structuration theory also conceptualizes workplace relationships as enabled and constrained by structures—structures that guide, yet limit, interaction that is appropriate for that particular relationship (e.g., employees typically communicate differently with their peer coworkers than with their supervisors or subordinate employees).

Given these assumptions and conceptualizations, workplace relationship research grounded in structuration theory would examine a number of interesting and important issues. Researchers could uncover the structures that enable and constrain various types of workplace relationships (e.g., what structures govern and distinguish supervisor–subordinate relationships from peer relationships?), the processes by which such structures transcend time and space (e.g., how are workplace relationship structures transported across countries in multinational organizations?), the processes by which workplace relationship structures become, or have become, institutionalized at the societal level (e.g., to what extent are workplace relationship dynamics replicated and reproduced across organizations and industries?), and the ways individuals (agents) transform, rather than reproduce, workplace relationship structures.

Conclusion

Workplace relationships are vital to both organizational and individual well-being. Despite their importance, the workplace relationship literature is comparatively underdeveloped. The bulk of research has focused on one type of relationship—the supervisor–subordinate relationship—and has relied largely on a single theoretical lens—postpositivism. While existing research is of great value, broadening our views and approaches toward organizations, communication, and relationships has the potential for greatly enriching both research and practice. In particular, social constructionism, critical theory, and structuration theory each conceptualize organizations, and organizational relationships, in unique and innovative ways. As the following chapters demonstrate, studying workplace relationships and approaching the phenomena in practice from each of these perspectives is essential to the growth and development of our field and to improved organizational and employee experiences.

2

Supervisor–Subordinate Relationships

Alan Robbins learned the difficulties of managing supervisor–subordinate relationships the hard way (Aeppel, 1998). When he started his own company that recycled glass and plastic containers into synthetic lumber products, Alan made it a point to develop close and friendly relationships with his employees. This involved him not only seeking employees' input on decisions, but also lending employees money, sharing beers with them at the end of shift, and tolerating tardiness and absenteeism. As time went on, Alan felt employees were taking advantage of him, and the organization became increasingly chaotic. After being sued by two employees he fired for engaging in a physical fight in the factory, Alan decided he needed to take control of the company. The first step was creating a substantial employee rule book (quite a shock to employees not used to rules), and the second step involved strict enforcement of those rules. Reclaiming control of the organization resulted in Alan ending friendships with his employees and instead distancing himself from the others. Although he missed the fun of those early years and the close relationships he had with his employees, Alan believed saving the business required these somewhat painful changes (Aeppel, 1998). Alan's experience highlights the complex, difficult, and even emotional nature of supervisor–subordinate relationships, a topic of much research attention.

Hierarchy is a defining characteristic of organizations. And as Alan's experience indicates, hierarchical relationships are of great consequence for employees and organization. Early formal theories of organization—bureaucratic theory and administrative management—held hierarchy at the core of management processes, emphasizing chain of command, order, control, and discipline. These and other important organizational processes occur in the context of supervisor–subordinate relationships. Despite recent moves toward participative and "flat" organizations, supervisor–subordinate relationships remain an important part of the fabric of contemporary organizations. One is hard pressed to identify an organization in which no one holds authority or is formally accountable for unit performance.

Overview

Supervisor–subordinate relationships are workplace relationships in which one partner (the supervisor) holds direct formal authority over the other (the subordinate employee). These are extremely important and consequential relationships, both from the perspective of the larger organization and for individuals whose working lives are so strongly impacted by their immediate supervisors and subordinate employees. Not surprisingly, supervisor–subordinate relationships are among the most frequently studied topics in organizational research.

In this chapter, I review the long tradition of supervisor–subordinate relationship research by discussing the functions of such relationships; the processes that guide the development, maintenance, and deterioration of supervisor–subordinate relationships; and the "outcomes" or consequences of supervisor–subordinate relationships for the relationship partners and the larger department and organization. I then offer alternative conceptualizations of supervisor–subordinate relationships that suggest new directions for research and practical understanding. At the end of the chapter, I provide a case and a series of discussion questions designed to help the reader apply the knowledge and principles discussed in this chapter about supervisor–subordinate relationships in an attempt to understand and address practical, real-world concerns. Table 2.1 provides a brief summary of research on these various themes.

Functions of Supervisor–Subordinate Relationships

LEADERSHIP

Early theory and research tended to treat *management/supervision* and *leadership* as synonymous terms. Both "processes" had to do with leaders (supervisors/managers) eliciting the optimal (i.e., most productive) attitudes and performance from followers (subordinate employees). In the early 1980s, scholars began to distinguish between *management/supervision,* which centers on day-to-day direction of departmental activities, and *leadership,* which centers on vision and organizational change (Bass, 1985). Toward this end, leadership is distinct from management in its focus on strategy and the future, rather than maintaining status quo conditions, and in its focus on crisis and innovation, rather than organizational stability (Bennis & Nanus, 1985; Hackman &

Table 2.1   Summary of Supervisor–Subordinate Relationship Research

Supervisor–Subordinate Relationship Functions

Leadership
- Trait theories
- Style and behavior theories
- Leader–member exchange (LMX) theory
- Leadership and gender

Information Exchange
- Supervisor as information source
- Subordinate as information source
- Relationship quality and information exchange

Feedback and Appraisal
- Downward feedback
- Upward feedback

Mentoring
- Formal and informal mentoring
- Dysfunctional mentoring relationships

Power and Influence
- Supervisory power and control
- Upward influence
- Relationship quality and influence
- Supervisor–subordinate relationships as site of abuse and dominance
- Employee resistance

Supervisor–Subordinate Relationship Development

Developmental Processes
Factors influencing relationship development
- Employee ability/job performance
- Supervisor ability/job performance
- Employee personality traits
- Supervisor personality traits
- Similarity and dissimilarity (attitudinal, personality, cognitive style, demographic)
- Communication

Outcomes and Consequences

Employee Adjustment
- Job satisfaction
- Communication satisfaction
- Commitment
- Intent to quit

Employee Performance and Behavior
- Job performance
- Citizenship behavior
- Creativity

Supervisor's Effectiveness

Johnson, 2003). A full discussion of leadership is beyond the scope of this chapter. However, many books have been written on the topic, and readers are encouraged to consult those for in-depth treatments of leadership (e.g., Bass, 1985; Burns, 1978). Here I discuss leadership research as it relates to the *relationships* between leaders (supervisors) and followers (subordinate employees).

Early studies of leadership and supervisor–subordinate relationships, conducted by both leadership and management scholars, tended to be unidirectional and focused on the functional aspects of such relationships. This research attempted to identify *leader/supervisor* qualities and behaviors that lead to improved employee attitudes, motivation, and job performance. The earliest leadership theories focused on leader "traits." Trait theories of leadership assumed "great leaders" possess particular personality traits that enhance leadership ability, such as charisma, intelligence, and courage (e.g., Ghiselli, 1963), assuming that leaders are born, not taught. The follower (subordinate) was largely irrelevant in these theories. A great leader could lead anyone effectively.

"Style" or "behavioral" theories of leadership focused on leader behaviors and skills, rather than traits, assuming that people can learn to be effective leaders. These theories assume that leaders/supervisors tend to adhere to a general supervisory style. The Ohio State Leadership studies, for example, indicated that leaders who exhibit a high level of consideration for employees (e.g., trust, warmth, respect) and a high level initiating structure (i.e., focus on the task) were the most effective (e.g., Hemphill, 1955).

Style and behavioral theories of leadership differed with respect to the role of the subordinate employees. Managerial grid theory (Blake & Mouton, 1964), for example, assumed effective leadership behaviors were universal; that is, all employees would respond similarly to leader behaviors, thus giving subordinate employees a passive role in the leadership/management relationship. Path-goal theory (e.g., House, 1971) and situational leadership theory (Hershey & Blanchard, 1982), in contrast, assumed certain leader behaviors would be effective only with certain types of employees. For example, research indicated that mature and confident employees respond best to a "delegating" leadership style while employees who lack maturity and confidence would respond best to a "telling" or more directive leadership style. In these theories, subordinate employees began to play a more active role in supervisor–subordinate relationship research. However, the effectiveness of the relationship was still conceptualized as being in the supervisor's control. The supervisor only had to determine which behaviors to use with which employees.

In the mid-1970s, Graen and colleagues introduced vertical dyad linkage (VDL) theory (e.g., Graen & Cashman, 1975), which has had an important and lasting impact on both leadership and supervisor–subordinate relationship research. VDL theory (later named "leader–member exchange theory") questioned the trait and average leadership style (ALS) theoretical assumptions that supervisors treat employees similarly and the generally passive role of subordinate employees in supervisor–subordinate relations. Instead, VDL theory maintained that supervisors form different types of relationships with their various employees and these relationships vary with respect to quality. In general, high-quality supervisor–subordinate relationships (also known as "in-group" relationships) are characterized by higher levels of mutual trust, respect, and obligation among the relationship partners than are low-quality relationships (also known as "out-group" relationships). In high-quality relationships, leaders and members rely on one another for support and encouragement. Such relationships function more as "partnerships" where "members move beyond their own self-interests to focus on larger mutual interests" (Graen & Uhl-Bien, 1995, p. 233).

According to VDL theory, leader–member relationships (i.e., supervisor–subordinate relationships) represent a type of "exchange" relationship in which *both* partners (supervisor and subordinate) negotiate their relationship on an ongoing basis. The name "vertical dyad linkage" theory eventually was replaced by the name "leader–member exchange" (LMX) theory to emphasize the negotiated nature of supervisor–subordinate relationships. Thus, LMX theory was the first to give an active role to the subordinate partner in the supervisor–subordinate relationship—employees and supervisors both influence the leader–member relationship. As will be seen in later sections of this chapter, LMX theory laid the foundation for much of the research on supervisor–subordinate relationships.

An important subtheme in leadership research addresses the notion of gender. This work tends to address two primary issues—the extent to which men and women are similar and/or different in their management styles and the ways in which the gender of both parties impacts their relationship. It is important to recognize that much, if not most, of this research treats gender and biological sex synonymously. The complexities of gender will be discussed later in this chapter when I address supervisor–subordinate relationships from the social construction and critical perspectives. For the time being, however, this section addresses biological sex (i.e., being a man or a woman) as it impacts supervisor–subordinate relationships.

A meta-analysis (Eagley, Karau, & Makhijani, 1995) revealed that women and men generally do not differ with respect to their managerial effectiveness (as indicated by the ability to motivate employees and employee and unit productivity). Several studies do indicate, however, that men and women may differ in their management styles and *relationships* with employees. In general, this research indicates that female managers tend to emphasize personal relations more than males, who are more likely to emphasize task accomplishment (Eagley & Johnson, 1990). Studies also indicate that women managers are more likely to be perceived as using a considerate, nurturing style; to engage in participative decision making; and to be inclusive, while male managers were more likely to be perceived of as directive, controlling, and task oriented

(Carless, 1998; Gibson, 1995). Many scholars theorize that these perceived managerial style differences may explain the relatively few women in upper management positions, arguing that females displaying such behavior are likely to be less valued in Western organizations that tend to value masculine characteristics such as individuality, competition, and assertiveness.

Parker (2001) provides a more complex view of gender, race, and leadership. Her interpretive study of African American female managers in organizations dominated by white male managers revealed that rather than adopting traditional masculine leadership practices, these leaders enacted a unique form of collaboration and control that redefined control as "interactive and personal, rather than competitive and distant" (p. 43). Specifically, these managers relied on five primary communication practices: interactive communication, challenging others to produce results, communication openness, participative decision making, and effective boundary spanning.

In sum, leadership theory, originally treated synonymously with management, evolved over time with respect to the relationship between leader/supervisor and follower/subordinate employee. Early theories (both trait and behavioral/style) gave employees a passive role in the relationship. Leaders (supervisors) were assumed to be in control of leader/follower relations, either by possessing specific traits, or by displaying particular behaviors. LMX theory, introduced in the mid-1970s, substantially reconceptualized supervisor–subordinate relationships from a unidirectional relationship controlled by the supervisor to a reciprocal relationship negotiated by supervisor and subordinate. LMX theory has informed much supervisor–subordinate relationship research in the past 30 years, as seen in the remaining sections of this chapter.

INFORMATION EXCHANGE

An employee's relationship with his or her supervisor has important implications for that employee's socialization into the organization and subsequent career progression (Jablin, 1987), as well as for the supervisor's ability to perform his or her tasks effectively and ensure optimal unit functioning. This is due, in large part, to information sharing between supervisors and subordinate employees. From their very first meeting, supervisors and subordinate employees are crucial sources of information for one another, and supervisors play an important role in the socialization of new employees. The supervisor's primary role during the "encounter" phase of employee socialization is to provide information and instruction regarding the organization, the department, and the new employee's tasks, assignments, and goals (Jablin, 1987, 2001).

New employees experience a great deal of uncertainty when they begin a new job—uncertainty about their tasks, or referent uncertainty; their ability to competently perform their tasks, or appraisal uncertainty; and relationships with their new coworkers and their role in the social network, or relational uncertainty (V. D. Miller & Jablin, 1991; Teboul, 1994). They rely on their supervisors as a primary source of information to reduce this uncertainty, using a variety of information-seeking tactics. Specifically, people use three primary types of tactics to obtain information at work—direct questions; indirect questions, such as hinting or asking a third party; and monitoring, for example, observing others' conversations and actions (V. D. Miller & Jablin, 1991).

New employees tend to seek information directly from their supervisors, especially during the first few months in their new job (Morrison, 1993; Teboul, 1994). Direct tactics are assumed to be the most effective with respect to employee job performance because misunderstandings are less likely to result from direct conversations than from indirect hinting, use of third parties, or observation (V. D. Miller & Jablin, 1991). As the "honeymoon" ends, employees become more concerned with their image and the impression they're making on others in the workplace. No longer "new" hires, employees worry about the social costs associated with asking too many questions—that is, asking questions may make them appear unconfident and incompetent, and so employees tend to decrease their use of direct information-seeking tactics and increase their use of indirect and monitoring tactics (Fedor, Rensvold, & Adams, 1992; Sias & Wyers, 2001).

Although most research on information seeking in organizations has focused on new employees, recent research indicates *veteran* employees continue to experience various types of uncertainty, depending on the organizational context. For example, veteran employees experience relational uncertainty whenever a new employee is hired (Gallagher & Sias, in press). They also experience uncertainty during times of organizational change or turmoil (Sias & Wyers, 2001), as well as uncertainty during mundane and everyday organizational functioning (Sias, 2005). These studies all indicate that supervisors are one of the most important sources of quality information for veteran employees, as well as newcomers. Along these lines, much research indicates that supervisors are important role models for subordinate employees. As primary sources of information, supervisors filter and interpret downward information for their employees, enabling them to strongly influence employees' perceptions of organizational, job-related, and performance issues (Jablin, 1987, 2001). Research also indicates subordinate employees learn management and supervisory communication behaviors from their supervisors and tend to imitate those behaviors in their own supervisory roles (Weiss, 1977).

As mentioned earlier, however, information sharing is a reciprocal event. Just as subordinates rely on supervisors for information, supervisors rely heavily on their subordinate employees for information so that they can make informed management decisions. The extent to which employees are willing to provide their supervisors with accurate, quality information or instead engage in "upward distortion" (i.e., distorting information provided to a supervisor either through lying or omission) depends on a number of factors. First, the more influence supervisors have over the career advancement of employees, the more likely employees are to filter information they provide to the supervisor. Second, employees are most likely to omit information that would reflect negatively on themselves, such as information about mistakes they make or poor performance. Third, the more employees trust their supervisor, the less likely they are to distort information provided to the supervisor (Jablin, 1979).

In a similar vein, research on "communication openness" also addresses the reciprocal nature of supervisor–subordinate information exchange. Essentially, studies show that individuals are more likely to provide information to those who provide information to them (Jablin, 1979). Thus, supervisors are most likely to receive quality information from employees when they also provide quality information to those employees (e.g., Ramaswami, Srinivasan, & Gorton, 1997). This work, taken with research on upward distortion, indicates that trusting and open supervisor–subordinate relationships are crucial to effective information exchange.

A recent study provides strong direct evidence of the link between supervisor–subordinate relationships and information exchange. Sias (2005) examined the link between LMX quality (defined as supportive, open, trusting relationships) and the amount and quality of information employees (both new hires and veteran employees) received from their supervisors. Results indicated that supervisor–subordinate relationship quality was positively related to both the amount and quality of information employees received from their immediate supervisor. In fact, relationship quality predicted more than half of the variance in quality of information employees reported receiving from their supervisors.

In sum, research over the years consistently demonstrates the importance of supervisor–subordinate relationships to effective information exchange. Supervisors and subordinate employees depend heavily on one another for quality information. The better the supervisor–subordinate relationship, the better informed the employees.

FEEDBACK AND APPRAISAL

Downward Feedback

One of the most important types of information supervisors provide to employees is *appraisal* information, or feedback about the employees' job performance. Providing positive feedback to employees can motivate and encourage continued good performance (Fedor, 1991). Providing negative feedback to employees, while considerably more difficult and uncomfortable, is crucial to employee development and organizational performance. Unfortunately, many supervisors either avoid providing negative feedback or provide it in destructive rather than constructive ways (Benedict & Levine, 1988; Jablin,

1979). As a result, employees are not made aware of performance deficiencies, are not motivated to improve their performance, and continue their poor job performance.

Supervisors are one of the most important sources of performance feedback for employees (Ashford, 1993; Fedor, 1991; Herold, Liden, & Leatherwood, 1987). Supervisors are responsible both for employee training and development and for monitoring, evaluating, disciplining, and rewarding employee performance. Not surprisingly, then, employees rely on supervisors for information about how well they are performing their jobs. The extent to which such feedback is effective has important implications for the employees' future performance, morale, and career progression (Fedor, 1991). Supervisors provide performance feedback to employees in two primary venues—day-to-day informal feedback provided via everyday conversation, and formal performance evaluation interviews typically conducted annually or semiannually. Both types of feedback are conducted in the context of supervisor–subordinate relationships, and the nature of those relationships has important implications for the feedback event.

Much research has focused on *feedback sign*—whether the feedback is positive or negative. Positive feedback, while not designed to change employee performance, can reinforce effective performance. Positive feedback is of limited utility, however. Ashford (1993) found that while employees reported using more positive feedback messages from their supervisors than negative messages to evaluate their own performance, they perceived the negative feedback to be more useful with respect to career advancement. In other words, positive feedback is helpful for informing employees as to their current performance, but negative feedback is crucial for eliciting *change* in employee performance, change that is essential for employee development and career advancement.

Negative feedback, although essential, is very difficult to provide. In fact, much research indicates that supervisors often avoid, delay, or misrepresent negative feedback to employees (Benedict & Levine, 1988; C. D. Fisher, 1979; Jablin, 1979). This is primarily due to fact that negative feedback is a face-threatening act (Goffman, 1959), and supervisors expect employees to be defensive when given negative feedback (Larson, 1989). A number of factors can "soften the blow" and make it more likely that employees actually listen to the negative feedback, make efforts to improve their performance, and develop positive attitudes toward their job and the organization. Leung, Su, and Morris (2001) found that employees were more likely to listen to, and accept, criticism from their supervisors when the supervisors provided that feedback in "constructive," rather than "destructive," ways. Specifically, their research indicates that when supervisors provided the feedback in a private location, listened to the employee's ideas, showed respect for the employee, and were supportive of the employee, the employee was more likely to accept the feedback and more willing to exert effort toward improving his or her performance. In addition, receiving this type of "constructive" negative feedback was positively associated with trust in, and satisfaction with, the supervisor. In contrast, employees who received negative feedback from supervisors who were disrespectful (i.e., interrupted the subordinate employee, made fun of the employee's ideas, and did not pay attention to the employee) were less likely to listen to and accept the feedback, and were more likely to report lower levels of trust in, and satisfaction with, the supervisor. Thus, providing "destructive" negative feedback does more harm than good—it does not improve employee performance and instead harms employee attitudes and the relationship between supervisor and employee. Relatedly, Steelman, and Rutkowski (2004) found that the source and delivery of feedback are important factors in the process. Specifically, their study indicated that employees are more motivated to improve their performance in response to negative feedback from the supervisor when they perceive the supervisor is knowledgeable about their performance and when the supervisor provides the feedback in a considerate, thoughtful manner.

In sum, employees attend to both positive and negative feedback. However, negative feedback appears to be more important for employee development and advancement. While much research indicates that supervisors often avoid, delay, or distort negative feedback to employees, recent studies show that trusting, respectful relationships between supervisor–subordinate enhance the delivery and effectiveness of constructive, negative feedback.

Upward Feedback

Perhaps because of the enduring hierarchical nature of organizations, research has focused primarily on downward feedback from supervisor to subordinate. Little attention has been given to upward feedback provided by subordinate employees to supervisors. The research that has been conducted focuses primarily on *formal* upward feedback, despite the fact that subordinate employees do provide supervisors with feedback during everyday informal conversation. Again, however, due to enduring structures of hierarchy and authority, informal upward feedback is likely less frequent than formal feedback due to the fact that formal feedback is organizationally sanctioned and often anonymous.

Research findings are mixed with respect to the effectiveness of formal upward feedback, with respect to supervisor attitudes and performance. Smither et al. (1995) found that supervisors who received upward feedback did show some subsequent improvement in their performance, although the improvement scores were highly variable, suggesting that other factors intervene in the relationship between upward feedback and performance. Atwater, Waldman, Atwater, and Carter (2000) identified two such moderating factors in their longitudinal study of supervisors in a police agency. Specifically, the supervisor's level of organizational cynicism (a general belief that one's organization lacks integrity and that honesty and fairness are "sacrificed" to expediency and self-interests) was negatively related to performance improvement after upward evaluation. Relatedly, they found that the extent to which the supervisor reacted positively to the upward feedback, and attempted to improve his or her performance, was positively related to actual performance improvement. Finally, the Atwater et al. study revealed that upward feedback processes can impact the supervisor–subordinate relationship itself. Specifically, supervisors who received positive feedback from their subordinate employees reported increased levels of commitment to the employees over time, while supervisors receiving negative ratings from employees reported lower levels of commitment to their subordinate employees. An interesting 5-year longitudinal study (Walker & Smither, 1999) found that supervisor–subordinate communication was a crucial moderator in the upward feedback–performance link. Their results indicated that supervisors who discussed their upward feedback scores with subordinate employees were more likely to show subsequent performance improvement than were supervisors who did not discuss the feedback with employees.

In sum, research on upward feedback indicates the important role of supervisor–subordinate relationships in upward feedback processes. The relationship between supervisor–subordinate impacts the effectiveness of the feedback (with respect to performance improvement) and the feedback process itself impacts the supervisor–subordinate relationship (with respect to the supervisor's commitment to subordinate employees).

MENTORING

A primary function of workplace relationships, including the supervisor–subordinate relationship, is mentoring. Mentoring includes the above-mentioned information sharing and feedback, but goes beyond those functions. *Mentoring* refers to a specific type of relationship in which the mentor functions as a type of "guide" for the development and career advancement of the protégé/mentee. Thus, mentoring relationships are unique from other types of workplace relationships in a couple of aspects. First, they are typically unidirectional rather than reciprocal; that is, the information sharing, feedback, and support flows one-way from mentor to protégé. Second, the focus of mentoring is on the protégé's career as a whole, rather than solely on specific tasks and performance. Relatedly, the goal of mentoring is career advancement for the mentee, rather than improved organizational productivity (although, individual career advancement is likely indirectly tied to improved organizational functioning).

Mentoring relationships develop between employees at all levels. Mentors can be people two or more hierarchical levels above the protégé (Raabe & Beehr, 2003), or can be their peer coworkers (Kram & Isabella, 1985). However, because of their position of authority and their proximity (both hierarchically and physically), supervisors often take on the role of mentor. In fact, research indicates that mentoring is an important component of the LMX relationship (Scandura & Schriesheim, 1994).

Mentoring research focuses on two primary forms of mentoring—formal and informal. Formal mentoring relationships are formally assigned "pairings" or relationships between one (the mentor) who is more experienced and knowledgeable than the other (the protégé). Formal mentoring programs are typically targeted toward new employees with the goal of facilitating their learning and their advancement in the organization. *Informal mentoring* refers to mentoring relationships that are not formally assigned, but rather develop naturally between the parties. These relationships tend to last "as long as the parties involved experience sufficient positive outcomes" (Jablin, 2001, p. 768). Jablin (2001) summarized research on formal and informal mentoring and reported the following conclusions. First, informal mentoring relationships are more likely to occur between individuals who are "visible" to one another and engage in frequent, regular communication. Thus, supervisors and peer coworkers are good candidates for informal mentors. Second, employees who are mentored (whether formally or informally) tend to experience more positive benefits than those who receive no mentoring. These benefits include greater understanding of organizational issues and higher levels of satisfaction. Third, although it is difficult to determine whether formal mentoring is more or less effective than informal mentoring overall, research indicates that protégés in informal mentoring relationships tend to receive more career-related information than those in formal mentoring relationships. Relatedly, research indicates a positive relationship between frequency of communication between mentor and protégés and the protégé's receipt of psychosocial benefits (e.g., adjustment, satisfaction), career guidance, and role modeling (Jablin, 2001, pp. 768–769).

While most research has focused on the positive aspects of mentoring, scholars have also addressed the potential negative side of the relationship. Ragins and Scandura (1997) and Scandura (1998), for example, note that mentoring relationships between supervisors and subordinate employees can become dysfunctional. Among the potential dysfunctional dynamics are sabotage, harassment, deception, and submissiveness. Mentoring relationships characterized by such dynamics, not surprisingly, result in negative consequences for the protégé such as lower self-esteem, decreased job satisfaction, higher absenteeism, and turnover. They can also have negative consequences for the mentor such as increased anxiety and jealousy. Along these lines, Ragins, Cotton, and Miller (2000) found that simply providing a mentor is not necessarily better for employees than not providing access to a mentor. Rather, mentoring effectiveness lies on a continuum, and the quality, rather than the quantity, of mentoring relationships in an organization is what determines the consequences of mentoring.

POWER AND INFLUENCE

Because hierarchy is a defining characteristic of the supervisor–subordinate relationship, much research has examined power and influence processes among supervisors and subordinate employees. Although a natural topic for critical research, relatively few studies have centered on critical examinations of power and influence in supervisor–subordinate relationships.

Early work in this area tended to be unidirectional, focusing on how supervisors control and influence employees. Early management theories conceptualized the supervisor–subordinate relationship as a power relationship in which the supervisor held legitimate authority to direct and control the subordinate employee's behavior (Fayol, 1949). Power was conceptualized as a relatively simplistic downward process in which supervisors gave orders to employees and employees were disciplined if they failed to carry out those orders effectively. Later theorists in the human resources movement, such as Mary Parker Follett and Rensis Likert, maintained that subordinate employees are more competent and knowledgeable than earlier theories suggested and not easily or effectively controlled through direct orders. They advocated participatory processes in which subordinates participated in decisions and exerted greater control over their tasks and work processes (e.g., Likert, 1961).

Conceptualizing subordinates as participants in power and control processes, many scholars have studied "upward influence" and identified several tactics subordinate employees use to influence their supervisors. The tactics fall into three broad categories: *hard* (e.g., assertiveness, upward appeals, coalitions), *soft* (e.g., ingratiation, self-promotion), and *rational* (e.g., providing rational evidence and arguments). A recent meta-analysis (C. Higgins, Judge, & Ferris, 2003) revealed that rationality and ingratiation tend to be the most effective tactics with respect to garnering positive performance assessments from supervisors and greater extrinsic success (i.e., salary increases and promotion). In a related line of research, Ferris and his colleagues identify impression management skills as a political tactic used by supervisors and employees to influence one another (Ferris, Hall, Royle, & Martocchio, 2004; Ferris & Judge, 1991).

Research also shows that employees with higher quality relationships with their supervisors have more influence on supervisors' decisions than do employees in lower quality relationships. Fairhurst (1993), for example, identified a number of communication patterns characteristic of high-quality LMX relationships that imbue the "in-group" employee with greater influence and power than the "out-group" employee. In particular, high-quality LMX communication patterns such as role negotiation, insider markers, and non-routine problem solving tend to minimize power distance between supervisors and employees. In contrast, communication patterns characterizing low-quality LMX relationships, such as performance monitoring, face-threatening acts, and power games, tended to maximize the power distance between leader and member. Fairhurst and Chandler (1989) similarly found employees in low-quality LMX relationships tended to rely more on powerless forms of speech than did employees in high-quality LMX relationships.

Scholars have examined the supervisor–subordinate relationship as a site of dominance and abuse. Research indicates that supervisors are perceived to be the most frequent perpetrators of workplace abuse (Hornstein, 1996; Keashly, Trott, & MacLean, 1994), including sexual harassment (Tangri, Burt, & Johnson, 1982). Much work in this area is grounded in critical theory. Several scholars have argued that sexual harassment from a (typically male) supervisor to a (typically female) subordinate is an act of power and control and carried out not for sexual purposes but to keep the women "in their place" (Bingham, 1994; Clair, 1993; Hearn & Parkin, 1987; Tancred-Sheriff, 1989).

As Sias, Krone, and Jablin (2002) noted in their summary of abusive supervision, workplace abuse refers to "abusive work interactions involving hostile verbal and nonverbal, nonphysical behaviors directed by one person toward another [Keashly et al., 1994; Tepper, 2000] with the primary purpose of undermining the other to ensure compliance [Keashly et al., 1994]" (p. 626). Specific abusive behaviors include intimidation (Keashly et al., 1994), public put-downs (Bies & Tripp, 1998; Tepper, 2000), being harsh in interaction and "hypercritical" of employees (Bies & Tripp, 1998), calling an employee "stupid," having unpredictable mood swings, and an obsession with obedience and loyalty (Bies & Tripp, 1998). Of particular relevance to this chapter, research generally indicates that employees perceive abuse as deriving from interpersonal interaction in the context of the supervisor–subordinate relationships (e.g., being put down), rather than from the larger organizational context (such as a high pressure climate).

Because the supervisor–subordinate relationship is a site of dominance, it is also often a site of resistance. Research in this area provides a number of insights into employee resistance to supervisory dominance and abuse. First, employees resist when an act of control or abuse threatens important components of the employee's identity (Ashforth & Mael, 1998). Whether or not resistance is effective with respect to ending the abuse or altering the situation, resisting represents a form of power that signals the resister's refusal to be victimized (Ashforth & Mael, 1998; Clair, 1998).

Research indicates that resistance rarely results in meaningful changes in the power relationships. However, the act of resistance is meaningful nonetheless. As Sias, Krone, and Jablin (2002) explained,

If what we resist persists, why bother resisting? What is at stake in a person's participation in the power-resistance "drama" [Clegg, 1994]? Identities are constituted in systems of power relations and supervisory relationships provide ideal places to examine the micropractices through which identities are formed, challenged, fought for, and sustained. In their everyday conversations, supervisors and subordinates make numerous identity claims that the other can honor or dispute. (p. 628)

Thus, resistance is an important form of identity construction for both the subordinate employee and the supervisor she or he resists.

The above sections discussed research on five important functions of the supervisor–subordinate relationship—leadership, information exchange, feedback, mentoring, and power and influence. Research in all of these areas is consistent in one way—the nature and quality of the supervisor–subordinate relationship strongly impacts, and is impacted by, these functions. The following section addresses how and why supervisor–subordinate relationships develop in different ways for different individuals.

Supervisor–Subordinate Relationship Development

The nature and quality of one's relationship with a supervisor or subordinate employee has important implications for both the individuals in the relationship and the organization as a whole. Employees with high-quality, trusting, open relationships with their supervisors tend to be better informed, obtain more useful feedback, and are more likely to receive useful career guidance than those with lower quality relationships. Supervisors who develop quality relationships with subordinate employees are better informed and receive more useful feedback than supervisors with lower quality subordinate relationships. The processes by which supervisors and subordinates develop their relationships are, therefore, important issues.

Studies of supervisor–subordinate relationship development began largely with the introduction of LMX theory, which maintains that supervisors form different types of relationships with their various subordinate employees (Graen & Scandura, 1987). Scholars sought insights into how and why some employees develop higher (or lower) quality relationships with their supervisors than do other employees. Such research indicates a process by which supervisor–subordinate relationships evolve from "stranger" to "acquaintance" to "maturity" status (Graen & Uhl-Bien, 1995). In the stranger phase, the relationship is characterized primarily by "role taking," wherein leaders/supervisors and members/employees behave strictly within the bounds of their prescribed jobs. After a time, one of the parties "offers" an improved relationship (e.g., the supervisor seeks employee input on a decision, or the employee shares increased information or performs tasks beyond his or her prescribed role).

Thus, role taking transforms to "role making," and the relationship moves from purely contractual (stranger phase) to a closer, more multifaceted relationship (the "acquaintance" phase). As the relationship grows closer, it enters the maturity, or "role routinization," phase where the relationship develops an emotional, rather than solely instrumental, quality. The supervisor and subordinate exhibit mutual trust, respect, and support for one another. Those who reach the maturity stage develop the high-quality LMX relationship discussed earlier. Sparrowe and Liden's (1997) model of LMX relationship development centers on social networks. According to their model, employees and supervisors who share a common social contact are more likely to develop high-quality LMX relationships because their shared contact implies a similarity between the leader and member.

Not all supervisor–subordinate relationships reach the maturity phase or develop into high-quality relationships, however, and scholars have examined the factors that impact this developmental process. These include individual characteristics such as ability, personality, race, and biological sex of the relationship partners. In addition, communication scholars have examined the role of factors that are discussed below.

ABILITY

Research indicates that the ability of employees to perform their tasks impacts their supervisor–subordinate relationships (Bauer & Green, 1996; Deluga & Perry, 1994; Wayne & Ferris, 1990). Together, these studies show that employees rated as better performers enjoy higher quality LMX relationships with their supervisors. Given the "social exchange" basis of LMX theory, such findings make sense. Employees exchange good performance for a good relationship with their bosses. Although fewer in number, studies indicate that the *supervisor's* performance and ability can also impact relationship quality. Bauer and Green (1996) found that the supervisor's ability to delegate was positively associated with LMX quality. Cogliser and Schriesheim (2000) found that the leader's ability to exert power was also associated with LMX relationship quality. Specifically, supervisors' expert power (e.g., having the expertise and knowledge to assist and train employees) and referent power (e.g., being perceived as competent) were positively associated with LMX quality. In contrast, coercive power, expressed via discipline and punishment, was negatively associated with LMX quality. Similarly, Farmer and Aguinis (2005) found the more power employees perceived their supervisors had, the higher the quality of their LMX relationships.

PERSONALITY

A number of studies have investigated the extent to which the personality of supervisors and subordinate employees impacts the quality of their relationships. Kinicki and Vecchio (1994), for example, found that employees with a high internal locus of control were more likely to develop high-quality relationships with their supervisors. Porter, Wrench, and Hoskinson (2007) found that a supervisor's "temperament" (or broad set of personality traits) was linked to employee perceptions of the supervisor's approachability.

Finkelstein, Protolipac, and Kulas (2000) found indirect evidence that subordinate employee authoritarianism is negatively associated with LMX quality. Specifically, they examined the extent to which employees engaged in "extra role" activities with their supervisor such as socializing outside the workplace. They found that the more authoritarian the employee, the less frequently the employee would engage in such activities with the supervisor. The authors reasoned that authoritarian personalities would be uncomfortable acting outside the boundaries of their traditional prescribed role. Given that one of the primary characteristics of "in-group" high-quality LMX relationships is role negotiation and change, the study of Finkelstein et al. suggests that authoritarian subordinate employees would be less likely to move to the "acquaintance" stage of LMX development because they would be uncomfortable accepting the supervisor's "offer" of role change.

M. A. Smith and Canger (2004) also found indirect evidence that supervisor personality is associated with supervisor–subordinate relations. They examined the extent to which supervisor ratings on the "Big Five" personality traits were associated with subordinates' satisfaction with their supervisors. The traits include agreeableness, emotional stability, extraversion, conscientiousness, and openness. Their results indicated that the more agreeable, emotionally stable, and extraverted the supervisor, the more satisfied subordinate employees were with the supervisor. In addition, they found that the less conscientious the supervisor, the more satisfied the subordinate was with the supervisor. The authors concluded that the links between agreeableness, emotional stability, and extraversion with satisfaction with the supervisor suggest employees prefer supervisors who do not "rant and rave." At the same time, the negative relationship between supervisor conscientiousness and satisfaction with the supervisor may "represent the profile of a popular, but unproductive, supervisor" (M. A. Smith & Canger, 2004, p. 477).

SIMILARITY AND DISSIMILARITY

While much supervisor–subordinate research has focused on the individual level of analysis (e.g., assessing the impact of individual performance, personality traits on relationship), a number of scholars have conceptualized and examined the *dyadic* nature of supervisor–subordinate relationships by examining the extent to which similarity or dissimilarity between the supervisor and subordinate on a number of cognitive and demographic factors is linked to relationship quality.

Engle and Lord (1997) examined the extent to which attitudinal similarity between supervisors and subordinates predicted relationship quality. They also examined congruence between supervisors and subordinates with respect to implicit theories/cognitive schemas regarding leadership (i.e., the extent to which they agree on prototypical leadership qualities such as intelligence, cooperativeness, etc.) and regarding performance (i.e., the extent to which they agree on prototypical performance criteria for subordinate employees such as hard working, honest, reliable, etc.). They found that congruence on these factors was positively associated with LMX relationship quality via the mediating effect of liking. That is, the more similar supervisors and subordinates were in their attitudes toward social issues, and the more similar they were in their views of appropriate leader and employee qualities, the more they liked each other, and as a consequence, the higher the quality of their relationship. They also found that the more congruent the supervisor and the subordinate were with respect to schemas regarding prototypical subordinate performance criteria (i.e., standards for good performance), the more the supervisor liked that employee and the higher the quality of their relationship. Thus, their study provides support for the notion that people like individuals who are attitudinally similar, and liking is an important predictor of LMX quality. Interestingly, they found that congruence regarding the *employee* prototypical performance criteria was more important than congruence regarding prototypical *leader* qualities in predicting liking and LMX quality, providing additional support for the previously mentioned notion that employee performance plays an important role in LMX relationship dynamics performance, and that "trait" theories of leadership are less useful.

Research also indicates that *dissimilarity*, particularly with respect to personality traits, between supervisors and subordinate employees can encourage positive relationships. In a study originally focused on similarity, Allinson, Armstrong, and Hayes (2001) examined the extent to which *cognitive style* similarity between supervisors and subordinates was associated with various aspects of the supervisor–subordinate relationship, including dominance and nurturing. Cognitive style refers to an individual's preferred way of organizing and processing information (Allinson et al., 2001, p. 203). Research indicates two primary cognitive styles. An "analytic" employee tends to "be compliant, prefer a structured approach to decision making, apply systematic methods of investigation, and be especially comfortable when handling problems requiring a step by step solution" (p. 203). An "intuitive" employee, in contrast, tends to "be relatively noncomformist, prefers a rapid, open-ended approach to decision making, rely on random methods of exploration, and work best on problems favouring a holistic approach" (Allinson et al., 2001, p. 204). Grounded in the attraction-similarity paradigm, the authors predicted that the more congruent the supervisors' and employees' personalities along these dimensions, the higher the quality of their relationships as indicated by measures including liking and respect for one another and the frequency with which they talked to each other. Their results indicated, instead, that the more dissimilar the partners on these personality traits, the more positive the outcomes. Specifically, they found that the more intuitive the supervisor was than the employee, the more the employee liked and respected the supervisor. The authors used complementary needs theory (Winch, Ktsanes, & Ktsanes, 1954) to interpret these results, explaining that "a successful relationship may be the product of reciprocal need gratification" (Allinson et al., 2001, p. 213).

Recent studies also indicate that personality dissimilarity is associated with higher quality supervisor–subordinate relationships. Glomb and Welsh (2005) examined personality congruence between supervisor and subordinate with respect to the "control" personality trait (i.e., the extent to which a person is passive and submissive or competitive and controlling). They found that the more "controlling" (as measured by personality tests) the supervisor was than the employee, the more satisfied that employee was with the supervisor. The authors reasoned that given the authoritarian and hierarchical nature of the supervisor–subordinate relationship, subordinate employees expect their supervisors to be more controlling than themselves and therefore are more satisfied when these expectations are met.

Finally, studies have examined links between demographic similarity and supervisor–subordinate relationships. Pelled and Xin (2000) found that gender (i.e., biological sex) and racial similarity between supervisors and subordinate employees were positively associated with LMX quality. However, age similarity was negatively associated with LMX quality, indicating that the greater the difference in age between supervisor and subordinate (specifically, the older the supervisor is than the employee), the higher the quality of the relationship. Similarly, Dow (1983) found individuals who were the same sex as their supervisor reported more trusting relationships with that supervisor than did individuals whose supervisor was of the opposite sex. More recently, Foley, Linnehan, Greenhaus, and Weer (2006) found that both gender and racial similarity between supervisors and subordinates were positively related to the extent to which the supervisor provided support (specifically, in the form of supporting subordinates' family-related needs) to employees. African American women, in particular, tend to experience lower quality (out-group) LMX relationships. The research on similarity helps explain this phenomenon. As Combs (2003) explained, African American women tend to have less access to the informal social networks that enhance one's ability to develop high-quality LMX relationships that extend beyond formal job requirements.

In sum, research indicates that supervisor–subordinate similarity with respect to performance, competence, and demographic factors is positively associated with relationship quality. However, *dissimilarity* with respect to personality traits can yield positive relational outcomes.

COMMUNICATION

Communication scholars conceptualize relationship development as a communicative process. As mentioned earlier, Gail Fairhurst and her colleagues demonstrated that supervisor–subordinate relationships are socially constructed during routine conversations. The differential nature of such conversations constructs differential relationships. Research indicates, for example, that high-quality relationships are characterized by communication in which supervisors and subordinates minimize power distance, using communication patterns such as insider talk, value convergence, and nonroutine problem solving. Low-quality relationships, in contrast, are constructed via conversations that emphasize power distance between the supervisor and subordinate, including communication patterns such as performance monitoring, face-threatening acts, and competitive conflict (Fairhurst & Chandler, 1989). Yrle, Hartman, and Galle (2003) also examined the ways communication patterns distinguish between various types of leader–member exchanges. Their results indicated two communication patterns that were positively associated with LMX quality—coordination and participation. *Coordination* refers to the extent to which managers coordinate activities with subordinates in a two-way rather than unidirectional manner, and *participation* refers to the extent to which supervisors invite employees to participate in decision making. These practices are consistent with those identified by Fairhurst (1993).

Communication also enables individuals to maintain stability in their supervisor–subordinate relationships. Strategy use varies depending on the quality of the supervisor–subordinate relationship (e.g., high or low quality). In general, in-group employees tend to rely on personal and direct communication tactics to maintain their leader–member relationship, while out-group employees rely more on "regulative" tactics, such as talking superficially, avoiding discussion of problems, and so on (J. Lee & Jablin, 1995; Waldron, 1991).

In a recent study that recognized the increased reliance of computer-mediated communication in the workplace, Huang (2002) examined the ways in which employee e-mail use was associated with LMX quality. Results of that study indicated a positive relationship between the frequency with which subordinate employees communicate with their supervisors via e-mail and their perceptions of the quality of their supervisor–subordinate relationships (as indicated by LMX quality).

Outcomes and Consequences of Supervisor–Subordinate Relationships

The nature and quality of supervisor–subordinate relationships is of great consequence, both for the individuals in the relationships and for the unit and organization in which the relationship is embedded. In general, research in this area examines the impact of supervisor–subordinate relationships on various indicators of employee adjustment (e.g., indicators of an employee's adjustment to the work environment such as satisfaction, commitment, turnover, etc.) and on employee performance and behavior.

EMPLOYEE ADJUSTMENT

The impact of supervisor–subordinate relationships on employee adjustment has been the focus of much research over the years. Research is generally consistent in demonstrating positive relationships between supervisor–subordinate relationship quality (typically measured as LMX quality or dimensions of LMX such as trust in the supervisor and perceived support from the supervisor) and *employee job satisfaction* (Gagnon & Michael, 2004; Graen, Liden, & Hoel, 1982; Turban, Jones, & Rozelle, 1990), *employee communication satisfaction* (Mueller & Lee, 2002), and *organizational commitment* (Gagnon & Michael, 2004). Research also indicates that supervisor–subordinate relationship quality is negatively associated with the employee's *intent to quit* his or her job (Graen et al., 1982; Vecchio, Griffeth, & Hom, 1986).

Recent research, however, suggests the relationships between LMX and these outcomes are not straightforward. Fix and Sias (2006), for example, found the relationship between LMX and employee job satisfaction a bit more complex. They examined the extent to which LMX is associated with *person-centered communication* (PCC), which refers to the extent to which one's communicative messages consider the perspectives of others. More specifically, PCC refers to messages in which the higher status party (e.g., supervisor) encourages the lower status party (e.g., employee) to reflect upon the complexities and contingencies in a given situation, define himself or herself and act as an autonomous, responsible agent, and develop methods for dealing with a situation (Burleson, Applegate, & Delia, 1995). These message characteristics are similar to the communication patterns Fairhurst (1993) identified as distinguishing high-quality LMX relationships. Fix and Sias (2006) found a strong positive relationship between employee perceptions of their supervisors' "person centeredness" in communication and LMX quality. Consistent with prior research, their results also indicated a positive relationship between LMX and employee job satisfaction. However, when PCC and LMX were both included in a regression model predicting job satisfaction, only PCC remained in the model as a significant predictor. This study, therefore, indicates that the previously identified association between LMX and employee job satisfaction is likely driven primarily by the communicative dimensions of LMX (i.e., PCC).

Recent studies by Harris and Kacmar (2006) indicate that the demonstrated negative association between LMX and intent to quit is also more complex than early research indicated. Specifically, they found while LMX was negatively related to turnover intentions for individuals in low-quality and mid-quality LMX relationships, the association was positive for high-LMX employees. In other words, employees who enjoyed high-quality relationships reported higher intentions to quit their jobs (Harris & Kacmar, 2006). According to the authors, this is likely due to the fact that high-LMX employees may be better performers, and receive more mentoring and career advice than those in low- to mid-level LMX relationships. Thus, high-LMX employees likely have more job and career alternatives and choices, many of which may be more attractive than their current positions. Low-LMX employees, in contrast, likely feel they have little option to improve but are motivated to quit their jobs to get out of what they perceive as unpleasant or even intolerable circumstances. Consistent with this, Morrow, Suzuki, Crum, Ruben, and Pautsch (2005) found a nonlinear relationship between LMX and *actual* employee turnover. Specifically, they found turnover was lowest with employees who reported "moderate" levels of LMX quality, and higher for those with low-quality and high-quality LMX relationships. Firth, Mellor, Moore, and Loquet (2004) also examined complexities in links between supervisor–subordinate relationships and turnover intentions. Their study indicated a negative relationship between supervisor support and employee intent to quit; however, they found that association was moderated by stress; specifically, supervisor support mediated the impact of stress on employee intent to quit.

In sum, while supervisor–subordinate relationship quality is associated with a number of important indicators of employee adjustment, those links appear to be impacted by other intervening factors, such as the supervisor's communication practices and the availability of job alternatives.

PERFORMANCE AND BEHAVIOR

Employee adjustment is linked to employee performance. Thus, it is not surprising that many studies have identified links between supervisor–subordinate relationships and employee performance and behavior. Studies also indicate that supervisor–subordinate relationships are also linked to supervisor performance and behavior. This research is discussed below.

A great deal of research indicates that LMX quality is positively associated with employee job performance, with performance assessed by both actual performance indicators and by performance evaluations and ratings (Brandes, Dharwadkar, & Wheatley, 2004; Graen et al., 1982; Keller & Dansereau, 1995, Vecchio & Gobdel, 1984). Relatedly, Michael, Leschinsky, and Gagnon (2006) found that employee performance was positively linked to the extent to which employees perceived their supervisors were supportive and provided the employees with frequent feedback. Similarly, Lester and Brower (2003) identified a positive relationship between employees' performance and the extent to which they felt their supervisors trusted them (another element of the LMX relationship).

Similar to research examining the link between relationships and employee adjustment, however, recent studies indicate the link between relationships and employee job performance is not necessarily straightforward. Dunegan, Uhl-Bien, and Duchon (2002) found that the LMX-employee performance link was moderated by different task-related factors in different ways. Specifically, low role conflict, high role ambiguity, and high intrinsic job task satisfaction enhanced the LMX-performance link. In contrast, high levels of role conflict "constrained" or reduced the LMX-performance link. In addition, low levels of role ambiguity and intrinsic task satisfaction "neutralized" the LMX-performance link, such that LMX was not associated in any way with performance in such situations. This study highlights the ways the supervisor–subordinate relationship, and its impact on various outcomes, is embedded in a meaningful social context.

Another study suggests that the link between supervisor–subordinate relationships (as indicated by employee perceptions of the supervisor's supportiveness and directive behaviors) and employee performance is moderated by the duration of the relationship. Mossholder, Neibuhr, and Norris (1990) found that the longer an employee worked for the same supervisor, the less impact the supervisor's behavior had on the employee's performance. The authors interpreted this from an LMX perspective, suggesting the LMX relationship has its greatest impact on employee performance during the early period when the employee is "learning the ropes," highlighting the important role of supervisor–subordinate relationships in the organizational socialization process.

Finally, scholars have examined links between supervisor–subordinate relationships and a variety of other behavioral outcomes, including employee citizenship behavior and creativity. *Organizational citizenship* refers to employee behavior that is extra-role, discretionary, and "above and beyond the call of duty" (Konovsky & Pugh, 1994). It includes altruistic helping of others, conscientiousness, "sportsmanship" or accepting frustrations without complaint, and the like. Konovsky and Pugh (1994) used a social exchange perspective to examine influences on employee citizenship behavior. Their results indicated that citizenship behavior was more likely to occur in superior–subordinate relationships characterized by high levels of social exchange (specifically, subordinate trust in the supervisor). Similarly, R. J. Deluga (1994) and Wayne and Green (1993) found that LMX quality was positively related to employee citizenship behavior. More recently, Bolino, Varela, Bande, and Turnley (2006) identified a positive relationship between employee citizenship and the extent to which the supervisor liked the employee (an element of LMX). Taken together, these studies suggest that employees in high-quality relationships with their supervisors are more likely to perform "above and beyond the call of duty." It is important to note, however, that all of this research uses self-report data and analyses based on correlation. Thus, it is unclear whether the relationship causes the citizenship behavior or the citizenship behavior causes positive relationship development.

Supervisor–subordinate relationships are also linked to employee creativity and innovation. Tierney, Farmer, and Graen (1999) found positive links between LMX quality and the creative performance of research and development employees. In addition, S. D. Williams (2004) examined the links between a supervisor's directiveness (measured as "initiating structure") and employee creativity and found that the more directive the supervisor (an element of low-quality LMX relationships), the more negative the employee's attitude toward divergent thinking. These studies suggest that supervisor–subordinate relationships can enhance or constrain employee creativity.

Finally, although the vast majority of research on links between supervisor–subordinate relationships and performance has focused on the subordinate employee's performance, some studies indicate that relationship quality is also linked to the *supervisor's* performance. R. J. Deluga (1998) found that LMX quality was positively associated with supervisor effectiveness. More recently, Varma, Srinivas, and Stroh (2005) found LMX quality was positively associated with subordinates' evaluations of their supervisors' effectiveness.

Theoretical Perspectives on Supervisor–Subordinate Relationships

Supervisor–subordinate relationships are among the most studied topics in organizational research. As the preceding review demonstrates, we know much about these important relationships. Researchers have examined various important functions of supervisor–subordinate relationships, including information exchange, feedback, and mentoring. This research provides knowledge regarding the important consequences of effective and ineffective relationships, for employees and the organization. Effective supervisor–subordinate relationships are linked to employee adjustment indicators such as job satisfaction, commitment, intent to quit, and career progression. They are also linked to subordinate employee job performance, citizenship, and creativity, as well as to the supervisor's performance and effectiveness. Finally, we have obtained some insights into the ways supervisor–subordinate relationships develop and are maintained over time and into various factors, such as personality, competence, and demographic factors, that are associated with supervisor–subordinate relationship development.

Consideration of existing research from the theoretical perspectives discussed in Chapter 1 reveals that while this large body of work has generated important knowledge about supervisor–subordinate relationships, it has been guided almost exclusively by a postpositivist approach. The following sections demonstrate how examining supervisor–subordinate relationships from other perspectives would greatly enrich our understanding of such relationships and their role in organizational processes. Table 2.2 provides a summary of the key assumptions and goals of the various theoretical perspectives.

POSTPOSITIVIST PERSPECTIVE

As noted in Table 2.2, postpositivist studies of workplace relationships assume human beings are observable physical objects who occupy a physical space or context (i.e., social relationships and the larger organization). These objects influence, and are influenced by, those contexts. Because the reality of the relationship and organization transcend our direct perceptions, researchers look to observable indicators of that reality via self-report data regarding attitudes and behavior. Thus, postpositivists examine observable indicators of reality such as self-report assessments, observations of communication, and the like. With few exceptions (e.g., Fairhurst, 1993), the studies reviewed above used self-report survey data to test hypotheses and examine research questions. The data include data regarding perceptions of the relationship (e.g., LMX measures) and self-reports of attitudes including job satisfaction, satisfaction with supervisor, commitment, motivation, and the like. Data also include indicators of performance, perceived effectiveness, and competence.

Consistent with postpositivist assumptions, many existing studies explicitly conceptualize supervisors and subordinate employees as physical objects and examine how the individuals' physical characteristics impact their relationships. Studies of gender in supervisor–subordinate relationships treat gender as an immutable physical characteristic, essentially using *gender* and *biological sex* as synonymous terms. Being a man or a woman or being of the same or different sex as your relationship partner has important implications for the quality of the relationship and the outcomes you may or may not garner. Studies examining the impact of age and race on supervisor–subordinate relationships are also grounded in the naturalist principle, conceptualizing individuals as physical objects that impact, and are impacted by, the physical context in which they operate.

The postpositivist line of research on supervisor–subordinate relationships tends to conceptualize such relationships as real, as transcending our perceptions, and as "indicated" by the data described above. Thus, to assess the reality of the relationship, researchers obtain self-report data from the relationship partners regarding their perceptions of the relationship. These perceptual data are treated as indicators of the "real" relationship. It is important to note that these types of data are valid in their own right. LMX measures, for

Table 2.2   Research Agenda for Supervisor–Subordinate Relationships

	Postpositivism	Social Construction	Critical Theory	Structuration Theory
Conceptualization of organizations	Real entities that exist beyond human perception "Contain" individuals Indicated by attitudes, behavior	Socially constructed Constituted in social practices Dynamic	Socially constructed Constituted in social practices Dynamic Systems of power, domination, and control	Socially constructed Constituted in social practices Dynamic Patterned social practices of organizational members across social systems
Conceptualization of communication	Occurs "inside" the relationship Indicates nature and status of the relationship	Constitutes social reality Constitutes relationships; as communication changes, so does the relationship	Constitutes social reality Constitutes relationships Essentializes and reifies organizational "realities" and relationships	Constitutes society and social systems Enables, produces, and reproduces structure Enabled and constrained by structure
Conceptualization of relationships	Real entities that exist beyond human perception "Contain" individuals Indicated by attitudes, communication behavior Predictive of outcomes (e.g., satisfaction, productivity, commitment) Influenced by physical environment	Socially constructed Exist in interaction Observable in interaction	Socially constructed Sites of power, domination, marginalization Sites of hegemonic, unobtrusive control	Socially constructed Constrained and enabled by structure

	Postpositivism	Social Construction	Critical Theory	Structuration Theory
Research goals	Measuring indicators of relationship quality and status Predicting outcomes of relationships	Understanding social construction process Understanding relationship development dynamics	Understanding social construction of power, reification, consent, hegemony, domination, marginalization	Understanding production, reproduction, and institutionalization of relationships
Sample research topics/questions		How do supervisors and subordinate employees socially construct LMX relationships over time? What "memorable messages" characterize movement from "stranger to acquaintance," and from "acquaintance to maturity" in LMX relationships? How do supervisors socially construct "invitations" to participate in high-quality LMX relationships? How do subordinate employees communicatively respond to such invitations?	How do supervisor–subordinate relationships become "reified?" What leads employees to perceive their relationships with supervisors as immutable and unchangeable? How do employees contribute (i.e., consent) to the construction and maintenance of abusive or dysfunctional supervisor–subordinate relationships? How does supervisor–subordinate interaction maintain managerial interests?	What is/are the prototypical qualities of effective and ineffective supervisor–subordinate relationships? How are these prototypes (i.e., structures) maintained, reproduced in leader–member interaction? How are these structures transported across time and context? What structures guide supervisor–subordinate interaction in different social contexts (e.g., different countries, industries, occupations, hierarchical levels), and how are those structures created, maintained, and transformed?

(Continued)

Table 2.2 (Continued)

	Postpositivism	Social Construction	Critical Theory	Structuration Theory
Sample research topics/questions (continued)		How do supervisors and subordinates communicatively transform an "instrumental" relationship focus to an "emotional" relationship focus? How do employees "accomplish" gender in their supervisor–subordinate relationships? To what extent, and how, do employees "match" their gender to that of their relationship partner? How do employees socially construct their "performance" for their supervisors? How do supervisors and subordinates communicatively increase/decrease semantic information distance? How do supervisors socially construct "leadership" for their employees?	How do supervisor–subordinate relationships reflect instrumental reasoning processes?	What structures constrain/enable same-sex and mixed-sex supervisor–subordinate relationships? How do institutionalized supervisor–subordinate relationship structures constrain and/or enable relationships between female supervisors and male subordinate employees? What structures constrain/enable gendered communication in supervisor–subordinate relationships? How do supervisor–subordinate relationship structures enable and reproduce gendered social systems?

example, assess the "quality" of supervisor–subordinate relationships, and quality is subjective, not objective.

Also consistent with postpositivism, the vast majority of supervisor–subordinate relationship research uses cross-sectional data, not longitudinal, repeated-measures data, offering a "snapshot" of the relationship at that single point in time. Such studies, consequently, either implicitly or explicitly conceptualize supervisor–subordinate relationships as static and unchanging. This is consistent with the postpositivist notion of a stable, immutable reality. Again, this critique does not mean the research is flawed or wrong. Indeed, such studies are valuable in that they provide important insights into the nature of supervisor–subordinate relationships and how they are associated with a variety of individual, dyadic, and organizational factors.

In sum, hundreds of studies over the past few decades have yielded valuable and important insights into supervisor–subordinate relationships. The vast majority of these studies are grounded in a postpositivist perspective and, therefore, informed and constrained by the assumptions of that perspective. Examining supervisor–subordinate relationships from multiple perspectives will greatly enrich our understanding of these important entities. The following sections detail a research agenda for the future using multiple theoretical foundations, including the social construction, critical, and structuration theoretical perspectives.

SOCIAL CONSTRUCTION PERSPECTIVE

The social construction perspective makes fundamentally different assumptions about reality and about human behavior than does postpositivism. These assumptions draw our attention to different aspects of supervisor–subordinate relationships and drive different types of research questions. As noted in Table 2.2, social construction theory conceptualizes reality as socially constructed. Thus, reality is not static, but dynamic. Social construction theory conceptualizes organizations as socially constructed, constituted by human behavior, and specifically by human interaction. Similarly, supervisor–subordinate relationships are socially constructed entities constituted in the interaction of the relationship partners. The relationship does not exist outside the supervisor and subordinate employee; it exists *in* their communication and is directly observable in the partners' communication.

Social construction research is concerned primarily with the social construction process—the process of creating, maintaining and transforming "reality." Accordingly, studies of supervisor–subordinate relationships grounded in social construction theory would provide unique and important insights into supervisor–subordinate relationship development processes and the ways supervisors and subordinates together socially construct organizational realities such as performance, evaluations, and the like. Social construction research would also provide important insights into the role of gender in supervisor–subordinate relationships that extant research on biological sex overlooks.

Extant research provides consistent evidence that supervisor–subordinate relationships are linked to a variety of important individual and organizational factors such as job performance, creativity, employee adjustment, and turnover. Accordingly, how and why supervisor–subordinate relationships develop in different ways for different people are very important research issues. Research guided by postpositivism indicates several factors are associated with different types of supervisor–subordinate relationships, such as biological sex, performance, supervisor power, similarity, and dissimilarity. This research, however, is based on cross-sectional samples and self-report data. Consequently, as noted earlier, we know only that these factors are associated, but we know nothing about the direction of the association, that is, what causes what. Even the work of Fairhurst and her colleagues (e.g., Fairhurst & Chandler, 1989), while grounded in the social construction notion that relationships are constituted in interaction and providing insights into the communication practices that distinguish high-quality supervisor–subordinate relationships from low-quality relationships, does not inform us as to whether the distinct communication practices cause relationships to be high or low quality, or whether the low versus high-quality nature of the relationship leads to unique communication patterns.

A number of social construction studies of supervisor–subordinate relationships could fill this void in our understanding. An ideal examination of relationship development processes would entail a longitudinal study of supervisor–subordinate interaction. In such a study, researchers would obtain interaction data (similar to the data collection process used in Fairhurst, 1993) at various points in time during an employee's first year on the job. Researchers may pay particular attention to data collected at those time periods. However, analytic attention should be drawn especially to points at which the supervisor–subordinate interaction becomes noticeably different; for example, at what point do supervisors become less directive in their interaction with employees, and at what point do employees begin to offer their own ideas, negotiate their roles, and participate in decisions. As important, from the social construction perspective, researchers would examine what such conversations entail, and how they "sound." Such data and analyses would provide rich insights into the *changing* communicative constitution of supervisor–subordinate relationships.

Additional insights could be obtained via protocol analysis. Protocol analysis involves having participants review their interaction (either video- or audiotaped conversations) and explain what happened in that interaction, what they were feeling at the time, and their interpretations and perceptions of the interaction event. In the study described here, researchers would have the supervisors and subordinate employees review their interactions (particularly at points where there is a noticeable change in the nature of their interactions). Participants would then provide their insights and interpretations of why their interactions changed and how that change impacted the quality of their relationships.

Given the many difficulties of conducting longitudinal studies (e.g., unrealistic time commitment from participants and attrition), researchers could address similar questions with different methods. One method is to analyze "memorable messages" that occur during relational turning points. As Graen and Cashman (1975) suggest, leader–member relationship development is marked by a series of phases moving from stranger to maturity. The move from "stranger" to "acquaintance" is marked by an invitation or offer of an improved relationship from one partner to the other. The move from "acquaintance" to "maturity" is marked by an emotional, rather than solely instrumental, quality, wherein the supervisor and subordinate exhibit mutual trust, respect, and support for one another. Social construction research could tell us what "invitations" to an improved relationship sound like and what type of communication moves a relationship from an instrumental to an emotional focus. To examine these dynamics, researchers could interview both parties regarding "turning points" in their relationship. Using the retrospective interviewing technique (Bullis & Bach, 1989; Sias & Cahill, 1998), participants would discuss the factors they feel caused the relationship to change at that point and the role of communication in accomplishing that transformation, that is, what memorable messages occurred to make that transition.

As noted earlier, many studies indicate that gender is associated with supervisor–subordinate relationships. Specifically, research indicates that employees with a supervisor of the same sex enjoy higher quality relationships than those of the opposite sex (Fix & Sias, 2006; Varma & Stroh, 2001). The postpositivist approach that informs such research, however, tends to equate gender and biological sex. Social construction scholars, in contrast, argue that gender itself is socially constructed. According to these scholars, gender is an accomplished performance (Allen, 2005), and organizational members perform femininity and masculinity in multiple ways in different organizations. Mumby (1998) for example contrasts the "technological masculinity" (characterized by technical knowledge, submission to authority, and workaholism) performed in an engineering organization with the "blue collar" masculinity required in a manufacturing plant (characterized by resistance and a clear separation between work and home). Liu and Buzzanell's (2006) case study of how a female employee who became pregnant negotiated her role, and gender, in the context of an already problematic relationship with her supervisor also highlights the socially constructed nature of both gender and organizations. Such approaches to gender highlight the ways men and women perform according societal and organizational expectations of gender role—expectations that are socially constructed and, therefore, socially transformable.

Social construction studies of gender and supervisor–subordinate relationships would provide important insights into the links between these two factors. For example, researchers could examine a concept akin to "gender matching," or the extent to which individuals perform gender based on the gender of the person with whom they are interacting. So, for example, a woman might "tone down" feminine behavior when interacting with a male supervisor or subordinate and "turn up" the feminine behavior when interacting with a female supervisor or employee. Similarly, men may "tone down" the masculine behavior with female counterparts and "turn up" the masculinity when interacting with men. Thus, a social construction conceptualization of gender as performance assumes men and women do not display gendered characteristics consistently. Instead, gender is dynamic and changes, perhaps slightly or to a large extent, across situations and across relationships. To examine these dynamics, scholars could obtain interaction data (video or audiotape recordings) of supervisors and their subordinate employees (similar to the Fairhurst methods) and compare those conversations with respect to gender stereotypical interaction patterns (e.g., feminine patterns such as hesitance, use of disclaimers vs. male patterns such as interruptions, certainty, etc.).

Social construction theory can also provide unique insights into the links between employee job performance and supervisor–subordinate relationships. With the exception of a few "objective" indicators of performance (e.g., sales data, productivity tallies), a supervisor's perceptions of an employee's performance are socially constructed. A supervisor's knowledge of how well an employee is performing his or her job depends in large part on what that employee, and others such as other employees, clients, and so on, tell the supervisor. As noted earlier, most supervisors and employees experience "semantic information distance," or a difference in perceptions of the employee's job performance and ability (Jablin, 1979). The larger the distance, the less congruent the perceptions. Many employees are responsible for providing information to their supervisors about their job performance (e.g., in the form of weekly or monthly reports, as well as informal updates). Most extant studies of the performance–relationship link are grounded in postpositivism and, consequently, either implicitly or explicitly conceptualize performance as objective and real. Using methods like those described above, our insights into these links would be greatly enriched by social construction studies that conceptualize performance as socially constructed.

In sum, social construction theory can broaden our conceptualizations of supervisor–subordinate relationships in a number of important ways. Studies of relationship dynamics and the socially constructed nature of gender and performance would greatly enrich our understanding of these important relationships. Grounded in social construction theory, critical approaches would lend even more unique insights, as discussed in the following section.

CRITICAL PERSPECTIVE

Critical theory and social construction theory share similar conceptualizations of social reality, organizations, relationships, and communication; that is, reality is socially constructed, and social entities such as organizations and interpersonal relationships are constituted in interaction. Critical theory expands on these notions by conceptualizing organizations as socially constructed systems of power and domination. The use and abuse of power and domination are the main concerns of critical research. The hierarchical nature of supervisor–subordinate relationships makes such issues particularly salient. Studies of such issues, however, are relatively rare (Sias, Krone, & Jablin, 2002).

As noted in Table 2.2 (and Chapter 1), critical theory addresses four primary themes—reification, consent, universalization of managerial interests, and dominance of technical/instrumental reasoning (Deetz, 2005). These themes suggest a number of important research ideas grounded in critical theory. Critical research could examine reification with respect to supervisor–subordinate relationships in a number of interesting ways. For example, current research indicates individuals are guided by "prototypes" of "appropriate" supervisor and employee traits and behaviors. The extent to which these prototypical qualities have become reified is a matter for critical research. As Mumby and Putnam (1992) pointed out, bureaucracy, and bureaucratic practices including rationality and control, have become so ingrained in organizational structure and practices that to "organize" differently is unthinkable or, at least, considered as wrong, flawed, and unacceptable. They argue that bureaucracy privileges masculinity and masculine behaviors and devalues femininity and feminine behaviors such as emotionality, collaboration, nurturing, and participation. This results in the marginalization of women, particularly from upper management positions. A critical study of supervisor–subordinate relationships addressing similar issues would lend insights into the evidence of many studies that women tend to report lower-quality relationships with their supervisors than do men, particularly if the supervisor is a man (Varma & Stroh, 2001), and men tend to report lower-quality relationships when the supervisor is a woman than when the supervisor is a man. If women are not portraying the proto-typical male behaviors expected of supervisors, they may be perceived as less competent and may be less "liked" by their employees.

Critical research could also examine how supervisor–subordinate relationships themselves become "reified" via the everyday communicative practices of the relationship partners. Such studies could examine a number of issues, such as the extent to which individuals perceive their relationships as static and unchangeable and how the communicative dynamics reinforce such reification. This is of particular concern for employees in low-quality supervisor–subordinate relationships. Examining the interactions of supervisors and subordinates, along with interview data of their perceptions, would provide insights into their understanding of the nature of their identity as a subordinate employee, their relationships, and the extent to which those understandings are considered to be "real" and "natural" and, therefore, immutable. Interaction data could reveal communication practices that reinforce, and reify, these perceptions. Knowledge obtained via such studies would provide important insights into the hopelessness individuals might feel regarding their relationships with supervisors and insights into ways such individuals might be able to transform those relationships and improve their situations.

Related is the critical concern with consent. While many employees find themselves in low-quality or problematic relationships with their supervisors, research and theory has not studied the extent to which employees co-construct those problematic relationships. Critical studies would conceptualize supervisor–subordinate relationships as dyadic phenomena socially constructed by both parties. Similar to the reification studies discussed above, interview and inter-action data would lend insights into the extent to which employees are unaware, or perhaps aware, of their consent to supervisor authority, and low-quality relations. Examination of interactions would reveal the communication practices that subordinate employees use to consent to the problematic relationship. Additional insights would be provided by macrolevel projects that investigate broader societal discursive formations that enable and engender employee consent to such relationships.

Critical theory can also guide examination of the ways supervisor–subordinate relationships serve managerial over individual interests. Research examining supervisor–subordinate interaction could provide insights into how communication between low-LMX employees may privilege organizational concerns, while interaction in high-quality LMX relationships may also consider the concerns and needs of the employee. Such dynamics are likely found in supervisor–subordinate interaction in the areas of feedback, appraisal, and information sharing. Supervisors, for example, may withhold information (e.g., rumors of layoffs or budgetary cuts) from out-group employees that may help the employee but harm the organization. The extent to which the sharing or withholding of such information empowers some employees and disempowers others is an issue for critical research. Comparative critical analyses of feedback and appraisal conversations between a supervisor and his or her various subordinate employees would be appropriate for such a study.

Relatedly, critical theory could inform examination of the privileging of instrumental over emotional reasoning in the context of the supervisor–subordinate relationship. Analysis of supervisory feedback, for example, may reveal how such forms of reasoning inform supervisors' perceptions and evaluations of employee performance, how such perceptions are communicated to the employee, and how that communication impacts future employee performance. Employees who are punished for demonstrating "emotional" rather than "rational" behavior at work, for instance, may be compelled to engage in greater control over their emotions (e.g., "emotional labor") in the future.

STRUCTURATION PERSPECTIVE

Like social construction theory, structuration theory conceptualizes society, and organizations, as constituted in human practices. Like critical theory, structuration theory addresses the processes by which structures and practices become embedded and function below the level of consciousness (i.e., reified). Structuration is unique, however, and studies of supervisor–subordinate relationships guided by structuration theory would provide a number of important and interesting insights to the current body of literature.

Table 2.2 summarizes the primary assumptions and goals of structuration and the types of supervisor–subordinate relationships research such a perspective enables. For example, a structuration study would conceptualize workplace relationships as *systems*, that is, as a pattern of social relations and structures that stretch across time and space. This conceptualization would guide an interesting examination of the supervisor–subordinate "prototypes" discussed earlier. Such a study would address questions such as what is/are the prototypical qualities of effective and ineffective supervisor–subordinate relationships (e.g., Fairhurst, 1993), how these prototypes (i.e., structures) are maintained and reproduced in leader–member interaction, and how these structures are transported across time and context. For example, LMX research indicates the stranger phase that marks the beginning stages of leader–member relationship development is characterized by relatively predictable communication patterns (e.g., task related, role bound, instrumental, directive). A structuration study would ask how supervisors and employees are "knowledgeable" enough to reproduce those patterns. Interviews would obtain data from the supervisors and subordinates asking what they perceive as appropriate interaction during the stranger phase, why such interaction is appropriate, and where they learned the prototype (e.g., from prior supervisors, from educational sources, from the media, etc.), and interaction data would reveal the structures supervisors and employees enact in their interaction with one another.

Structuration theory would also address system construction via the concepts of *time–space distanciation,* leading to research questions such as: To what extent are supervisor–subordinate structures (e.g., prototypes) transferable or context bound? What structures guide supervisor–subordinate interaction in different social contexts (e.g., different countries, industries, occupations, hierarchical levels), and how are those structures created, maintained, and transformed? Such examinations could provide new insights into the persistence of a number of organizational practices and patterns such as institutionalized power structures and gendered supervisor–subordinate interaction and relational patterns. Studies addressing these issues require obtaining data from individuals in different organizations and social contexts and at different points in time. Particularly interesting would be comparisons of management and organizational communication textbooks and popular press books over the past several decades to determine which management behaviors and skills have spanned time and space and which have been left by the wayside.

Conclusion

Literally hundreds of studies have examined supervisor–subordinate relationships. As perhaps the most frequently studied organizational topic, our body of knowledge about these important entities is vast. Yet given the limited theoretical lens used to examine supervisor–subordinates, we have much left to learn. This chapter has provided a lengthy, but certainly not exhaustive, research agenda for the future guided by multiple theoretical perspectives that will enhance and complement our current understanding of supervisor–subordinate relationships.

As noted in the preface, considering supervisor–subordinate relationships from a variety of theoretical perspectives is not only beneficial for researchers. It also draws practitioners' attention to various aspects of actual workplace issues and problems involving supervisor–subordinate relationships, enabling a richer and more complex understanding of those issues. Such understanding can help employees and managers address relationship problems in more substantive and effective ways. The following "Practicing Theory" case is designed to highlight the practical implications of multiple theoretical perspectives.

"Equal but Not Equitable"

When Rachel started her job as a financial analyst for the state one year ago, she was part of a cohort of six employees all beginning at the same time. They went through orientation and training together and developed a collegial and friendly work environment. Their supervisor, Brandon, was pleased with this group and the generally pleasant climate of the office. Of all the employees, however, Rachel was a standout. She worked harder and longer hours than anyone else in the office, and her work was the highest quality. Her competence was recognized and admired by her coworkers, who often came to her for advice and help with their own projects. She was a team player, and helped in any way she could. She loved her job and her department and was willing to go the extra mile to help the department.

March was the month for annual reviews of all employees. At that time, supervisors prepared detailed performance evaluations for all of their direct reports and made decisions regarding raises, promotions, or disciplinary actions, if necessary. And supervisors met with each employee individually to discuss their evaluations and decisions.

Rachel and her colleagues anxiously anticipated their appraisal meetings with Brandon. All felt they would receive good evaluations and, hopefully, decent salary increases. They all had different expectations for Rachel, however. Because her performance had clearly been head and shoulders above the rest, the group expected Rachel to not just receive a raise, but she was the natural choice for promotion to the next level, specifically, account manager. This position would present a variety of new challenges for Rachel, combining financial expertise with management responsibilities. Given that she was perceived as the informal group leader of her department, it would be a wise decision for Brandon, and well deserved by Rachel. Although her colleagues assured Rachel that this was a "no-brainer," Rachel modestly told them she had no such expectations, but would be thrilled with such a promotion.

The appraisal meetings with Brandon took place over 2 days during the third week of March. One by one, employees went to their meetings and returned generally pleased—each received good evaluations and a modest salary increase. Rachel was the last meeting scheduled. Everyone took this as a sign that her evaluation would be special. They were so confident, in fact, that they planned to go out and celebrate after work that day—drinks would be on Rachel, of course!

Rachel went into Brandon's office and sat down. The meeting went pretty much as expected. Brandon praised Rachel's performance, attitude, collegiality, and work ethic. He showed her the evaluation form he prepared on which he gave her "superior" ratings throughout. He told Rachel that she was, by far, the best employee in the department and, in fact, the best employee he'd ever supervised. Rachel was pleased and excited. Then Brandon told her that she was getting a salary increase. Rachel was shocked, however, when she heard the amount—the exact same raise that everyone else in the department received. There was no mention of a promotion. Seeing the look of disappointment on Rachel's face, Brandon explained, "Rachel, I know you deserve more, but if I gave you a bigger raise than everyone else, they might get mad and it could hurt morale in the department. I'm really sorry, but I'm sure you can see how this is best for the department."

Rachel left Brandon's office in shock. When she walked out of his office, her colleagues were waiting, anxious to hear the good news. She just looked at them in tears and walked out of the office. When she told them the next day about what happened, they were furious at Brandon and sad for Rachel. Rachel told them not to worry about her. As she explained, her meeting with Brandon made one thing perfectly clear: "Working hard gets you nowhere around here. My life just became a whole lot easier; I won't be working extra hours anymore. I'll just do the minimum expected, since it doesn't matter anyway."

Two weeks later, Rachel left the department for an account manager position in a private investment firm.

Discussion Questions

1. Why did Brandon treat all employees the same? Did that help or hurt the department?

2. Why did Brandon think Rachel's coworkers would be upset if she received a promotion and larger salary increase? Why didn't he know how they actually felt about Rachel and her performance?

3. If Brandon really believed Rachel deserved a raise and promotion, how might he have handled the situation differently?

4. What do Brandon's actions say about his relationships with the various employees?

5. Consider this case from a structuration perspective. What structures constrained Brandon's approach to employee evaluations? Rachel took a new management position. How might her experience with Brandon influence her own management style and decisions?

6. Consider this case from a critical perspective. How were management's and the employees' needs addressed? How instrumental and "rational" was Brandon's decision-making process? How did the employees contribute to what happened to Rachel?

3

Peer Coworker Relationships

While interviewing people for one of my studies, a participant, Dan, spoke about one of his coworkers, Luke. Luke had been dealing with serious marital problems. While Dan sympathized with his coworker, he also noted that Luke's preoccupation with these problems began to seriously distract him from his duties, both by causing Luke to miss work more frequently and also by distracting Luke from his tasks when he was at work. This, of course, forced Luke's coworkers, including Dan, to pick up the slack. In addition, because Luke's tasks affected the rest of the workgroup, Luke's distractions also began to harm the work of the entire group. Dan really began to resent the situation and this resentment eventually took a toll on his relationship with Luke. As Dan stated, "I lost all respect for him and even when he got his personal life back together I could never look at him the same way again." In fact, Dan began to complete tasks in different locations just to avoid contact with Luke. This, of course, made it difficult for both of them to do their jobs effectively.

Most people have one supervisor and several peer coworkers. Consequently, most of us spend more time with our peer coworkers than with anyone else at work (Comer, 1991). And many of us spend more time with our peer coworkers than we spend with our family and friends. The bulk of organizing, therefore, occurs in the context of coworker relationships. As Dan's story suggests, the quality and effectiveness of coworker relationships has important implications for the quality and effectiveness of employees' experiences and the organization as a whole.

Given their ubiquitous nature, it is unfortunate that these relationships have received relatively little research attention. The enduring hierarchical and authoritarian nature of contemporary organizations is likely responsible for the overwhelming predominance of supervisor–subordinate relationship research over peer relationship research. This is unfortunate because, as this chapter demonstrates, peer coworker relationships are of great importance to both organizations and the individuals who participate in these relationships.

Overview

Peer coworker relationships refer to relationships between employees at the same hierarchical level who have no formal authority over one another. The term *coworker* can refer to any individual with whom one works (including supervisors and subordinate employees). However, coworker relationships are often assumed to refer specifically to relationships among peer employees. For clarity, and ease of reading, I use the term *peer relationships* for the remainder of this chapter.

Peer relationships were largely ignored in early formal theories of management. Bureaucratic theory (Weber, 1946) and administrative management theory (Fayol, 1949) focused almost solely on hierarchy, authority, and, consequently, supervisors. Effective communication was prescribed as downward and formal, focusing on supervisors instructing, controlling, and disciplining subordinate employees. Lateral relationships and lateral communication among peers was considered largely unnecessary. Fayol (1949) granted that peer communication was sometimes a necessary evil to be used only in emergency situations via "Fayol's bridge," which referred to links between peers, if necessary. Otherwise, peer communication was assumed to be "chitchat" and unrelated to work. As discussed in this chapter, subsequent research reveals that non-work-related communication is *not* non-work related; rather, such communication in the context of peer relationships is strongly associated with work and a number of important organizational and individual factors.

The famous Hawthorne studies represented a major turning point in our thinking about peer relationships. These studies began as a typical "Tayloresque" efficiency study of production processes at the General Electric plant in Hawthorne, Illinois. Through a series of studies, Elton Mayo and his team made some surprising discoveries regarding peer communication. First, they found that individuals are motivated to work for intrinsic rewards such as satisfaction, enjoyment, and development, and these rewards are derived, in part, via communication with their coworkers. Second, when observing workgroups actually carrying out their work (in this case, installing wiring in banks), they found that employee performance was impacted primarily by informal communication among the group members, rather than by formal rules and job descriptions. Thus, the Hawthorne studies revealed what most employees already knew—people like to interact with their peers, and peer communication is one of the most important influences on employee behavior and performance (Roethlisberger & Dickson, 1939).

The Hawthorne studies sparked a great many "new" management theories that placed interpersonal relationships at the center of organizational processes. Human relations theorists such as Maslow (1954) and McGregor (1960) highlighted the links between peer relationships and employee morale. Human resources theorists such as Likert (1961) highlighted the ways employees each bring a unique set of competencies to the workplace and how, via interpersonal relationships, organizations could effectively "tap" their human resources to their fullest potential. Together, these two sets of theories placed peer relationships at the center of organizational processes and sparked a stream of research in the broad area of peer communication and, in particular, the ways peer communication was associated with a variety of individual and organizational "outcomes" such as satisfaction, commitment, productivity, and employee turnover.

It was not until 1985, however, that scholars explicitly examined peer *relationships.* In an examination of mentoring alternatives for employees, Kram and Isabella (1985) identified three primary types of peer relationships—the information peer, the collegial peer, and the special peer. Their study was the first to empirically examine peer *relationships,* rather than simply peer *relations* (in the form of peer communication) and the first to categorize different types of peer relationships. The Kram and Isabella (1985) study spawned further research in the area of peer relationships and provides the foundation for many studies reviewed in this chapter. It is described in detail in a later section.

In this chapter, I discuss peer relationship research according to three primary areas—functions of peer relationships, peer relationship developmental processes, and outcomes and consequences of peer relationships. I then forward a research agenda conceptualizing peer relationships from alternative theoretical perspectives. Finally, an applied case is provided at the end of the chapter to help the reader appreciate the practical implications of considering organizational issues from different perspectives. Table 3.1 provides a brief summary of research on these various themes.

Functions of Peer Relationships

Peer relationships provide a variety of important functions for the individuals involved in the relationship and for the organization in which the relationships exists. These functions include mentoring, information exchange, and social support.

MENTORING

As mentioned earlier, peer relationships are an important mentoring "alternative" to the traditional supervisor–subordinate mentoring relationship (Kram & Isabella, 1985). Kram and Isabella (1985) noted that at the time of their study, researchers tended to assume mentoring relationships developed between a young protégé and a more experienced, higher ranking mentor. They argued that a number of other relationships in organizations could provide

Table 3.1   Summary of Peer Relationship Research

Peer Relationship Functions

Mentoring
- Factors influencing mentoring relationships (sex, race, technology)
- Mentoring networks

Information Exchange
- Information-seeking tactics
- Peer relationship quality and information exchange

Power, Control, and Influence
- Coworker talk and control
- Peer relationships and concertive control
- Bullying and mobbing

Social Support
- Peer relationships as sites of instrumental, informational, and emotional support

Peer Relationship Development

Factors Influencing Peer Relationship Development
- Individual/personal factors
    Personality
    Similarity (demographic, attitudinal)
    Sex and sex composition of dyad
- Contextual
    Organizational climate
    Organizational culture
    Proximity
    Shared tasks
    Work-related problems
    Extra-organizational socializing
    Life events
    Sex composition of the organization

Communication in Peer Relationship Development
- Increased frequency
- Increased breadth
- Increased intimacy
- Decreased caution

Outcomes and Consequences

Employee Adjustment and Behavior
- Motivation
- Professional satisfaction
- Job satisfaction
- Organizational commitment
- Self-esteem
- Stress
- Turnover

alternatives to these traditional types of mentoring relationships, which tended to be relatively rare and difficult to access. In particular, they focused their study on peers at work. Their study revealed three primary types of peer relationships, distinguished primarily by the nature of communication between the relationship partners. *Information peer relationships* exist at a superficial level. Communication among information peers reflects a low level of intimacy and low levels of self-disclosure and trust and is limited to work-related topics. Information peers communicate primarily as required by their tasks and work responsibilities. *Collegial peer relationships* are characterized by moderate levels of trust, intimacy, emotional support, and self-disclosure. Collegial peers discuss a broader array of topics regarding work and nonwork issues. Collegial peers combine coworker and friendship roles in their relationship (Bridge & Baxter, 1992; Odden & Sias, 1997). *Special peer relationships* are characterized by high levels of trust, intimacy, self-disclosure, and support. Kram and Isabella (1985) describe the special peer as equivalent to a "best friend." Special peers talk about virtually any topic and at high levels of openness and intimacy.

These relationships provide distinct types of developmental *mentoring* functions and these functions vary as one's career progresses. The primary function of information peers, as the name indicates, is information sharing. In the early stages of an individual's career, information peers are key to helping the new employee "learn the ropes" and accomplish necessary tasks. As the individual's career advances, maintaining contact with information peers ensures that the employee obtains information and, therefore, is perceived by others as a knowledgeable employee, which helps that employee maintain visibility to higher ups. Although the information peer relationship tends to be rather superficial and limited in its scope, these relationships are crucial for an employee's ability to "network," "stay in the loop," and be an informed and competent decision maker; all of which are needed for career success.

Collegial peer relationships are more complex and multifaceted than information peers. Beyond providing work- and organization-related information, collegial peers provide feedback and emotional support to one another. In the early career phase, conversations among collegial peers deal with "evolving professional roles and job performance" (Kram & Isabella, 1985, p. 125). Receiving feedback from a collegial peer helps an employee develop professionally, rather than just stay informed. As an individual's career progresses, collegial peers engage in career strategizing and help one another gain recognition and identify "realistic advancement options" (Kram & Isabella, 1985, p. 126).

Special peer relationships fulfill the information sharing, feedback, support, and strategizing functions of the information and collegial peer relationships. They also, however, are characterized by higher levels of trust, self-disclosure, and intimacy and are even more multifaceted than the collegial peer in the breadth and depth of conversation. Although such relationships are rare in the early stages of an individual's career (Odden & Sias, 1997), special peers help at this stage by providing "confirmation, emotional support, personal feedback, and friendship," which helps the individual "acquire competence and confidence" (Kram & Isabella, 1985, p. 126). As the individual's career advances, the multifaceted nature of the special peer is particularly important in helping the individual deal with "work/family conflicts and with concerns about their potential and the extent to which they are willing to make commitments and conform to the demands of the organization" (Kram & Isabella, 1985, p. 126). Special peers also help one another manage "fears of obsolescence and processes of reassessment and redirection" that can occur as one's career progresses over the years (p. 126).

Having relationships of all three types provides individuals with multifaceted and multidimensional mentoring. A subsequent study by Hill, Bahniuk, Dobos, and Rouner (1989) supported the value of multidimensional mentoring. Their study of mentoring in an academic setting revealed that the traditional "mentor/protégé" relationship between an individual and someone of higher hierarchical status (e.g., a supervisor) comprises only part of an employee's mentoring and support network. Employees also benefit from receiving "collegial task" and "collegial social" support from their peer coworkers. *Collegial task* support refers to engaging in the exchange of ideas and working together on joint projects (e.g., coauthoring papers). *Collegial social* support refers to the exchange of confidences, consideration, and constructive criticism, as well as devoting more time and sharing confidential personal information with one another. As Hill et al. point out, the collegial task function is consistent with the collegial peer role, and the collegial social support function is consistent with the collegial and special peer roles identified by Kram and Isabella (1985). Taken together, these studies highlight the value of multidimensional mentoring from a variety of sources.

M. C. Higgins and Kram (2001) recently revisited the topic of multidimensional mentoring by developing the concept of "developmental networks." A *developmental network* refers to "the set of people a protégé names as taking an active interest in and action to advance the protégé's career by providing developmental assistance" (p. 268). This conceptualization broadens mentoring beyond a single relationship with the protégé's organization. Their conceptualization includes both career support (e.g., advice, sponsorship, exposure, and protection) and psychosocial support (e.g., friendship, counseling, confirmation, etc.). The authors theorize that employees' developmental networks vary on a variety of dimensions. *Network diversity* refers to the extent to which a protégé receives developmental support from different types of mentors, such as mentors from different areas of the organization and different areas of the protégé's social environment. *Network strength* refers to the extent to which the tie between an individual and that individual's relationship partner is reciprocal such that each provides support to the other.

Varying combinations of these two dimensions result in four distinct types of developmental networks. A network of a few weak ties (low strength) from the same social context (low diversity) comprises a *receptive* network in which the protégé is open or receptive to receiving support from a limited number of mentors but does not actively cultivate developmental relationships. A network with a large number of diverse yet weak (low-strength) ties comprises the *opportunistic* network in which a protégé is open to receiving assistance from various sources but is largely passive toward cultivating these relationships. A network of a few or even just one (low-diversity) mentor in which the mentor(s) and protégé exchange mutual respect, trust, and sharing (high strength) comprises the *traditional* network. Finally, a highly diverse network of strong ties comprises the *entrepreneurial* network of mentors who are "highly motivated to act on behalf of a protégé and who collectively provide access to a wide array of information" (M. C. Higgins & Kram, 2001, p. 271).

The above indicate that peer mentoring is important to an individual's career experience and progression. Access to mentors, and in particular to a variety of mentoring sources, is therefore crucial. Not all employees, however, have such access to peer mentoring. A number of studies have examined factors that are associated with access to peer mentoring, including individual factors such as personality, gender, and race, and the workplace contextual factors such as task requirements and technology.

Individual Factors

Research on gender and mentoring indicates the relationship between the two is complex. Many studies indicate that women are more likely than men to develop intimate, trusting, close relationships with their peers characterized by friendship (Cahill & Sias, 1997; Fritz, 1997; Odden & Sias, 1997). In addition, most of these close relationships are with other women (Sias, Smith, & Avdeyeva, 2003).

Because such characteristics comprise collegial and special peer relationships that are important mentoring sources, one might think women have an advantage over men with respect to access to mentoring. This advantage is mitigated, however, by the "glass ceiling," which refers to the difficulty women experience in attempting to "break through" to higher levels of management such that women remain largely unrepresented at the higher levels of management in U.S. organizations (Veale & Gold, 1998). Consequently, a female employee's network of mentors is largely limited to lower hierarchical levels. Men, on the other hand, have access to mentors at higher hierarchical levels, and as male employees' careers progress together, their peer mentoring continues. Thus, while men may have fewer close mentoring relationships, they are more likely to have more mentors at higher hierarchical levels. Accordingly, cross-gender mentoring relationships are important.

Such relationships are difficult to negotiate, however. Hurley (1996) identified some dangers associated with cross-gender mentoring. First, individuals involved in such relationships sometimes have difficulty maintaining appropriate levels of intimacy and instead cross the line into sexual harassment. Second, even when the relationship remains appropriate, others in the organization may misinterpret the relationship as romantic, rather than simply a close mentoring relationship. These perceptions can cause a many of problems for the relationship partners. As a consequence, individuals appear to be quite cautious about developing cross-gender mentoring relationships, and functional relationships of this type are relatively rare (Sias, Smith, & Avdeyeva, 2003).

Work Context Factors

The environment in which a mentoring relationship is embedded can impact that relationship in a number of ways. M. C. Higgins and Kram (2001) argue that communication technology, or the lack of such technology, can either enhance or hinder an individual's ability to cultivate and maintain effective mentoring networks by providing, or limiting, access to potential mentors. Physical proximity may also be of consequence. Employees who are physically isolated from others at work will have more difficulty developing relationships than those who are near their peers (M. C. Higgins & Kram, 2001). In sum, research indicates the peer mentoring relationships and mentoring networks are very important for employee development and advancement. Related to the information sharing component of mentoring, the following section discusses information exchange as a primary function of peer relationships.

INFORMATION EXCHANGE

As seen in the discussion of mentoring above, peer relationships are crucial sites of information exchange. A large body of work has addressed employee needs for information and the tactics and strategies employees use to obtain information. The bulk of this work centers on the experience of new employees. Grounded primarily in uncertainty reduction theory (C. Berger & Calabrese, 1975), these studies posit that new employees experience a great deal of uncertainty when they enter an organization. Many experience uncertainty about the nature and requirements of their new job (referent uncertainty). For example, a new faculty member may understand her teaching assignment but be unsure about other faculty duties such as committee work, advising, and the like. New employees also experience uncertainty about their ability to competently perform the tasks required in their new job (appraisal uncertainty). For example, a new faculty member may be clear about her teaching assignment, but unsure about her ability to teach those classes competently. Finally, new employees typically experience uncertainty about their relationships with their new peers and their ability to fit into the social network of the organization (relational uncertainty). According to uncertainty reduction theory, when individuals experience uncertainty, they seek information to reduce that uncertainty. Studies consistently identify peer coworkers as one of the most important information sources. Peers typically are the most knowledgeable about the tasks themselves. They also have greater opportunity to observe the new employee performing his or her tasks so they are likely the most accurate sources of appraisal information. Finally, peers are likely the most knowledgeable about the social network. Accordingly, much research addresses how and why new hires seek information from their peers.

In general, and similar to information exchange in supervisor–subordinate relationships (see Chapter 2), new employees rely on direct and indirect tactics when seeking information from their peers. *Direct tactics* refer to overt questions to peers while *indirect tactics* refer to a variety of methods, including indirect questions, hinting, observation, and the like. Regardless of the tactics used, new hires typically find peers to be among the most informative sources in the organization, particularly with respect to information about tasks and the social relationships of the workgroup (Comer, 1991; Morrison, 1993; Teboul, 1994). Research also indicates that, at least early on, new employees rely primarily on direct tactics when seeking information from peers. After a time, however, the new employees become increasingly concerned that continued questioning of peers may make the new employees appear incompetent and unconfident (i.e., seeking information incurs "social costs"). Consequently, new employees turn to more indirect information seeking (V. D. Miller & Jablin, 1991).

Information exchange among peers does not apply only to new employees, and it does not cease when a new employee becomes a veteran in the organization. Information exchange is a crucial part of the organizing process, and being well informed is necessary for both individual and organizational effectiveness (Spillan, Mino, & Rowles, 2002). Accordingly, information exchange is an important and *ongoing* function of peer relationships. The nature of information exchange among peers varies, however, according the nature of the relationship between those peers. As noted in an earlier section, information, collegial, and special peer relationships are distinct from one another primarily with respect to the communication that occurs in those relationships (Kram & Isabella, 1985). More specifically, the type of information exchanged and the nature of that exchange process vary. Information peers, as the name indicates, primarily exchange work-related information that is superficial, rather than intimate. These peers do not share personal information or personal feedback. Information exchange in the context of these relationships is limited to that required to accomplish tasks. Collegial peers exchange information in a substantially different way. Information exchange among these peers is task related, but also extends to nonwork and personal information exchange. Collegial peers share information with one another regarding their personal life. They also provide one another with feedback, both with respect to personal and work-related events. In particular, collegial peers will often exchange information regarding problems at work, rather than simply information needed for task accomplishment (Sias & Cahill, 1998). Special peers have unique information exchange characteristics as well. The information shared among special peers is virtually limitless, dealing with any topic—work or personal. These peers share intimate information regarding their personal lives and work lives. Special peers freely share their opinions and feelings about work-related issues such as problems with a supervisor or other peers (Sias & Jablin, 1995).

Not only does the type of information shared vary in different types of peer relationship, but so does the quality of that information. Using the Kram and Isabella (1985) peer coworker typology, Sias (2005) examined links between the quality of peer relationships and the amount and quality of information shared in the context of those relationships. Information quality refers to the extent to which individuals perceive that the information they receive is accurate, timely, and useful. Results indicated that employees with higher proportions of information peer relationships reported receiving lower quality information than those with higher proportions of collegial peers. Consistent with Kram and Isabella's (1985) claim that collegial peers tend to engage in higher amounts of trust and self-disclosure than do information peers, collegial peers appear to be more forthcoming with information; therefore, the information they provide to one another is perceived as more accurate, useful, and timely than information received from the more superficial and role-bounded information peers. These results indicate that employees with primarily information peer relationships are at an information disadvantage relative to their colleagues.

Interestingly, the Sias (2005) study found that special peer relationships were unrelated to information quality. Thus, although collegial and special peer relationships are similar in many ways, they also have distinct characteristics. A possible reason for this comes from research that indicates special peer relationships are often associated with problematic work environments. Sias and Jablin (1995), for example, found that special peers can become isolated from a problem supervisor, thus increasing the social distance between employees and supervisor. In a similar vein, Sias and Cahill (1998) found that work-related problems (e.g., an inconsiderate supervisor) can draw peer coworkers into closer relationships as their communication about the problems becomes more intimate and more frequent. As communication between the supervisor and employees decreases, information sharing between supervisor and those employees likely decreases as well. As a consequence, these employees likely receive less, and less accurate, information from their supervisor that they can subsequently share with one another. Thus, "As special peers isolate themselves from their supervisor, they may also isolate themselves from information, harming the quality of information they share with one another" (Sias, 2005, p. 390).

In sum, peer relationships are important sites of information exchange throughout one's career. The nature of an individual's relationships with peers is associated with both the type of information and the quality of those peers' exchanges.

POWER, CONTROL, AND INFLUENCE

While supervisors are assumed to exert control and influence via legitimate authority, hierarchy, and bureaucratic structures, scholars have also examined the ways power and control are embedded in peer coworker relationships. This line of research began, of course, with the Hawthorne bank wiring studies mentioned above, which were the first to reveal the power of informal group communication and norms over employee behavior. Subsequent research focused on relatively overt forms of power and control, such as French and Raven's (1959) typology of power sources including coercive, reward, legitimate, referent, and expert power. Pfeffer's (1981) resource dependency theory conceptualized power as control over critical resources such as money and budgets, prestige, rewards, sanctions, and expertise. With the exception of expertise, these theories privilege supervisors and others in positions of authority. It was not until the "interpretive turn" in the early 1980s (Putnam & Pacanowsky, 1983) that scholars began to focus on power outside the obvious authority holders, that is, unobtrusive forms of control and influence that operate in the "deep structure" of the organization. This move brought attention back to informal power and control.

Interpretive scholars study organizational power by focusing on "the relationships among communication, power and meaning" (Mumby, 2001, p. 595). *Power*, therefore, refers to the ability to manage meaning and is exerted through communication. In contrast to earlier conceptualizations of power as control over resources (e.g., Pfeffer, 1981), power is conceptualized as control over meaning. Kunda's (1992) study of engineers exemplifies this approach and is particularly relevant to peer relationships. He examined how employees create and manage meaning in their everyday conversations. His analysis revealed that these conversations, rather than being simply idle chitchat, are important sites of meaning creation and meaning management, in other words, organizational power. Kunda's study shows "how organizing is produced in the moment to moment, as members 'do' meetings, engage in hallway talk, and tell stories" (Mumby, 2001, p. 595). As peers engage in such interaction, they develop and maintain relationships. From this perspective, exerting control requires access to these sites of organizing; or, put differently, exerting control requires participating in peer relationships.

Barker (1993) examined control and influence in self-managing teams. In particular, he examined how a self-managing team developed normative rules that functioned as forms of *concertive control*. In contrast to bureaucratic, authoritarian, and technological forms of control, concertive control emerges from the employees. As Barker explains, "Workers achieve concertive control by reaching a negotiated consensus on how to shape their behavior according to a set of core values found in a corporate vision statement. In a sense, concertive control reflects the adoption of a new substantive rationality, a new set of consensual values, by the organization and its members" (p. 411). Concertive control, then, is a particularly powerful form of control created and maintained by the workers themselves via socially constructed normative rules and "rationalities." Barker's ethnographic study followed a self-managing team as it developed such rules over three phases. Phase 1 involved *consolidation and value consensus*. In this phase, employees explicitly articulated mission and value statements, and over several conversations, the coworkers achieved consensual agreement on these rules. Phase 2 represented the *emergence of normative rules*. During this phase, employees focused on enforcing the normative rules, rather than on creating and building consensus around those rules. This phase involved "peer pressure" among the coworkers to ensure adherence to the norms. Phase 3 represented *stabilization and formalization of rules*. In this phase, the previously informal normative rules became rigid and formalized, essentially "bureaucratized." This study reveals the control embedded in peer relationships as the peers socially construct normative rules and "substantive rationalities" via their interaction with one another.

Finally, scholars have increasingly turned their attention to the abuse of power in peer relationships by examining workplace bullying and "mobbing." *Bullying* is a dyadic phenomenon in which a bully repeatedly continually harasses and abuses a specific victim. Such abusive behaviors include verbal abuse, undermining the victim's work, and belittling the victim (R. T. Lee & Brotheridge, 2006). *Mobbing* is basically a group version of bullying that involves a group of people "ganging up" on a victim. Employees who mob a coworker actively seek out communication with the victim with the intent to torment, hurt, and frustrate, rather than simply ignore, the victim (Einarsen, 2000). Moreover, mobbing is a "long-lasting, escalated conflict with frequent harassing actions systematically aimed at a target person" (Zapf, 1999, p. 70). Mobbing occurs in many forms, including threats to the victim's professional status (e.g., belittlement), threats to the target's personal status (e.g., teasing and humiliation), intentional marginalization and isolation, and destabilization, such as repeatedly mentioning mistakes or blunders (Djurkovic, McCormack, & Casimir, 2005; Girardi, Monaco, Prestigiacomo, & Talamo, 2007).

A number of factors are associated with the likelihood an employee will be bullied or mobbed by his or her coworkers. Research suggests that homosexual employees are among the more likely targets of ostracism, and these individuals experience a great deal of anxiety regarding whether or not to "come out" at work (Day & Schoenrade, 1997; Embrick, Walther, & Wickens, 2007). Employees from ethnic and racial minorities are more vulnerable to ostracism than are majority employees, particularly in the form of mobbing. One of the reasons for this is that mobbing can be motivated by racism. However, as Hodson, Roscigno, and Lopez (2006) explain, "Workplace bullies often attempt to socially isolate and ostracize their victims. This may be easier in the case of minority workers because these workers already face a certain degree of isolation from majority groups" (p. 386). For similar reasons, employees are often ostracized because of a physical disability (Zapf, 1999).

Various elements of the organizational context can enable or even encourage ostracism bullying and mobbing. Zapf (1999), for example, found that employees who reported working in conditions of *organizational uncertainty* and high levels of *work stress* were significantly more likely to report being bullied or mobbed than those working in healthier environments. Hodson et al. (2006) likened some organizational environments to "pressure cookers" in which mobbing can thrive. In particular, organizations characterized by high levels of *job insecurity* and uncertainty can decrease trust among employees and increase feeling of powerlessness and conflict. These, in turn, can lead to intimidation and bullying among those employees (Hearn & Parkin, 1987; Hodson et al., 2006). *Chaotic* organizations also provide fertile environments for ostracism in the form of bullying and mobbing. Chaotic organizations are those in which production processes lack coherence, are not well integrated, and in which all processes lack organization. Such environments tend to "depress citizenship and spark worker revolt" (Hodson et al., 2006, p. 388). As Hodson et al. (2006) explain, "in the chaotic workplace, bullies may feel free to intimidate and belittle others at will" (p. 388). Similarly, Leymann (1996) notes that mobbing can thrive in organizations with poorly organized production processes and oversight.

Adopting a critical and structuration stance, Lutgen-Sandvik (2006) examined the ways victims enacted their agency and resisted bullying. Her analysis of narratives obtained from bullying victims revealed five primary forms of resistance. *Exodus* refers to quitting, threatening to quit, or requesting a transfer. *Collective voice* refers to talking with other coworkers and seeking advice on how to deal with the situation. In these conversations, employees socially constructed the bully as cruel, crazy, and/or unfair. Thus, these conversations produced both knowledge (in the form of advice) and support. *Reverse discourse* "turned repressive practices and language to liberating advantages" (Lutgen-Sandvik, 2006, p. 416). With this strategy, victims appropriated or co-opted controls or labels by producing alternative meanings. For example, victims referred to themselves as "troublemakers," as a preferred identity (e.g., someone who stands up for what she or he believes in). Other tactics under this category included making use of formal and informal grievance procedures, and seeking help from others who were influential or experts (e.g., lawyers, EEOC staff, etc.). Finally, retaining written documentation of bullying incidents empowered victims as they pursued a positive outcome.

SOCIAL SUPPORT

Organizational life can be stressful. Beyond bullying and mobbing, individuals experience stress from a number of sources, including the work itself and the organizational environment. Work overload or underload, role ambiguity, and role conflict are just a few of the stressors employees experience from their tasks (K. I. Miller, Ellis, Zook, & Lyles, 1990). Emotional labor is another source of task-related stress. *Emotional labor* refers to work in which employees are required to display certain mandated emotions and, in contrast, hide nonmandated emotions (Hochschild, 1983). Flight attendants, for example, are required to display a calm and pleasant demeanor, regardless of whether or not they feel calm and pleasant (Murphy, 1998). Such management of emotions is stressful and can result in mental and physical exhaustion (Rafaeli & Sutton, 1987). Stress also comes from the work environment as employees deal with workplace politics, conflict, change, and uncertainty (Frost, 2004; Persoff & Siegel, 1998).

Regardless of its source, workplace stress is associated with a number of negative consequences, including low morale, physical and mental health problems, absenteeism, turnover, and decreased productivity (Blau, 1981; LaRocco, House, & French, 1980). Consequently, employees attempt to relieve stress by seeking social support from others. *Social support* refers to verbal and nonverbal communication between receiver and provider that reduces uncertainty about a situation, one's self, another, or a relationship, and enhances the perception of control over one's life (Albrecht & Adelman, 1987). Research indicates individuals rely on three primary types of social support. *Instrumental support* refers to more tangible forms of help such as providing services and material assistance (e.g., helping someone find the copy machine on their first day of work). *Informational support* refers to providing information and advice. *Emotional support* refers to venting or providing consolation to someone, for example, helping a peer get through a difficult time with a boss by listening and offering support and consolation (House, 1971).

Having access to sufficient support is important for individual and organizational well-being. As Eisenberg and Goodall (2004) note, access to a network of support is necessary for dealing with work-related stress. Research consistently demonstrates that peers are among the most effective support sources for organizational members. Peers offer a unique type of support—support that a family member cannot provide with the same knowledge and understanding and, in fact, when faced with a work-related problem, employees often turn to peers first for support (Cahill & Sias, 1997).

One's access to social support is dependent, however, on one's relationships with peers. As seen in the preceding section, peers are important sources of informational support as they provide crucial information to one another. Peers of all types provide information; however, as Sias (2005) found, the quality of that information is strongly associated with the quality of the peers' relationships. Similarly, the quality of informational support an employee receives from peers depends on the quality of that employee's relationships with those peers. While information peers provide task-related information to one another, collegial and special peers provide more intimate, multifaceted, and substantial information to one another (Kram & Isabella, 1985). Not surprisingly, then, providing informational, and in particular emotional, support are important functions of the collegial and special peer relationships.

Persoff & Siegel (1998) found peer relationships to be crucial sites of support for employees experiencing stress resulting from a corporate merger. Their results provide interesting insights into the role of peer relationships during times of uncertainty. Specifically, they found peer relationships play a pivotal role in reducing stress via information exchange (i.e., informational support). They also found, however, that peer relationships provided a number of "psychosocial" functions that were of even greater value in helping employees deal with the stress of the merger. Among these psychosocial functions were mutual support, collaboration, confirmation, and the provision of emotional support. This social support resulted in decreased stress and anxiety, and increased learning for the employees (Persoff & Siegel, 1998).

In sum, peer relationships fulfill a number of functions, including mentoring, information exchange, and social support. The effectiveness of those functions is associated with the quality of the relationships. Understanding how and why peer relationships develop is, therefore, an important concern. These developmental processes are discussed in the following section.

Peer Relationship Development

The nature and quality of one's relationships with peers has important implications for both the individuals in the relationship and the organization as a whole. As discussed above, employees with high-quality and functional peer relationships are more likely to receive effective mentoring, are better informed, and have greater access to effective networks of support in the workplace. The processes by which peers develop relationships with one another is, therefore, an important issue.

As noted earlier, virtually all peer relationships begin as *information peer* relationships. However, not all peer relationships remain information peer relationships. Many develop into more intimate, multifaceted relationships such as collegial or special peer relationships. Research indicates that an individual employee's highest proportion of peer relationships is likely comprised of information peers. Collegial peers are typically the second highest proportion, and special peer relationships are the most rare (Fritz, 1997; Odden &

Sias, 1997). This is likely due to the fact that time and effort are required to develop and maintain collegial and special peer relationships.

Odden and Sias (1997) used the Kram and Isabella typology to examine links between peer relationship development and the organizational climate. Results indicated that climates perceived as highly "cohesive" were related to larger proportions of collegial and special peer relationships, and lower proportions of information peer relationships. Thus, a high proportion of collegial and special peer relationships may be indicative of an organization in which employees like one another, get along well, and help each other out. "Supervisor consideration" (i.e., the extent to which employees perceived their supervisor to be supportive, trustworthy, and fair) was negatively related to special peer relationships. In other words, higher proportions of special peer relationships were more likely to be found in organizations with problematic supervisors.

Along these lines, Sias and Jablin (1995) found that peers often increased their interaction and became closer when their supervisor treated employees unfairly. Thus, while Kram and Isabella (1985) suggest that special peers act as "sounding boards" or places in which to vent problems, in particular, special peers may act as confidantes with whom to discuss troubling dimensions of the superior–subordinate relationship and may, therefore, be likely to develop in problematic work environments (Odden & Sias, 1997; Sias & Jablin, 1995).

Sias and Cahill (1998) examined the ways peers become friends. Although this study is not grounded in the Kram and Isabella (1985) typology, it does provide some insights into how information peers develop the friendly characteristics of collegial peers and the close friendship that characterizes special peer relationships (see also Chapter 4 of this volume). Sias and Cahill (1998) found that peer relationships develop into friendships due to individual and contextual factors. Specifically, individuals became closer when they perceived they were demographically and/or attitudinally similar to one another and when they enjoyed each other's personalities (although research has not yet identified specific personality factors associated with peer relationship development). Peers who worked in close physical proximity (e.g., had desks, offices, or work stations near each other) or who worked on projects together were also more likely to become friends. Finally, consistent with the research discussed in the preceding paragraphs, Sias and Cahill (1998) also found that work-related problems, such as problems with the supervisor or other peers, often propelled peer relationships toward closer levels.

As Sias and Cahill (1998) noted, proximity and shared tasks provided the coworkers opportunities for interaction. Perceptions of similarity and liking provided the coworkers with motivation to interact with one another. And work-related problems created stress and uncertainty for employees for which they sought support via interaction with peers. As the peers interacted, their communication changed. Specifically, as their relationship developed, communication among peers became broader, more likely to address nonwork topics, be more intimate, and be less cautious. The changes in communication effectively changed the relationship.

In an interesting study that examined peer relationships through a critical lens, Ashcraft (2000) examined relationships in a "feminist" organization—that is, an organization comprised primarily of female employees with an explicit commitment to "feminine" ways of organizing values such as collaboration and emphasizing interpersonal relationships, in contrast to bureaucratic and more masculine approaches such as rationality and the bifurcation of work and personal relationships. The study examined how the culture of the organization strongly encouraged the formation of close personal relationships among employees. However, a variety of consequences associated with those relationships (e.g., politics, competition, favoritism) resulted in the organization embracing a more bureaucratic approach that explicitly banned friendships and romantic relationships among staff members. This study highlighted the ways peer relationships both influence, and are influenced by, the organizational culture.

In addition to the relational and contextual factors discussed above, a number of individual characteristics are associated with peer relationship development, including gender, race, physical ability, and employment status. Odden and Sias (1997) found that women tend to have higher proportions of collegial peer relationships than do men. In contrast, men appear more likely to have higher proportions of information peer relationships than do women (Fritz, 1997; Odden & Sias, 1997). Similarly, in their study of work-related stress and social support, Cahill and Sias (1997) found that women were more likely to talk to their peer coworkers about work-related problems than were men, and that women thought talking with peers about these problems was more important than did men. Moreover, Fritz (1997) found that women and men differed with respect to peer relationship functions. Women rated socioemotional functions such as emotional support as more important than did men who, in contrast, rated engaging in outside activities as more important than socioemotional functions. Taken together, these studies suggest women and men approach workplace relationships with different orientations and, consequently, form different types of relationships with their peers.

A more recent study indicates the complexity of links between biological sex and peer relationship development. Sias, Smith, and Avdeyeva (2003) examined links between sex and *sex composition* (i.e., same-sex versus different-sex dyads) and peer friendship development. Results indicated that men and women did not differ significantly with respect to the reasons their peer relationships grew closer (e.g., information to collegial and special peers). However, the sex composition of the dyad did distinguish respondents' relational trajectories. Specifically, same-sex peer relationships were more likely to result from factors outside the organizational context such as important events in the partners' personal lives and socializing outside the workplace. Cross-sex relationships, in contrast, were more likely to result from workplace factors such as working together on projects and physical proximity. Thus, while same-sex friendships extend beyond the organizational boundary, cross-sex friendships tend to exist primarily within the workplace context.

At an even broader level, Ely (1994) examined how women's peer relationships were associated not with the individual's sex, nor with the sex composition of the dyad, but with the sex composition of the organization itself. Their results indicated that women in male-dominated companies were more likely to perceive their relationships with female peers as competitive, while women in sex-integrated companies (e.g., greater numbers of women in managerial positions) were more likely to perceive their relationships with female peers as supportive. This study and the Sias et al. (2003) study indicate that links between gender/sex and peer relationships are more complex than simply male/female differences in relationship orientation and development. Dyadic and organizational factors appear to be important components in these developmental processes.

Relatedly, Teboul, and Cole (2005) developed an evolutionary psychological model of workplace relationship development. This model suggests that humans' natural tendencies toward similar others, along with their needs and instincts for survival, adjustment, and adaptation, lead them to develop relationships with "high-preference partners" or HPPs. Characteristics of HPPs include similarity as well as placement and integration in prestigious hierarchies. Thus, individuals are motivated to develop closer relationships with people like themselves and who the individual perceives are well placed in prestigious and important social networks.

Outcomes and Consequences of Peer Relationships

The nature and quality of peer relationships is consequential for the relationship partners as well as the organization in which the relationship is embedded. Individual outcomes include indicators of employee adjustment such as satisfaction, commitment, and stress. Organizational outcomes include employee performance, citizenship, and turnover.

EMPLOYEE ADJUSTMENT

Peer relationships are linked to employee adjustment in a number of ways. Bottger and Chew (1986) found that the more satisfied employees were with their peer relationships, the more motivated they were and the more satisfied they were with their professional development and growth. Similarly, Sias (2005) found that employees' perceptions of the quality of their peer relationships were positively associated with employee job satisfaction and commitment.

Kirsch (2000) also found that positive relationships were associated with employee satisfaction and self-esteem.

Interestingly, just as peer relationships are helpful in coping with stress, these relationships can also be a *source* of stress. Such stress results from problems that emerge from the peer dyad itself, not from sources external to the dyad such as the task or workplace environment. Waldron (2000) identified several ways in which workplace relationships create rather than relieve stress, including tensions related to balancing public and private issues at work, "emotional buzzing" or the ways in which emotions regarding organizational problems and issues spread to employees via relational communication, and the conflicting loyalties individuals experience as they attempt to balance multiple peer relationships.

Fritz (2002) identified eight "troublesome" types of peers, all of whom were perceived by study participants to be unpleasant and create stress for the participant. These troublesome peers include peers who focus excessively on their personal problems to the point that their talk about those problems distracts from their work (the "soap opera star"). The "adolescent" is a demanding, controlling, self-promoting, and unprofessional peer who, in Fritz's words is "the prototype of an employee who has not reached professional maturity as a functioning member of an organization and whose focus is on the security and comfort of the self rather than on the community" (p. 427). Similar to the adolescent is the "self-protector" whose primary concern is his or her own advancement and self-interests. The "bully," the "rebellious playgirl or playboy," and the "abrasive, incompetent harasser" are all types of workplace bullies who cause a great deal of stress for employees. The "bully" is controlling and rebellious. This peer is also a type of "hustler" who gets other peers to do the bully's work. The "playgirl/boy" gives peers unwanted attention that is considered sexually harassing. Similarly, the "abrasive, incompetent harasser" is a peer who fears for his or her own job, sexually harasses others, and is perceived by peers as incompetent, unprofessional, distracting, and bossy (Fritz, 2002, p. 427). All of these types of peers contribute to a difficult, unpleasant, and stressful work environment. Thus, as mentioned earlier, while peer relationships are crucial mechanisms for coping with stress, they can often be the source of stress.

Related research on "social undermining" also indicates peer relationships can be a source of stress. Social undermining refers to "behavior intended to hinder, over time, a worker's ability to establish and maintain positive interpersonal relationships, work-related success, and favorable reputation" (Duffy, Ganster, Shaw, Johnson, & Pagon, 2006). Such behaviors include putdowns, insults, belittling, shunning and silent treatment, refusing to help the employee, talking behind the employee's back, and similar acts. Duffy et al. (2006) found employees who suffered such undermining behavior were more likely to suffer depression, lower job satisfaction, and higher intent to quit.

Research also indicates that peer relationships are associated with behavioral outcomes. Many studies suggest peer relationships impact employee turnover. Scott, Connaughton, Diaz-Saenz, and Maguire (1999) found peer relationship strength (assessed with measures of peer communication) was negatively associated with employee turnover. Similarly, Sias and Cahill (1998) found that employees with close peer relationships often chose to remain in highly dysfunctional work environments because they did not want to leave their coworkers. These two studies suggest that high-quality peer relationships are effective employee retention mechanisms, regardless of whether staying in the job is the best thing for the employee. In contrast, Cox (1999) found that peers also encourage one another to quit their jobs in a number of antisocial (e.g., berating peers, criticizing their work) and prosocial (e.g., informing them of better job opportunities, assisting peers with job transitions) ways.

In sum, research demonstrates that peer relationships are associated with employee attitudes, experiences, and behavior. The relationships an employee has with his or her peers can make organizations pleasant or miserable, and can "tie" that employee to the organization, whether staying in the same job is good for the employee or not.

Theoretical Perspectives on Peer Relationships

Despite the fact that most workplace relationships are peer relationships, relatively little research has focused on these important entities. Likely due to the hierarchical nature of contemporary organizations, scholarship has instead centered on supervisor–subordinate relationships. Those who have examined peer relationships have made important contributions to our understanding of peer relationships. Extant research provides insights into the types of relationships employees form with their peers (e.g., Fritz, 2002; Kram & Isabella, 1985) and the primary functions of peer relationships such as mentoring (e.g., Kram & Isabella, 1985), information exchange (e.g., V. D. Miller & Jablin, 1991), power and influence (e.g., Kunda, 1992), and social support (e.g., Persoff & Siegel, 1998). We have also developed a useful understanding of how and why peer relationships develop in particular ways (e.g., Sias & Cahill, 1998) and the consequences and outcomes associated with engaging in various types of peer relationships (e.g., Bottger & Chew, 1986).

Consideration of existing peer relationship research from the theoretical perspectives outlined in Chapter 1 reveals that, similar to supervisor–subordinate relationship research, peer relationship research is grounded largely in postpositivism. Consideration and examination of peer relationships from other perspectives would provide a much richer and more multifaceted understanding, as seen below. Table 3.2 summarizes these theoretical perspectives and an agenda for future research.

Table 3.2   Research Agenda for Peer Relationships

	Postpositivism	Social Construction	Critical Theory	Structuration Theory
Conceptualization of organizations	Real entities that exist beyond human perception "Contain" individuals Indicated by attitudes, behavior	Socially constructed Constituted in social practices Dynamic	Socially constructed Constituted in social practices Dynamic Systems of power, domination, and control	Socially constructed Constituted in social practices Dynamic Patterned social practices of organizational members across social systems
Conceptualization of communication	Occurs "inside" the relationship Indicates nature and status of the relationship	Constitutes social reality Constitutes relationships; as communication changes, so does the relationship	Constitutes social reality Constitutes relationships Essentializes and reifies organizational "realities" and relationships	Constitutes society and social systems Enables, produces, and reproduces structure Enabled and constrained by structure
Conceptualization of relationships	Real entities that exist beyond human perception "Contain" individuals Indicated by attitudes, communication behavior Predictive of outcomes (e.g., satisfaction, productivity, commitment) Influenced by physical environment	Socially constructed Exist in interaction Observable in interaction	Socially constructed Sites of power, domination, marginalization Sites of hegemonic, unobtrusive control	Socially constructed Constrained and enabled by structure

(Continued)

77

Table 3.2 (Continued)

	Postpositivism	Social Construction	Critical Theory	Structuration Theory
Research goals	Measuring indicators of relationship quality and status Predicting outcomes of relationships	Understanding social construction process Understanding relationship development dynamics	Understanding social construction of power, marginalization, reification, consent, domination, universalism of managerial interests and rationality	Understanding production, reproduction, and institutionalization of relationships
Sample research topics/questions		How do peers socially construct relationships over time? How do peers socially construct the relationships of other employees? How do peers socially construct "performance"? How do peers socially construct social support? What are the characteristics of effective and ineffective social support communication?	How do peer relationships become "reified"? How do peer relationships contribute to employee consent to concertive control? How do "victims" contribute/consent to peer "bullies"? How is workplace bullying socially constructed? How do peer relationships contribute to managerial concerns and interests?	What structures guide peer relationships? What structures guide information exchange, mentoring, and social support among peers? What structures constrain/enable same-sex and mixed-sex supervisor–subordinate relationships? What structures constrain/enable gendered communication in peer relationships?

	Postpositivism	Social Construction	Critical Theory	Structuration Theory
Sample research topics/questions (continued)		How do peers in cross-sex dyads socially construct boundaries between personal and work spheres? How do peers perform gender in the context of peer relationships?		How do employees become knowledgeable about peer relationship structures? What peer relationship structures span time and social context? How do peer relationship structures become institutionalized across time and space? How do current institutionalized peer relationship structures compare to those of the past? How do the media contribute to the institutionalization of peer relationship structures?

POSTPOSITIVIST PERSPECTIVE

Similar to research on other types of workplace relationships, peer relationship research is grounded largely in postpositivism, typically conceptualizing employees as separate from the organization and as physical objects who can be observed and who occupy and operate in the physical world (e.g., the organizational "container"). Postpositivists assume reality exists outside our direct perceptions, and tend to examine observable indicators of reality such as self-report assessments, observations of communication, and the like (Corman, 2005). As seen in the above summary of extant literature, the vast majority of peer relationship research relies on self-report survey data to test hypotheses and examine research questions. The data provide information about employee perceptions, attitudes, and self-reported behavior (e.g., peer relationship quality, job satisfaction, and performance), which, in turn, "indicate" the "reality" of the relationship.

Similar to research on supervisor–subordinate relationships, peer relationship studies also often explicitly conceptualize employees as physical objects and examine how the individuals' physical characteristics impact their relationships. This is particularly notable in studies of "gender" and peer relationships in which gender is treated as an immutable physical characteristic by operationalizing gender as biological sex. Several of the studies reviewed indicate that being a man or a woman, or being of the same or different sex as your relationship partner, has important implications for the quality of the relationship and the outcomes you may or may not garner. These studies, grounded in the naturalist principle, conceptualize individuals as physical objects that impact, and are impacted by, the physical context in which they operate. The naturalist principle is also illustrated in the many studies that rely on cross-sectional, rather than longitudinal, data to obtain an assessment or "snapshot" of the relationship at that single point in time. This method, at least implicitly, conceptualizes relationships as static and unchanging, consistent with the postpositivist notion of a stable, immutable reality. While such research provides useful insights into a number of important issues, it prevents thinking about and studying peer relationship dynamics and change.

In sum, while peer relationship research has yielded an important and useful body of knowledge and understanding of these relationships and their role in organizational processes, the literature is grounded primarily in a postpositivist perspective, and consequently, our understanding is constrained by the assumptions of that perspective. The remainder of this chapter discusses alternative conceptualizations and approaches to peer relationships that could guide innovative research that will enrich our understanding of these important entities.

SOCIAL CONSTRUCTION PERSPECTIVE

As summarized in Table 3.2, the social construction perspective conceptualizes organizations and relationships in a number of ways that contrast
with postpositivism, and these unique conceptualizations and goals suggest a
number of important topics for future research in the area of peer relationships. For example, social construction research would provide important
insights into how peers socially construct not only their own relationships,
but other organizational "realities." Using the joint conversation reconstruction (JCR) method (Sias & Odden, 1996), Sias (1996) examined how peer
coworkers socially constructed "differential treatment" and perceptions of
fairness in their workgroups. Using this method, the researchers had dyads or
small groups of coworkers reconstruct past conversations they held with one
another regarding differential treatment. Analysis of these conversations
revealed that employees typically constructed these issues as being the fault
of their peers, not the supervisor, and these perceptions had important consequences for their peer relationships. Studies using similar methods could
obtain knowledge regarding a host of other issues, such as how employees
socially construct the relationships of other employees in their workgroup.
Research could also reveal how employees construct the performance of
other employees, and themselves, which would have important implications
for formal evaluations and the potential for promotion and career advancement. During times of change and uncertainty (e.g., a merger or layoffs),
social construction research would be useful in understanding how employees construct those realities in their conversations with one another, which in
turn impacts attitudes and behavior such as absenteeism and turnover.
Similarly, Lutgen-Sandvik (2006) found that coworkers often discuss the
workplace "bully" with one another as a form of resistance. Social construction research could provide important insights into the communicative
nature of bullying, addressing questions such as how people interact in ways
that bring bullying relationships into being, how employees communicatively make sense of bullies and victims, and the communicative strategies
employees use to effectively deal with bullying.

Much research indicates that peer relationships are important sites of
social support. However, we have little understanding of what social support
"sounds like." Nor do we have an understanding of the communicative nature
of effective support and ineffective support. Many of my own studies (e.g.,
Odden & Sias, 1997; Sias, 1996; Sias & Jablin, 1995) indicate that peers often
turn to one another for support when dealing with a problematic work environment; however, the results of that support vary greatly. Sometimes such
support results in employees quitting their jobs, while other times, the relationships forged via such interaction essentially "chain" employees to the very

work environments they should escape. Examination of social support conversations would provide rich insights into why and how social support functions differently across situations and dyads.

Finally, as noted above, many studies indicate that gender/biological sex is associated with peer relationships in a number of ways. That research is limited in that it equates gender with biological sex, ignoring the socially constructed nature of gender and gender-specific roles. Our understanding of the links between gender and peer relationships would be greatly enriched by research grounded in social construction theory. Such studies could, for example, illuminate the ways peers in cross-sex relationships socially construct the "boundary" between work and personal spheres noted by Sias and Cahill (1998) and how that boundary may, or may not, limit the complexity of those relationships and the outcomes, negative or positive, of those relationships.

In sum, examination of peer relationships from a social construction perspective would guide scholars toward the study of a variety of peer relationship dynamics that have been largely overlooked to date. Critical theory, grounded in large part in social construction concepts, would provide further important insights. This is discussed in the following section.

CRITICAL PERSPECTIVE

Table 3.2 summarizes the ways critical theory conceptualizes workplace relationships as socially constructed sites of power and domination. Despite the fact that peers are equal with respect to *formal* authority, power, influence, and control are nonetheless important dynamics in peer relationships, making these relationships an important area for critical research. As in my discussion of supervisor–subordinate relationships (Chapter 2), I organize the application of critical theory to peer relationship research by referencing three of the themes of critical theory explained in Chapter 1—reification, consent, and universalization of managerial interests.

The process of *reification* refers to the ways in which socially constructed phenomena become naturalized and unquestioned. Critical research could examine reification with respect to peer relationships by examining how such relationships themselves become reified via the partners' everyday interaction. Such studies could, for example, examine the ways in which Fritz's (2002) various types of "troublesome peers" become reified—how does peer conversation consistently reproduce the "harasser," and how does such interaction prevent employees from considering that peer in different ways? That is, if one is "typecast" as a certain type of peer, to what extent, and via what processes, is that typecast unchangeable? Revealing the socially constructed nature of these "stereotypes" would be useful in liberating and transforming employees, in this case, liberating both the harassed employee and the harasser who may feel trapped by the bully identity and unable to imagine change.

Critical studies could examine a number of other issues such as the extent to which individuals perceive their relationships as static and unchangeable. To what extent, and in what ways, do employees with primarily information peer relationships perceive and reinforce those relationships as immutable, thus reinforcing their isolated role in the social network of the organization? Examining peer interaction, along with interview data of their perceptions, would provide insights into their understanding of the nature of their relationships, and the extent to which those understandings are considered to be "real" and "natural" and, therefore, permanent.

Related is the critical concern with consent. Concertive control is effective because employees work in *concert* with one another to exert control and discipline. By necessity, then, employees consent to concertive control by their willingness to engage in the processes described by Barker (1993) and others. Those studies reveal concertive control is enabled by communicative and discursive practices that encourage employees' consent to discipline and power. Critical scholars could examine a variety of other peer relationship issues through the lens of consent. For example, scholars have not studied the extent to which employees co-construct problematic relationships with their peers. For example, while scholars have identified characteristics of the workplace "bully" (Seigne, Coyne, Randall, & Parker, 2007), and of the bully's victim (Salin, 2003), no research in this area has examined bullying from a dyadic or relational perspective. Individual-centered approaches assume, either implicitly or explicitly, that a bully is a bully across contexts, and across relationships. Every bully requires a victim, however. Critical research could examine the dyadic dimensions and dynamics of the bully–victim *relationship* by addressing issues such as how bully and victim socially construct their problematic relationship, how bully and victim co-construct that relationship, and the communicative practices by which the victim consents and participates in his or her own victimization. Similar to the reification studies discussed above, interview and interaction data would lend insights into the extent to which employees are unaware, or perhaps aware, of their consent to bullying and other problematic and dysfunctional peer relationships.

Another theme of critical research that applies to workplace relationships is the managerial bias, or the notion that what's good for the organization/management is good for employees. Similar to supervisor–subordinate research (see Chapter 2 of this volume), much research has examined the "outcomes" of peer relationships, and the vast majority of those outcomes represent managerial concerns such as turnover, performance, and productivity. Even in the studies of employee adjustment, in which the concern is ostensibly with the employee, the assumption is that employee satisfaction, morale, and commitment ultimately benefit the organization. Critical scholars should question these goals and our understanding of the consequences of peer relationships. For example, while the ability of close peer relationships to "chain" employees to dysfunctional work environments may help organizations prevent turnover, it is likely very harmful to the employee. Critical research that privileges the individual over the organization would be very useful in "unpacking" these problematic dynamics.

STRUCTURATION PERSPECTIVE

Grounded in both social construction and critical theory, structuration theory conceptualizes society, and organizations, as constituted in human practices. In particular, structuration theory focuses on the processes by which social structures and practices are produced and reproduced via human action and, in the process, become embedded and function below the level of consciousness (i.e., reified). Studies of peer relationships guided by structuration theory would provide important and interesting insights to the current body of literature.

Considering the duality of structure as it is enacted in peer workplace relationships suggests a variety of interesting avenues for research. For example, scholars could examine how peers produce and reproduce the structures that simultaneously enable and constrain their interaction. New employee socialization research indicates that new employees enter the organization with a variety of "structures" that both enable and constrain their interaction with veteran employees. Such structures both inhibit (via perceptions of social costs) and encourage information seeking on the part of the newcomer. A structuration study could examine how new and veteran employees are "knowledgeable" about the structures that guide information seeking communication. Studies grounded in structuration theory would enrich our understanding of these processes by examining the structures expressed via conversations among new hires and veteran peers.

Structuration theory conceptualization of workplace relationships as systems or patterns of social relations that stretch across time and space could guide an interesting examination of the various peer relationship "types" reviewed above. Such a study would address issues such as identifying the prototypical qualities of information, collegial, and special peers and how these typical relationships, in the form of structures, are maintained and reproduced in peer communication.

Using the concept of time–space distanciation, structuration research could also investigate the extent to which these structures are transported across time and context, that is, the extent to which peer relationship types span organizations. Structuration research could also address issues such as how peer relationship structures today compare to those in the past and how and why peer relationship structures changed over time. A number of types of data could be obtained to answer such a question. Interviews could obtain data from the peers regarding what they perceive as appropriate interaction at the information, collegial, and special levels stranger phase, why such interaction is appropriate, where they learned the prototype (e.g., from prior experience, from educational sources, from the media, etc.), to what extent peer relationship structures (e.g., prototypes) are transferable or context-bound, what structures guide peer interaction in different social contexts (e.g., different countries, industries, occupations, hierarchical levels), and how those structures are created, maintained, and transformed. Data addressing such questions could be obtained from a variety of sources including interviews, observation, and texts such as textbooks, popular press books, television, film, and novels.

Conclusion

Peer relationships are the most plentiful, yet also among the most understudied workplace relationships. These relationships perform many important functions including mentoring, information exchange, social support, and control and influence. Like research on other types of workplace relationships, our understanding of peer dynamics in organizations is limited by reliance on a single theoretical lens. Examination of peer relationships from social construction, critical, and structuration perspectives will provide insights into important issues such as how peers socially construct their relationships, their performance, and other organizational "realities," how employees contribute to the reification of dysfunctional peer relationships, how peer relationship structures transcend time and context, and a variety of other exciting, interesting, and useful elements of peer relationship dynamics. Understanding peer relationships from multiple perspectives can also inform practice by encouraging practitioners to consider specific situations and problems in broader, richer, and more complex ways. Such consideration will cause practitioners to ask questions about the situation they may not otherwise consider and suggest alternative solutions. Toward that end, the following "Practicing Theory" case illustrates the practical benefits of multiple theoretical perspectives.

Strata Tech

Josh joined Strata Tech 6 months ago as a software designer. Strata Tech is a leading software manufacturer, specializing in inventory control software programs. Josh, a recent graduate from Boston College, was very excited to begin his first "real job" and looked forward to getting to know his coworkers—all young, bright "techies." His workgroup is comprised of five software designers, all of whom report to Sara, the department supervisor.

In general, Josh likes his coworkers. As the new person, they were all helpful when he first started at Strata. They helped him learn the ropes of the organization, understand the task assignment and completion processes, and showed him how to deal with occasional (and somewhat ironic) software glitches.

Josh has had trouble developing relationships with his colleagues however. One reason has to do with the pressure of the job and the business overall. All of the designers experience heavy workloads and work under serious and challenging (some might say unrealistic) deadlines. Josh typically finds himself working 10–12 hours per day and eating lunch at his desk. The idea of having a "break" is laughable. On the one hand, Josh likes the excitement, adrenaline rush, and even the anxiety associated with the job. He finds every day and every project a challenge and has learned lot in a just a few months—a lot of things he didn't learn in college. And although he rarely sees his supervisor, Sara has given Josh positive feedback about his work performance. On the other hand, Josh realizes he really doesn't know his colleagues very well. In fact, the other day, he realized that he spoke to only two of his coworkers the entire day, and that was only to briefly ask about a memo regarding health benefits that he had trouble understanding.

Josh is becoming concerned with the fact that he actually knows very little about his coworkers and about their projects. He doesn't know at any given time what anyone else is working on, how their projects might, or might not, relate to his, or how their performance compares to his own. He knows some basic information about their personal lives—Ashley is a newlywed and looks to be about Josh's age; Kevin is perhaps 5 or 6 years older than Josh, married, and has two kids in elementary school; he thinks Mike and Lorie are both single. But beyond that, they are a bit of a mystery.

Andrew is troubling to Josh, but in a different way. Andrew started working at Strata around the same time as Josh. They both appear to have a lot in common—around the same age, recent college graduates, single, intelligent, and hardworking. At the beginning, Josh liked Andrew and, given all they had in common, he assumed he and Andrew would become good friends. That friendship never developed, however.

Since both began working at Strata, Andrew has asked Josh a lot of questions about his work progress, his work experience, his productivity, and how many hours he works each day. Josh senses these questions are not friendly nor are they intended to build a relationship—typically Andrew enters Josh's office unannounced, asks the questions, and then leaves. And Andrew never talks with Josh about nonwork topics.

The other day Andrew approached Josh when he was getting a cup of coffee in the breakroom. He asked Josh some questions about how he was organizing material for a presentation on a new software design that Josh was due to provide in a couple of weeks. Josh obliged, describing to Andrew the format of his presentation, the organizing system he planned to use, and so on. Andrew seemed impressed by Josh's plan, and Josh was pleased with himself and motivated to finish the presentation. The next week, however, he overheard his supervisor, Sara, praising Andrew for his "fantastic presentation." Apparently, Andrew had presented his latest project to management that morning. As Josh listened to Sara singing Andrew's praises, he realized that Andrew had used the exact format and organization that Josh planned to use for his presentation the very next week! Josh couldn't believe it when later that day, Andrew came by with a big smile on his face and asked Josh if he wanted to go out for a drink after work, saying, "I've had a great day; wanna go celebrate?" Josh just glared at Andrew and said, "No, I'm busy tonight."

Josh is extremely frustrated and angry by what happened. And he doesn't know who to talk to, and what to do. He's concerned that if he tells Sara, he'll appear self-serving or, even worse, she may think he is trying to steal Andrew's ideas. He doesn't know his other coworkers well enough to know who he can trust with this information or who might actually be able to help him. So far, all he's done is stop talking to Andrew, which has done little to improve his mood or the situation.

Discussion Questions

1. What factors have impacted Josh's relationships with his coworkers? Why doesn't he know much about them? Why does it matter? Which functions of coworker relationships are effective in Josh's department? Which are not?

2. This case presents Josh's side of the story; in other words, the "reality" that Josh perceives. What might Andrew have to say about this situation? What factors might suggest he perceives a different reality?

3. Consider this case from a critical perspective—how are management and employee interests attended to at Strata? How do these biases impact the individual employee's experiences? How do the employees consent to management interests? How might they overcome these biases?

4. Consider this case from the four theoretical perspectives discussed throughout this book. How would you conceptualize Josh's relationships with his colleagues and supervisor from each perspective? What advice would you give Josh for dealing with this situation, guided by the different perspectives?

4

Workplace Friendship

Michael Eisner, CEO of the Walt Disney Company, and Michael Ovitz, the company's former president, enjoyed a long and close friendship—that is, until they started working together. Their friendship was one of the main reasons Eisner decided to hire Ovitz as Disney president. Their friendship was also one of the main reasons Eisner's decision to fire Ovitz 14 months later was so difficult and painful for the former friends. Eisner claimed that Ovitz's incompetence led to the painful decision to let him go. Ovitz was stunned by the decision, explaining, "I loved this guy like a brother. . . . I'm a fantastic loyal friend and I am a horrible enemy. . . . But I was this guy's friend" (Madigan, 2004, pp. 9-1, 9-6).

Friendships among coworkers are unique types of relationships. They develop both between peers and between supervisors and subordinates. They develop between people within the same organization unit and in different organizational units. They involve unique functions and developmental processes. They differ, for example, from other workplace relationships in that they are voluntary, rather than imposed—we do not typically choose our coworkers, but we do choose which of those coworkers to befriend. They also differ from nonwork friendships in a number of ways. For example, as Michael Eisner can attest, workplace friends must negotiate the very difficult boundaries between friendly supportiveness and the organizational requirements of objectivity. Moreover, when an individual ends a nonwork friendship, she or he typically has the option of never having to see the former friend again. Coworkers have no such luxury—unless one of the partners quits or is transferred, they must continue to interact with their former friend for several hours every day. Many of us have heard people make statements like Ovitz's when disappointed by the actions of a friend at work. Perhaps we've even been the one to exclaim to a coworker, "But I thought we were friends!"

In this chapter, I discuss the relatively recent scholarship on workplace friendship. First, I provide an overview of workplace friendship, explaining the defining characteristics of friendship and the general role of workplace friendship in scholarly work. Next, I discuss research focused on the functions, developmental processes, and outcomes associated with workplace friendship. I then conceptualize workplace friendship from the various theoretical perspectives that underlie this book and develop a research agenda for the future. Finally, I provide a case at the end of the chapter to help readers apply various theoretical perspectives to real-world situations.

Overview

Workplace friendships are both ubiquitous and unique. Developing friendships with others at work is a common, some might say natural, occurrence. In virtually any workplace, you are likely to find employees who consider themselves friends (Marks, 1994). Workplace friendships develop at all levels of an organization, from frontline employees to top level management (Bridge & Baxter, 1992). In fact, it is easy to come up with a list of famous and infamous workplace friendships, such as Eisner and Ovitz, Ben and Jerry, Jobs and Wozniak, Bush and Cheney, to name but a few.

For many individuals, having friends is essential to their work experience as an important source of intrinsic reward (Sias & Cahill, 1998) and as an important source of information and support (Rawlins, 1992). Others, in contrast, feel that making friends with coworkers is dangerous and potentially harmful to productivity. These are often people who had a bad prior experience with workplace friendship (Sias & Cahill, 1998). Regardless of one's current perspective on workplace friendship, almost all employees have experienced this relationship, either by participating in workplace friendships or by observing, and being affected by, the friendships of other employees at work.

So what is workplace friendship and how are such relationships unique from other types of relationships? Workplace friendships are unique in two primary ways. First, workplace friendships are *voluntary*, not imposed. We may not be able to choose our supervisor or our coworkers, but we do choose which of those individuals we befriend. We voluntarily spend more time with our workplace friends than is required by our organizational role (Sias & Cahill, 1998). We voluntarily share information and provide support to our friends beyond that required by our organizational role (Fine, 1986; Sias, 2005).

Second, workplace friendships have a *personalistic focus* that other workplace relationships lack (Sias & Cahill, 1998). Workplace friends understand and communicate with one another as whole persons, not simply work role occupants. This personalistic focus is reflected in, and constructed by, the partners' interaction with one another. Workplace friends talk about a variety of topics other than work, and their communication is characterized by greater intimacy, frankness, and depth than coworkers who are simply coworkers (Sias & Cahill, 1998). This characteristic also makes workplace friendship distinct in that these relationships blur the boundaries between the public work role and the private personal realm (Marks, 1994). Workplace friendships blend the coworker and friend roles in unique and consequential ways (Bridge & Baxter, 1992).

While unique, workplace friendships develop and flourish in all types of organizations, at all hierarchical levels, and between all types of employees. The "in-group" or "high-quality" relationships in leader–member exchange (LMX) theory (Graen & Scandura, 1987) discussed in Chapter 2 are characterized in part by friendship. The "collegial" and "special" peer relationships (Kram & Isabella, 1985) discussed in Chapter 3 are also characterized, in part, by friendship. Friendships develop between men and women, between younger and older employees, and between line and staff employees. The benefits and challenges of these various types of workplace friendships, however, are somewhat unique, as seen in the following discussion of research.

Although not always explicitly labeled research on workplace "friendship," these relationships have received a great deal of research attention, studied under a variety of topics, including social networks, social capital, human capital, informal networks, expressive networks, informal communication, informal relationships, and informal behavior. The variety of these topic labels highlights the multiplex and complex role of friendship in organizational processes.

Friendships are crucial to organizational functioning, having important consequences, both positive and negative. Friendships are frequently conceptualized as important forms of "capital" resources for both individuals and the organizations in which the friendships are embedded. As Lincoln and Miller (1979) explained, friendship networks are "systems for making decisions, mobilizing resources, concealing or transmitting information, and performing other functions closely allied with work behavior and interaction" (p. 196). For individual employees, friends provide crucial information and function as a "second set of eyes and ears" for employees (Rawlins, 1992). Others have noted the important role of friends in providing invaluable support and advice, easing stress, and preventing employee burnout (Sias & Bartoo, 2007). At the same time, scholars note the difficulties involved in negotiating friendship at work, difficulties that often result in the friendship itself being a source of stress (Ray, 1993). For organizations, friendships can reduce turnover, improve morale, and increase creativity and innovation. They can also contribute to unethical behavior, conflict, and organizational politics.

This chapter discusses the body of knowledge regarding workplace friendship developed to date. Similar to other types of relationships, workplace friendship research has focused on three primary areas: functions of workplace friendship, developmental processes associated with workplace friendship, and the outcomes and consequences associated with workplace friendship. Table 4.1 provides a brief summary of research on these various themes.

Table 4.1   Summary of Workplace Friendship Research

Workplace Friendship Functions

Information Exchange
- Information quantity
- Information quality
- Gossip

Organizational Change Processes
- Informal network conditions for change
- Trust, identity, and support

Social Support
- Friends as sources of instrumental, informational, and emotional support
- Friendship networks as "holding" environments
- Factors enhancing support/helping intentions
- Expressive/friendship ties
- Task/outcome interdependence

Power and Influence
- Informal networks as sites of information exchange
- Network centrality and power
- Gossip as social capital

Workplace Friendship Development

Factors Influencing Friendship Development
- *Individual/Personal Factors*
     Personality
         Attitude similarity
         Demographic similarity (age, sex, race, hierarchical level)

- *Contextual Factors*
     Life events
     Extra-organizational socializing
     Physical proximity
     Tasks (autonomy, participation)
     Shared tasks and projects
     Technology
     Work-related problems
     Organizational culture

- *Communication Changes*
     Increased frequency
     Increased breadth (work and personal topics)
     Increased intimacy
     Decreased caution

Workplace Friendship Deterioration

Causes of Deterioration
- Dialectical tensions
- Conflicting expectations

- Problem personality
- Distracting life events
- Betrayal
- Promotion

Disengagement Tactics
- Depersonalization
- Withdrawal
- Cost escalation

Outcomes and Consequences

Employee Adjustment
- Job satisfaction
- Organizational commitment
- Stress
- Perceptions of psychological contract
- Perceptions of organizational justice

Employee Behavior and Performance
- Knowledge
- Learning
- Innovation
- Decision making
- Task performance
- Career success and advancement

Functions of Workplace Friendship

Much research on workplace friendship focuses on the functions of such relationships for employees and the organization in which the friendship exists. These functions include information exchange, support, and power, control, and influence. While these functions are similar to those of the supervisor–subordinate and peer relationships discussed in Chapters 2 and 3, they operate quite differently in the context of workplace friendships.

INFORMATION EXCHANGE

Most people have heard the saying, "It's not what you know; it's who you know that matters." This is often the case, but the reasons are complex. For example, having friends at work enhances the likelihood that one will receive important and accurate information. Thus, who you know often determines what you know. As with other types of workplace relationships, a primary function of workplace friendships is information exchange. Information exchange among friends is distinct, however, from information exchange among coworkers who are not friends. For example, Chapters 2 and 3 emphasized the importance of supervisor–subordinate and peer relationships for new employees as they enter the organization, experience uncertainty, and seek information from others to reduce that uncertainty. In general, none of a newcomer's workplace relationships are friendships; thus, the information exchanged among new employees and coworkers tends to be work related and relatively superficial. It is not until after the new employee has been on the job for a while and begun to develop closer relationships with others that friendship begins to function as an important site of information exchange.

Sias and Cahill (1998) found that as employee friendships grow closer (i.e., move from acquaintance to friend, friend to close friend, and close friend to best friend), their communication becomes broader, more focused on non-work topics, more intimate, less cautious, and more frequently regarding work-related problems. Thus, workplace friends tend to share more sensitive, discretionary information with one another, and tend to be franker in their communication than coworkers who are simply acquaintances. Workplace friends, therefore, function as valuable sources of information that provide timely, accurate, and useful information to one another. Along these lines, Sias (2005) found that employees who considered their supervisors to be friends (i.e., high-LMX relationships) received higher quality (i.e., more timely, accurate, and useful) information than employees who had lower quality relationships with their supervisors. Similarly, that study revealed that employees received higher quality information from their "collegial peers" (e.g., peer coworkers whom they considered as friends) than from their "information peers" (e.g., peer coworkers whom they considered as simply coworkers, not as friends).

A particular type of information shared among friends is gossip. *Gossip* refers to "informal and evaluative talk in an organization, usually among no more than a few individuals, about another member of that organization who is not present" (Kurland & Pelled, 2000, p. 429). Distinct from *rumors*, which refer to general uncertainty such as layoffs or downsizing, gossip refers to "specific, often trivial, particulars about other people's lives" (Hafen, 2004, p. 224). Although gossip can, and often is, exchanged among acquaintances, it finds particular currency among friends. In fact, the exchange of gossip can contribute to the maintenance of friendship by broadening the topics discussed and expressing trust in one another by providing discretionary information (Gluckman, 1963). As noted earlier, workplace friends are considered to function as a "second set of eyes and ears" for one another (Rawlins, 1992). Having friends at work means being well informed and being in touch with the goings-on at work. Being informed or uninformed has important consequences for employees and the organization, as seen later in this chapter.

ORGANIZATIONAL CHANGE PROCESSES

Many scholars have examined the ways workplace friendship enhances, or hinders, organizational change processes. In general, this body of work indicates that friendship ties and friendship networks play important roles in the management of organizational change primarily due to the trust and cohesiveness that characterizes friendship. Ledford and Mohrman (1993) found that "friendship networks" that spanned plant boundaries in a large manufacturing organization were important for the successful implementation of a major multiyear reengineering program. McGrath and Krackhardt (2003) developed a model of the "network conditions" that enhance organizational change efforts. A key component of their model is workplace friendship. Specifically, they found that workplace friendship enabled organizational change by "fostering trust and shared identity" (p. 301). The trust and identity shared by friends enhanced the diffusion of innovation by easing the anxiety induced by the potential change and making employees "more willing to engage in cooperative and altruistic behaviors necessary to make the change work for the organization" (McGrath & Krackhardt, 2003, p. 326). Kahn, Cross, and Parker (2003) examined the role of social networks in implementing change in a residential treatment clinic. Their analysis revealed that social networks impacted the organizational change efforts. In particular, their results demonstrated that friendships were important in helping employees make sense of the changes and that these sensemaking processes were impacted by the trust and support provided by workplace friends.

In sum, these studies indicate that the high level of trust that characterizes workplace friendships makes these relationships important factors in the implementation of organizational change. As many of these scholars suggest, change implementers are well advised to develop an understanding of an organization's friendship networks before beginning change efforts, as these networks can impact the success or failure of those efforts.

SOCIAL SUPPORT

Organizational change, uncertainty, politics, and task requirements are among the many causes of stress and anxiety for employees, and workplace friends are among the first people to whom employees turn to deal with such stress (Cahill & Sias, 1997). Thus, one of the primary functions of workplace friendship is social support. In fact, support is a defining characteristic of high-quality LMX friendships among supervisors and subordinates (Graen & Cashman, 1975) and a defining characteristic of collegial and special peer relationships that incorporate friendship (Kram & Isabella, 1985).

As noted in previous chapters, *social support* refers to verbal and nonverbal communication between receiver and provider that reduces uncertainty about a situation, one's self, another, or a relationship, and enhances the perception of control over one's life (Albrecht & Adelman, 1987). Workplace friends provide instrumental support to one another when they provide tangible forms of help such as providing information, as described in the preceding section, when they help one another with tasks, and other types of services. Friends provide emotional support to one another when they act as a "shoulder to cry on," a site for venting, and when they provide consolation and understanding to one another (House, 1981).

As scholars point out, workplace friends provide a unique, and uniquely useful, form of support in that they have an understanding and appreciation for workplace issues that other support sources, such as family members and nonwork friends, do not (Cahill & Sias, 1997; Ray, 1993). At the same time, because of their personalistic focus, workplace friends also become an important source of support for those dealing with stress and anxiety in their personal lives. Marks (1994) found that employees perceive workplace friends as important sites of intimacy and support. Specifically, workplace friends are those with whom employees discuss important work-related and personal matters. These discussions function as both instrumental support (e.g., providing information and advice for dealing with such problems) and emotional support (e.g., providing consolation and a sympathetic ear). Similarly, Sias and Cahill (1998) found that close friends at work were important to individuals dealing with major life events such as divorce and illness, as well as problems at work such as an inconsiderate supervisor or problematic coworkers.

Kahn (2001) developed a theoretical framework linking workplace relationships and social support in his model of "holding environments." Holding environments refer to "interpersonal or group-based relationships that enable self-reliant workers to manage situations that trigger potentially debilitating anxiety" (p. 260). The term *holding* is a metaphorical reference to the literal experience of being held in comfort. Effective holding environments rely largely on trust among coworkers, and although being friends is not necessarily required for a holding environment, friendship strengthens holding environments. As Kahn explains, "What ideally occurs between coworkers is similar to what occurs between sophisticated adult friends when one turns to the other for support" (Kahn, 2001, p. 265). Along these lines, Kruger, Bernstein, and Botman (1995) found friendships among residential counselors were instrumental in helping the counselors avoid burnout and emotional exhaustion.

While the above studies demonstrate workplace friendship is linked to social support generally, recent studies have examined complexities in those links. Lin (2006) studied factors that influence employees' likelihood of helping one another. Similar to other research, they found that employees are motivated to help coworkers whom they consider to be friends (i.e., with whom they have "expressive ties"). Lin also found, however, that helping intentions are impacted by "outcome interdependence" or the extent to which coworkers' positive job performance benefits one another. Such interdependence is indicative of a cooperative, rather than competitive, environment. Specifically, the study revealed that the higher the outcome interdependence of workplace friends, the more likely those friends were to help one another. According to the author, this result suggests the benefits of teamwork and shared projects. As the author explains, "A corporate spirit that values interdependent teamwork and guides employees to experience and receive organizational values will likely yield better expressive and instrumental ties, leading to a stronger willingness to help each other" (Lin, 2006, p. 180).

In contrast to the above, in a study of social support among supervisors for employees experiencing personal problems such as substance abuse, Hopkins (1997) found that friendship can sometimes hinder the provision of social support. Instead, her results indicated that supervisors sometimes found their friendship with an employee prevented them from offering help to a troubled employee because they did not want to risk harming their friendship by interfering in the problem.

POWER AND INFLUENCE

Another common notion is the importance of having "friends in high places." While having friends enhances one's ability to obtain important information of high quality, having friends at work benefits employees beyond information exchange. Friends are also important sources of influence and power. Certainly, friends in high places can help individuals with career advancement and success. As the research discussed in this section indicates, however, power derives from having friends at multiple levels and areas of the organization. Thus, a more accurate notion is that it is important to have "friends in all places" of the organization.

Many scholars have examined links between workplace friendship and power, particularly with the respect to career advancement and decision making. Access to informal friendship networks enhances employees' ability to perform their jobs and to advance their careers. As Kanter noted in her seminal book, lack of access to such networks is a primary reason women have trouble breaking through the glass ceiling (i.e., the difficulty and barriers that often prevent women from "breaking through" levels of hierarchy) and advancing to higher levels of management (Kanter, 1977). At the same time, informal friendship networks (e.g., "old boys" networks) are a primary mechanism supporting the overwhelming majority of white males at the top of corporate hierarchies.

The power derived from workplace friendship results from a variety of factors. As noted above, friendship networks are crucial sites of information exchange. To the extent that "information is power," participation in workplace friendships can imbue employees with power by ensuring they have important, often discretionary or proprietary information that they need to make decisions and perform their jobs competently. The least powerful people in organizations tend to be those uninformed employees who are marginalized from friendship networks and, consequently, are "out of the loop" (Kanter, 1977).

Brass and Burkhardt (1993) examined the links between information and social networks in their study of network centrality. Networks, in their study, were conceptualized as communication networks and, specifically, information distribution networks. Although their study did not explicitly examine friendships, it can be assumed that individuals who were active participants in these networks also participated in friendships with at least some of the other network members. Results indicated that individuals who played central roles in these social networks were perceived by others to be powerful and to wield influence in the organization. Although this study did not explicitly examine how network centrality was linked to power, the authors suggest that occupying a central role in the network means that such individuals receive more information than more distant employees, and they may use such information in various influence attempts.

Hafen (2004) examined links between friendship, power, and a specific type of information—gossip. Conceptualizing gossip as a type of "social capital" (i.e., a type of currency employees use in the workplace to accomplish goals), Hafen obtained narrative accounts of employees' experiences with gossip. These narratives revealed how gossip both supports organizational control and enables employee resistance to organizational control by encouraging workplace deviance. Specifically, the narrative accounts revealed that gossip, like other types of information, often served to preserve and strengthen social groups, such as friendship groups. Furthermore, the links between gossip and power were enabled by what the author termed the "gossip-information revolving door" via which gossip was legitimized and became information or information was illegitimized and became gossip. As the author explained, "Gossip used to regulate by organizational authority was done through the use of 'HR investigations' or through the dissemination of stories of heroes and cautionary tales. Gossip used to resist organizational efficacy was done through humor, nostalgia for the 'good ol' times,' and interpersonal maneuvers and forays" (Hafen, 2004, p. 236). According to this study, then, gossip exchanged among employees, including workplace friends, both enabled and hindered organizational control and individual resistance and deviance. Thus, gossip is a form of social capital for both organizations and individual employees.

Power does not derive from friendship via information exchange alone, however. Simply holding a position in friendship networks can provide employees with power via their perceived connections with others. These connections provide those employees with referent and legitimate power (Lamertz & Aquino, 2004). In other words, sometimes "who you know" is what matters. Along these lines, Lamertz and Aquino (2004) examined links between an employee's position in organizational friendship networks (i.e., expressive networks) and victimization, defined as "the extent to which individuals perceived themselves to be the target of negative or aggressive behaviors by others" (Lamertz & Aquino, 2004, p. 795). Their results indicated that employees occupying central positions in the friendship network had access to referent and legitimate power. This access reduced the likelihood of perceiving victimization by others via a variety of social dynamics, including protection, patronage, and social influence.

In sum, research indicates that friendship is linked to power via both information exchange and power derived from social status. In other words, it's both who you know and what they tell you.

Workplace Friendship Development

As seen above, workplace friendships have a number of important organizational functions. Participating in these relationships provides employees with important advantages, including access to discretionary and high-quality information, access to power, and support that mitigates anxiety and stress. Not surprisingly, many scholars have examined developmental processes associated with workplace friendship. This body of work addresses why and how employees develop workplace friendships, challenges that threaten the maintenance of such relationships, and why and how workplace friendships deteriorate.

WHY AND HOW WORKPLACE FRIENDSHIPS DEVELOP

As mentioned earlier, workplace friendships develop among all types of coworkers in all types of occupations and at all hierarchical levels. Scholars have examined relational development from a variety of perspectives, addressing the important questions of why and how employees develop friendships with one another. In particular, studies have focused on friendship development between supervisors and their subordinate employees, between peer coworkers, and between men and women.

Grounding their work in LMX theory (see Chapter 2), Boyd and Taylor (1998) developed a model of friendship development between supervisors and their subordinate employees. Characterizing high-quality LMX relationships as friendships, the authors developed a four-stage model of friendship development. The first stage is characterized by exploration. At this point, the partners consider the potential of their relationships for friendship. This potential is impacted by similarity with respect to attitudes and demographic factors, as well as physical proximity. Thus, the greatest potential for friendship development is for supervisors and subordinates who perceive themselves to be similar and who work near each other and, thus, are in frequent contact. During the second stage, the relationship partners increase their communication and begin to explore friendship potential with greater intent, albeit carefully. This stage is characterized by cautious and tentative orienting communication during which similarities and value congruence among the partners begin to emerge, along with greater liking of one another. In the third stage, the supervisor and subordinate employee engage in "casual friendship." The friendship is fairly superficial and low in intimacy at this stage and exists as a "medium LMX" relationship. These medium-LMX relationships develop into high-LMX relationships in Stage 4. In this stage, the relationship develops into a close friendship characterized by the qualities that are distinct in high-LMX relationships, including mutual support, open communication, and high levels of trust and self-disclosure.

While the Boyd and Taylor (1998) model identifies the stages of friendship development, and the characteristics that distinguish each stage, it does not explicitly identify specific factors that are associated with friendship development beyond Stage 1. In other words, it does not address the reasons or factors that propel a relationship from Stage 1 to Stage 2 and so on. It is likely, however, that factors discussed in Chapter 2 influencing LMX relationship development also apply to the development of LMX friendships, including the employee's ability, personality, similarity, and communication patterns. Along these lines, one's position in the organization's social network may impact development of LMX friendships. As Sparrowe and Liden's (1997) model suggests, employees and supervisors who share a common relationship with a third party in the social networks are more likely to develop the friendships characteristic of high-quality LMX relationships than those without common social contacts.

My colleagues and I have examined friendship development processes among peer coworkers. Our research focuses on identifying phases of relational development and identifying the factors that "drive" these relationship changes. Our studies indicate peer coworker friendships experience up to three primary relationship transitions—acquaintance to friend, friend to close friend, and close friend to (almost) best friend. Not all relationships make it through the three stages. Many remain at the "friend" level; others do not progress past the close friend stage. Few relationships actually reach the closest level of friendship due to the time and effort required to reach and maintain relationships at this level, as discussed below (Sias & Cahill, 1998).

Our research indicates peer workplace friendship development is "driven" by three primary types of developmental factors. *Individual* factors are those that derive from the individuals in the relationship. These include personality and perceived similarity. Contextual factors derive from the context in which the relationship develops. Two types of contextual factors emerged in our analyses. One type, labeled *contextual factors,* includes life events (i.e., important events in the individual's personal life such as marriage, divorce, illness, etc.) and nonwork socializing. The other, labeled *workplace contextual factors,* includes factors derived specifically from the workplace itself, including physical proximity, work-related problems, and shared tasks (Sias & Cahill, 1998; Sias, Smith, & Avdeyeva, 2003).

Our studies indicate that the influence of these developmental factors varies across the three transitions. The initial phase is impacted primarily by personality and perceived similarity. At this point, coworkers develop an affinity for one another that propels them toward conversations on a broader spectrum of topics both work and nonwork related. These opportunities for interaction are provided by physical proximity, shared tasks and projects, and socializing outside of work (e.g., having lunch together). Thus, contextual factors also impact the development of friendships at the early stages.

Different factors drive the move from friend to close friend. Specifically, individual factors become less important, and contextual factors such as life events and work-related problems become more important. Employees experiencing important events in their lives (e.g., marital problems, illness, etc.) and/or problems at work (e.g., problems with a supervisor or with other coworkers) turn to one another for support and advice. Their communication at this point becomes more intimate, less cautious, and more open, which serves to deepen and strengthen the friendship. Moving to the third and closest stage of friendship also results from work-related problems and life events. In addition, the mere passage of time brings friends closer together as they become reliable, dependable sources of support, affinity, advice, and affection.

A number of other studies also indicate the impact of individual and contextual factors on workplace friendship development. Among these factors are individual factors such as biological sex, age, race, and personality, and contextual factors such as task, technology, hierarchical level, proximity, organizational culture, and climate. This body of work is detailed below.

Individual Developmental Factors

Many studies have examined the role of biological sex/gender in workplace friendship development. Some studies in this area examined the nature of women's social networks in organizations. Kanter (1977), for example, found women were largely excluded from informal friendship groups and that this exclusion was one barrier to women's career advancement. Ibarra (1993b) argued that the friendship networks of women and minorities can constrain the ability of these minority employees to advance in their careers. Hultin and Szulkin (2003) found the restricted access of women to informal social networks is a "mechanism of inequality" that contributes to salary inequality among men and women.

Much work in this area is grounded in the "homophily principle," or the principle that individuals seek ties with similar others (Lazarsfeld & Merton, 1954; McPherson, Smith-Lovin, & Cook, 2001). The preference for similar others means minority employee networks are most likely comprised of similar others (i.e., women and racial minority employees) who are not hierarchically well placed to provide the help, information, and sponsorship needed to move up the corporate hierarchy. A more recent study found similar results. Graves and Elsass (2005) examined social exchanges among men and women in ongoing teams. They found that women reported lower levels of social exchanges (e.g., exchanges that provide support, trust, and friendship) than did men. Moreover, women reported higher levels of task contributions than did men. These results support the notion that women tend to be excluded from, or at least are less likely to participate in, friendship networks than are men.

Other scholars have done comparative studies examining differences and similarities between men's and women's workplace friendship networks. Burke, Rothstein, and Bristor (1995), for example, found that women's networks were comprised of a greater proportion of women than were men's networks. Similarly, Markiewicz, Devine, and Kausilas (2000) found men's and women's friendship networks were most likely to be comprised of same-sex relationship partners.

Using the Kram and Isabella (1985) typology of information, collegial, and special peers (see Chapter 3), Fritz (1997) found that while men and women did not differ significantly in the quantity of these relationships, they did differ with respect to the functions of those relationships. Specifically, men's information peer relationships (the least intimate and not characterized by friendship) were rated higher in honesty, mutual dependence, and social activity than were women's. At the same time, women's special peer relationships (characterized by close friendship) were rated higher in self-disclosure, mutual dependence, irreplaceability, and emotional support than were men's. These results indicate that "women's relationships in organizations, similar to what appears to be the case in non-organizational contexts, have the potential to be stronger, and, among very close friends, are characterized by greater strength. However, they are similar to men's in terms of functions or instrumentality" (Fritz, 1997, p. 41).

Others have taken the friendship dyad, rather than the individual, as the unit of analysis and explored the links between *sex composition* (i.e., same-sex or cross-sex dyads) and workplace friendship development. Sias et al. (2003) examined the Sias and Cahill (1998) friendship development model described earlier with respect to sex and sex composition and found general support for the Sias and Cahill (1998) three-stage model as applied to same-sex friendships. Cross-sex friendship differed significantly, however. Specifically, while the impact of workplace contextual influences such as proximity and shared tasks decreased as same-sex friendships developed over time, these influences retained their importance for cross-sex friendships as those relationships grew closer. In fact, at the third "close-friend to almost best-friend" stage, life events and socializing were among the most important developmental influences for same-sex dyads. For cross-sex dyads, in contrast, proximity and shared tasks were the most important developmental influences at Stage 3. These findings suggest that cross-sex friendships are more likely to remain defined by the workplace context than are same same-sex friendships. This is likely due to a number of factors, including concerns by the dyad that others may misinterpret the friendship as something more intimate such as a romantic relationship, and concerns by the individuals in the relationship that their partner may misinterpret the social exchange as a romantic exchange. Along these lines, Elsesser and Peplau (2006) examined obstacles and barriers to cross-sex friendship development, including concerns that "their cross-sex friends would misinterpret their friendliness as romantic or sexual interest, that their coworkers would misinterpret their friendliness to a cross-sex friend, and that their humor and conversational topics might be perceived by a cross-sex friend as sexual harassment" (p. 1077). These studies indicate the difficulties in negotiating cross-sex relationships at work. As noted earlier in this chapter, the glass ceiling prevents women from advancing to high-level management positions. Exclusion from informal social networks is one contributor to the glass ceiling (Kanter, 1977). However, breaking into these social networks requires forming and developing cross-sex friendships. Thus, women face unique challenges and difficulties.

Women are not the only minority employees faced with challenges in accessing friendship networks. Many studies indicate the difficulties faced by employees who are members of racial and ethnic minorities. Like women, most of these challenges result from the "homophily principle" and social identity theory (Tajfel, 1974), which describes the preference of individuals to bond with similar individuals with whom they identify. Ibarra (1995), for example, found that minority managers had fewer intimate network relationships than did majority managers. They also reportedly enjoyed less "access to career benefits" via social networks than did white majority managers. Schneider and Northcraft (1999) describe "dilemmas" of diversity in organizations, including the ways in which social identity influences employees to organize their interactions along social identity lines. The resulting segregation into homogeneous social networks creates a variety of "traps" and "fences" that prevent employees and organizations from developing and reaping the benefits of workplace diversity.

More recently, Mollica, Gray, and Trevino (2003) examined the formation of friendships among organizational newcomers (specifically, first-year MBA students). They found that, as predicted by the homophily principle, even though racial minorities had fewer "same-race ties" to choose from than did white students, "their friendship networks demonstrated greater homophily than those of whites" both early on and after 3 months. These results indicate that mutual support may be more salient to minority newcomers than the access to resources and information that could be obtained via friendship ties with majority and higher ranking individuals, highlighting the substantial stress and anxiety experienced by newly hired minority employees. In a similar vein, Mehra, Kilduff, and Brass (1998) used "distinctiveness theory" to examine friendship preferences among minority employees. Distinctiveness theory posits that rarity of members of a particular social group will lead such individuals to form relationships with others in that group for shared identity and interaction. They found that members of racial minorities were more likely than majority employees to make "within-group" friendship choices, and the authors note, such friendship choices contribute to the marginalization of racial minorities within the larger organization.

An individual hierarchical level may also be associated with employees' friendship development. Mao (2006) compared friendships between employees at different hierarchical levels and found that employees at higher hierarchical levels reported participating in fewer workplace friendships than those at lower levels. This finding might suggest that while friendships are useful in helping employees move up the organizational hierarchy, the usefulness of those relationships, and the difficulties high-level managers experience in maintaining workplace friendships may lead to the deterioration of such relationships. These issues are discussed in greater detail in subsequent sections.

As the preceding indicates, many individual-level factors impact the development of workplace friendships, including sex, race, task, and hierarchical level. Workplace relationships do not exist in isolation from the workplace itself, however, and studies indicate the ways in which the workplace context impacts friendships among employees. These are discussed in the following section.

Workplace Context Developmental Factors

Workplace friendships are literally defined by the context in which they exist—the workplace. It is not surprising, then, that the nature of the workplace is associated with the nature of the organization's friendship network. Factors such as physical proximity, tasks, technology, and the organizational culture all have been shown to impact friendships among employees. As noted earlier, employees are more likely to develop friendships with proximal coworkers. Simply working near someone increases the likelihood you will become friends with them (Hodson, 1996; Sias & Cahill, 1998). This is likely due to the fact that physical proximity provides opportunities for interaction (Sias & Cahill, 1998).

The tasks employees perform also can impact friendship development. Hodson (1996) compared friendship ties of employees in different types of occupations. His study suggests that tasks such as assembly-line production that require close supervision hinder the formation and maintenance of workplace friendships. In contrast, jobs that invite and require worker participation enhance friendship ties among employees. This is likely due to the fact that the former types of jobs limit interaction, while the latter, participatory jobs, require and encourage employee interaction. Shah (1998) found operations employees in a national brokerage firm were more likely to engage in workplace friendships than were brokers and sales assistants. This finding likely resulted from the fact that operations personnel worked in close proximity on highly interdependent tasks, while brokers and sales assistants were more likely to conduct their work independently. These findings echo those of Sias and Cahill (1998) who found that physical proximity and shared tasks were important contributors to workplace friendship development among peers. Again, employee participation and shared tasks provide opportunities for interaction that further the development of relationships among employees.

Given the importance of physical proximity and task interdependence, some scholars have questioned the impact new communication technologies may have on workplace friendships. New technologies enable a variety of innovative work practices, including flextime, telecommuting, and virtual workplaces. Communicating with other employees via technology removes the necessity of physical proximity and face-to-face interaction, creating concerns about decreased collegiality and friendship among employees. More optimistically, the burgeoning number of "virtual friends" and "virtual relationships" emerging on chat rooms of various types indicates that individuals may be capable of forming and maintaining "virtual" workplace friendships. Fehr (1996), for instance, argues that new computer-mediated communication technologies (e.g., e-mail, computer networks) may make physical proximity less important to friendship development as the new technologies "[open] up whole new worlds of friendship possibilities" (p. 45). Because such technologies increase the "field of available" coworkers with whom one may become friends, Fehr (1996) suggests "the historical emphasis on proximity as a prerequisite for the development of friendship ultimately may be revised in light of new technology" (p. 46). Similarly, Sias and Cahill (1998) argue that technology may not hinder workplace friendship development; virtual friendships may just follow different developmental trajectories than traditional, face-to-face friendships.

Recent theoretical work has addressed these issues. Hinds and Bailey (2003) developed a theory explaining how the geographical distribution of teams via communication technology is harmful to workplace friendship development. Basing their theory, in large part, on the well-documented importance of physical proximity to friendship development, the authors suggest that the lack of proximity in distant teams will prevent the development of friendships among team members. To counteract this deleterious effect, the authors suggest practitioners ensure team members recognize the potential impact of the technology on their relationships so that they can monitor their interaction in ways that prevent, for example, unduly harsh or curt language. The authors also recommend occasional face-to-face team meetings, particularly in the early stages of team development. Empirical work in this area sheds light on these issues. Reinsch (1997) examined the effects of telecommuting on supervisor–subordinate relationships. Grounding the study in LMX theory, his results indicated that the longer an employee had telecommuted, the lower the quality of his or her LMX relationship.

Research also indicates that *work-related problems* can draw coworkers closer together. Sias and Jablin (1995) found that when employees perceived their supervisor was treating a group member unfairly, the relationships among those employees became closer. Specifically, when employees perceived a coworker received unwarranted favoritism from the supervisor, they turned to one another to make sense of the differential treatment and developed closer friendships with one another. The target of the differential treatment (i.e., the "boss's pet"), in contrast, became isolated from the social network. The boss's victims, however (i.e., those receiving unwarranted negative treatment from the supervisor), were viewed sympathetically and drawn into closer relationships with the other employees. Other studies found similar evidence of the tendency for inconsiderate and/or unfair supervision to draw employees closer together (Odden & Sias, 1997; Sias, 1996).

An interesting study, and one of the few guided by a critical perspective, revealed how the workplace *culture* is associated with friendship development among employees. In this study, Ashcraft (2000) examined relationships in an organization comprised primarily of female employees with an explicit commitment to "feminine" ways of organizing values such as collaboration and emphasizing close interpersonal relationships. This organization was structured explicitly to contrast bureaucratic, and more masculine, approaches such as rationality and the bifurcation of work and personal relationships. As part of the "feminine" structure, the organization leaders explicitly encouraged the formation and development of close friendships among employees. Employees willingly obliged and grew quite close to one another, forming friendships and, in some cases, romantic relationships, characterized by high levels of trust, intimacy, and affinity. These relationships had some surprising consequences, however, in that employees began to complain about favoritism and unfair treatment resulting from these friendships and romantic relationships. Thus, the close relationships that were the core of the organization's "feminine" approach to organizing instead caused competition, jealousy, and political strife. The organization's leaders responded, quite ironically, by developing explicit, bureaucratic policies forbidding friendships and romantic relationships among staff members without the expressed permission of management.

As seen in the preceding examples, many scholars have examined the factors associated with the development of workplace friendships. These developmental influences include individual factors such as personality and perceived similarity, along with contextual influences such as proximity, tasks, technology, work-related problems, and workplace culture. Comparatively fewer studies have focused on the processes and factors associated with workplace friendship deterioration. This important area of research is discussed in the following section.

WORKPLACE FRIENDSHIP DETERIORATION

Despite their many rewards, workplace friendships are complex and difficult to maintain. These unique "blended" relationships combine the coworker role with the friend role. Often the expectations of the two different roles conflict with one another. As Bridge and Baxter (1992) noted, these conflicting role expectations create tensions for the relationship partners, and if those tensions are not managed, the relationship is harmed or even terminated. Using dialectic theory, Bridge and Baxter (1992) identified dialectical tensions that individuals experience in their workplace friendships. As I noted in a recent review,

> These dialectics derive from the politics inherent to the blending of these roles—individuals in any organization constantly negotiate their own goals and interests and the goals and interests of their workgroup and the larger organization as they go about their work. To the extent that these goals and interests conflict, the resulting tensions challenge the relationship and, if not effectively managed, can destroy the relationship. (Sias, 2006, p. 71)

Specifically, Bridge and Baxter (1992) identified five dialectical tensions inherent to workplace friendships. The *equality–inequality* tension refers to tensions between the friendship norms of equality and workplace constraints and expectations that constitute inequality (e.g., rank and hierarchy). The *impartiality and favoritism* tension refers to organizational norms of impartial and objective treatment of employees and friendship expectations of unconditional support. *Openness and closedness* refers to expectations of openness and honesty among friends on the one hand, and organizational expectations of confidentiality and caution about information sharing on the other. *Autonomy and connection* refers to the benefits of contact for friends and the possibility that ongoing and daily contact among coworkers may provide little autonomy for the relationship partners, "jeopardizing their friendship through excessive connection" (Bridge & Baxter, 1992, p. 204). The *judgment and acceptance* tension refers to expectations of mutual affirmation and acceptance among friends, and organizational requirements of critical evaluation (Bridge & Baxter, 1992; Sias, 2005). As mentioned earlier, if relationship partners are unable to manage these tensions (e.g., by setting guidelines and ground rules for their relationship such as not discussing work outside the workplace, or not discussing personal topics while at work), the relationship cannot survive. In such cases, the individuals either terminate the work relationship by one of them quitting their job or, more often, terminate the friendship and returning their relationship to that of "just coworkers" (Sias, Heath, Perry, Silva, & Fix, 2004).

My colleagues and I have examined the processes associated with those friendships that do not survive in the workplace, specifically focusing on the reasons for the friendship deterioration and how the relationship partners communicatively transform their relationship from a friendship to a strictly working relationship. Our studies indicate five primary causes of friendship deterioration. *Conflicting expectations* refer to events in which coworkers find their expectations regarding appropriate behavior conflict with one another (e.g., one partner asking the other to share confidential organizational information or a subordinate employee expecting, but not receiving, special treatment from a friend/supervisor—similar to the situation of Eisner and Ovitz described at the beginning of this chapter). Such events typically represent the openness–closedness and favoritism–impartiality tensions described above. Litwin and Hallstein (2007) identified a similar dynamic in their study of difficulties women face at work. Participants in their study reported being surprised when a female coworker violated their idealized notions about friendships among women by not acting "feminine" or not acting "like a female friend" and instead favoring organizational concerns over the relationship.

A *problem personality* can cause coworkers to end their friendship because one partner finds he or she can no longer tolerate an annoying personality trait exhibited by the other. Workplace friendships also deteriorate when one of the coworkers experiences *distracting life events,* or incidents that involve the excessive intrusion of the individual's personal problems (e.g., marital problems, health issues) into the workplace such that the employee is no longer carrying his or her fair share of the workload and/or distracting others from performing their tasks. Given the importance of trust to friendship, it is not surprising that *betrayal* (e.g., situations in which one of the partners feels that coworkers have betrayed his or her trust, typically by sharing with others information a partner has shared in confidence) can irreparably damage friendships. Elangovan and Shapiro (1998) also found betrayal can lead to the end of friendship. Finally, termination of a workplace friendship can also result from the *promotion* of one of the relationship partners to a position of formal authority over the other. In such cases, the equality–inequality and favoritism–impartiality tensions become particularly salient (Sias et al., 2004).

Grounding our research in the social construction perspective, we also examined how coworkers communicatively transform their relationships. Our qualitative (Sias et al., 2004) and quantitative (Sias & Perry, 2004) studies reveal that individuals rely on three primary communication tactics to disengage from a workplace friendship—cost escalation, depersonalization, and state-of-the-relationship talk. *Cost escalation* refers to tactics in which an individual behaves in an intentionally negative way toward the partner (e.g., using a snide, snappy, or condescending tone of voice; interrupting or insulting the partner; talking about the coworker negatively behind the coworker's back). *Depersonalization* refers to individuals intentionally avoiding interaction regarding personal issues with a coworker and avoiding socializing with that coworker outside of work. This functions to communicatively construct a clear boundary between the work and personal spheres. *State-of-the-relationship talk* involves direct and explicit discussion of the relationship transformation. In such conversations, the partners agree to terminate the friendship aspect of their relationship to preserve a functional coworker relationship. Our studies indicate that individuals rely primarily on the depersonalization tactic. As we note, "This strategy may be particularly effective for workplace relationship deterioration because it serves to remove the 'personalistic focus' that tends to characterize close workplace friendships, while maintaining the relationship at a functional level," as this tactic allows the employees to both disengage from the friendship, yet continue communication about work-related issues (Sias & Perry, 2004, p. 597).

Outcomes and Consequences of Workplace Friendship

As seen in the preceding, workplace friendships are unique and complex relationships that fulfill a number of important functions, yet are difficult for some individuals to develop and challenging to maintain. Workplace friendship is consequential for the relationship partners as well as for the organization in which the relationship is embedded. In this section, I discuss the various individual and organizational outcomes and consequences of workplace friendship. Similar to previous chapters, these represent two primary types of outcomes—employee adjustment and employee/organizational performance.

EMPLOYEE ADJUSTMENT

Because of their many functions and multiplex nature, workplace friendships are associated with employee adjustment in several ways. Like other types of workplace relationships, workplace friendships are linked to job satisfaction and commitment to the organization (Olk & Elvira, 2001; Sias & Cahill, 1998). The links between friendship and satisfaction are complex, however. As Sias and Cahill (1998) noted, close friendships sometimes flourish in problematic workplaces in which employees are not satisfied with their jobs, supervisors, or other aspects of their work. In such cases, employees turn to one another for sensemaking and emotional support. These interactions cause the relationship to develop into a closer, more intimate friendship. Odden and Sias (1997) also found that close friendships (i.e., "special peer" relationships) were associated with organizational climates characterized by problematic or "inconsiderate" supervision.

As discussed earlier, social support is an important function of workplace friendships. Friendships with coworkers help employees cope with uncertainty, anxiety, and stress (Lin, 2006; Sias & Cahill, 1998). Workplace friendships can also, however, *cause* stress and anxiety. The many challenges facing workplace friends create stress for employees as they attempt to manage those challenges (Bridge & Baxter, 1992). When employees fail to manage these challenges, the friendship deteriorates or even terminates. This, as noted by Sias et al. (2004), is a very traumatic emotional experience. Results of that study indicate the stress inherent in friendship deterioration impacts employees' morale, and can even detract from their task performance. Thus, with respect to stress and anxiety, workplace friendship is a double-edged sword. It can both relieve stress and create stress.

Studies also indicate friendships are associated with employees' perceptions of their psychological contract with the organization (Ho & Levesque, 2005; Ho, Rousseau, & Levesque, 2006). A *psychological contract* refers to "an individual's beliefs about the terms of an exchange agreement between the individual and the organization" (Ho & Levesque, 2005, p. 275). The extent to which an employee perceives the agreement has been fulfilled is associated with other adjustment outcomes such as satisfaction and commitment. Ho and Levesque (2005) found workplace friends are important referents for employees assessing their psychological contracts. Specifically, they found significant congruence among friends when it came to their psychological contract perceptions with respect to the fulfillment of organization-wide promises such as a relaxed environment or work–life balance and job-related promises such as salary. The impact of friends appeared to be strongest for organization-related promises, however, and as the authors explain, this may be due to the more competitive nature of job-related issues such as salary. Ho, Rousseau, and Levesque (2006) found that cohesive friendship networks were associated with employee perceptions that the organization owed the employees more balanced (e.g., opportunities for dynamic and challenging performance) and transactional obligations (e.g., pay, staffing needs). Somewhat related, Umphress, Labianca, Brass, Kass, and Scholten (2003) found friendship ties were associated with similarity in employee perceptions of organizational justice. Similarly, Gibbons (2004) found friendship networks facilitated the teaching and inculcation of organizational values.

PERFORMANCE

Workplace friendships are associated with a number of employee and organization-related performance outcomes. These include knowledge and learning, innovation, decision making, task performance, and career success and advancement.

Krackhardt and Stern (1998) found information sharing among friends across departmental boundaries helped organizations adapt to uncertainty and changing environments. Floyd and Woolridge's (1999) model of knowledge creation places social networks at the center of the process. According to the model, the information shared in relational contexts facilitates learning and knowledge creation throughout the organization. Meyers and Wilemon (1989) found that informal interaction in the context of friendship ties was more important to knowledge transfer and learning than were formal ties. Madhavan and Grover (1998) similarly argue that the information shared informally between friends is an important mechanism in transforming knowledge that is "embedded" in employees' cognition into knowledge that is "embodied" in new products. Relatedly, Ibarra (1993a) found that centrality in the organization's social network was strongly associated with involvement in administrative innovation.

Research also indicates workplace friendships can influence decisions. Halpern (1994) found that real estate agents, particularly more experienced agents, who were friends with one another found their friendships facilitated their business transactions. The author explains that this impact derived largely from the trust inherent in the friendships, as well as the cognitive scripts friends develop over time. In a critical study of friendship and decisions, Morgen (1994) examined the ways friendship can complicate decision making and make the process more stressful and emotional. Similar to the Ashcraft (2000) study, Morgen focused on a "feminist" organization that explicitly incorporated collectivist, nonbureaucratic/masculine structures and policies. As Morgen (1994) explained,

> Instead of basing personnel decisions (hiring, remuneration, advancement, and job separation) solely or primarily on criteria such as specialized training or certification, previous job/career experience, seniority, or meritorious job performance as evaluated by a superior, collectivist workplaces often replace or supplement these criteria with others that are more personal or political (e.g., friendship, a person's need for a job, affirmative action, and other social-political values). Rather than insisting that workers leave their personal concerns or needs at home, collectivist, and especially feminist, workplaces tend to encourage workers to express their needs, values, and ideas in a context that is supportive and nurturing. (p. 65)

Morgen's analysis of decision making in this organization revealed that "personalizing" personnel decisions led to emotionally charged processes, conflict, and trauma for all parties involved. While some decision makers simply reverted back to bureaucratic practices (as was the case in the Ashcraft, 2000, study), others rationalized their nonbureaucratic decision practices by emphasizing the political ends (advancing of feminist values) over the nonbureaucratic means (emotionally charged, often traumatic decision-making processes).

Given the information sharing, knowledge creation, and learning that derive from workplace friendship, it is not surprising that these relationships are associated with task performance and career success. Much of the research in this area is grounded in a "social capital" conceptualization of friendship. *Social capital* refers to the social resources (e.g., networks and institutional memberships) that individuals can use to enhance their positions (Bellieveau, O'Reilly, & Wade, 1996). As mentioned earlier, involvement in friendship networks provides individuals with such "capital" via the legitimacy and social cache derived from connections with powerful others, as well as from the important, often discretionary, information individuals obtain via network members. Social capital derived from friendship network involvement and centrality has been associated with higher pay (Belliveau et al., 1996), task performance (Baldwin, Bedell, & Johnson, 1997; Brandes, Dharwadkar, & Wheatley, 2004; Francis & Sandberg, 2000; Mehra, Dixon, Brass, & Robertson, 2006), and career success (Bozionelos, 2003; Matheson, 1999; Podolny & Baron, 1997; Seibert, Kraimer, & Liden, 2001).

In sum, research on workplace friendship demonstrates the unique nature of these important relationships. Although workplace friendships are not part of an organization's formal structure and are not formally sanctioned or mandated by management, these informal relationships and networks flourish in all types of organizations, at all hierarchical levels, and in all occupations. They are relationships of consequence for employees and for the organizations in which the friendships are embedded. Extant research provides insights into the primary functions of peer relationships such as information exchange (e.g., Sias, 2005), organizational change processes (e.g., McGrath & Krackhardt, 2003), social support (e.g., Kahn, 2001), and power and influence (e.g., Lamertz & Aquino, 2004). Research also provides understanding of workplace friendship development (e.g., Boyd & Taylor, 1998; Sias & Cahill, 1998), friendship deterioration (e.g., Sias et al., 2004), and the consequences and outcomes associated with engaging in workplace friendships (e.g., Meyers & Wilemon, 1989).

Theoretical Perspectives on Workplace Friendship

Similar to the research examined in Chapters 2 and 3, workplace friendship research is primarily guided by the postpositivist perspective, and our knowledge and understanding of these relationships would profit from consideration workplace friendship from multiple perspectives. Table 4.2 summarizes the various theoretical perspectives discussed in Chapter 1, along with a research agenda for the future informed by these perspectives.

Table 4.2 Theoretical Perspectives on Workplace Friendship

	Postpositivism	Social Construction	Critical Theory	Structuration Theory
Conceptualization of organizations	Real entities that exist beyond human perception "Contain" individuals Indicated by attitudes, behavior	Socially constructed Constituted in social practices Dynamic	Socially constructed Constituted in social practices Dynamic Systems of power, domination, and control	Socially constructed Constituted in social practices Dynamic Patterned social practices of organizational members across social systems
Conceptualization of communication	Occurs "inside" the relationship Indicates nature and status of the relationship	Constitutes social reality Constitutes relationships; as communication changes, so does the relationship	Constitutes social reality Constitutes relationships Essentializes and reifies organizational "realities" and relationships	Constitutes society and social systems Enables, produces, and reproduces structure Enabled and constrained by structure
Conceptualization of relationships	Real entities that exist beyond human perception "Contain" individuals Indicated by attitudes, communication behavior Predictive of outcomes (e.g., satisfaction, productivity, commitment) Influenced by physical environment	Socially constructed Exist in interaction Observable in interaction	Socially constructed Sites of power, domination, marginalization Sites of hegemonic, unobtrusive control	Socially constructed Constrained and enabled by structure

(Continued)

113

Table 4.2 (Continued)

	Postpositivism	Social Construction	Critical Theory	Structuration Theory
Research goals	Measuring indicators of relationship quality and status Predicting outcomes of relationships	Understanding social construction process Understanding relationship development dynamics	Understanding social construction of power, marginalization, reification, consent, domination, universalism of managerial interests and rationality	Understanding production, reproduction, and institutionalization of relationships
Sample research topics/questions		How do friends socially construct knowledge and innovation in their conversations with one another? What does knowledge creation "sound like" between workplace friends? How is innovation communicatively "diffused" via workplace friendship networks?	How do workplace friendships become reified? How do workplace friendship networks become reified? How do workplace friendship networks communicatively marginalize/include various employees? What discursive structures hinder the voluntary nature of workplace friendship?	What structures constrain/enable workplace friendships? What structures enable/constrain cross-sex workplace friendships? What structures guide workplace friendship deterioration? How do employees become knowledgeable about workplace friendship structures?

	Postpositivism	Social Construction	Critical Theory	Structuration Theory
Sample research topics/questions (continued)		How do friends socially construct social support with one another? How do friends "perform" gender in their relationships with one another? How does the performance of gender in same-sex friendships compare with performance of gender in cross-sex friendships?	How do minority employees participate in their marginalization from central friendship networks? How does the commodification of workplace friendship contribute to managerial interests? How does workplace friendship contribute to employee consent to concertive control?	What workplace friendship structures span time and social context? How do workplace friendship structures become institutionalized across time and space? How do the media contribute to the institutionalization of workplace friendship structures?

POSTPOSITIVIST PERSPECTIVE

The above discussion of workplace friendship research indicates that the majority of research in this area is grounded in postpositivism. Most studies rely, for example, on self-report survey data to test hypotheses and examine research questions. The data obtained via these methods indicate the "reality" of workplace friendship. Relatedly, the nature of the data results in analyses based primarily on correlation analyses (e.g., correlations, regressions, and analyses of variance). While such analyses identify associations between variables, they cannot provide insights into what direction and why the variables are associated.

Similar to research on peer and supervisor–subordinate relationships, existing research adopts a naturalist stance by conceptualizing employees involved in workplace friendships as physical objects. This is exemplified in research examining "individual differences" in workplace friendships such as age, race, and of course gender, which, like other research, tends to treat gender and biological sex synonymously, ignoring the dynamic nature of gender highlighted by social construction scholars. Research on workplace friendship instead operationalizes gender as a relatively simple, immutable physical characteristic (i.e., an individual is either a man or a woman). This method, while providing a number of important insights, limits our understanding of the ways gender is associated with workplace friendship, as discussed in more detail below. The naturalist principle is also illustrated in the many studies that rely on cross-sectional, rather than longitudinal, data to obtain an assessment or "snapshot" of the relationship at that single point in time. This method, at least implicitly, conceptualizes workplace friendships and limits our understanding of relational change and dynamism.

In sum, existing research on workplace friendships provides a great deal of understanding of the functions of such relationships, processes and factors associated with their development and deterioration, and consequences of these relationships for both individuals and organizations. Because of the substantial postpositivist bias of this research, however, our understanding is constrained by that perspective, leaving much to learn about workplace friendships. We can greatly expand our knowledge by conceptualizing, and studying, workplace friendships from multiple perspectives, as detailed in the remainder of this chapter.

SOCIAL CONSTRUCTION PERSPECTIVE

The assumptions of social construction theory direct researchers to consider workplace relationships as dynamic, socially constructed entities, and therefore, research focuses on issues of process; specifically, the process of creating, maintaining, and transforming "reality." Several studies of workplace friendship are grounded in such an approach and provide insights into how employees socially construct workplace friendships (Sias & Cahill, 1998; Sias et al., 2004) and how employees transform friendships into coworker-only relationships (Sias et al., 2004).

Some of the work discussed earlier, such as the social network research of Ibarra, is guided by social information processing (Salancik & Pfeffer, 1978), which shares assumptions similar to social construction theory, namely, that employees' perceptions and understanding of their social environment are constructed and influenced by interaction with others in their social network. While these studies are grounded in social construction assumptions, the *processes* by which employee perceptions of organization realities are created are unexamined. Instead, such research assesses employee network involvement (i.e., who talks to whom, how often) and links those quantitative measures with a variety of variables such as sex and race. These studies are very useful and provide insights into important issues related to workplace friendship.

We can learn much more, however, by examining social construction processes directly. Social construction research would provide important insights into how workplace friends socially construct not only their friendships, but other organizational "realities." For example, as discussed earlier, scholars have identified quantitative links between friendship network involvement and knowledge creation and learning and innovation (Ibarra, 1993a; Meyers & Wilemon, 1989). Social construction studies could provide rich insights by uncovering the interaction processes that underlie this link. The joint conversation reconstruction method described in Chapter 3 would be useful in obtaining data regarding conversations that occur between friends regarding new ideas, innovations, and new knowledge. Scholars could analyze these conversations to identify communication patterns (e.g., intimacy, trust, insider markers, etc.) that would indicate why such conversations are more likely to occur between friends than between acquaintances. In addition, tracing conversations as they are passed through the friendship network would provide very rich and useful insights into the communicative nature of diffusion of innovation. In other words, current research tells us that learning and innovation is enabled by friendship networks; social construction research would tell us why and how this occurs.

Similarly, studies indicate that social support is an important function of workplace friendships, but as with peer relationships (see Chapter 3), we have little understanding of what such effective and ineffective social support "sounds like." As noted in Chapter 2, some of my own studies (Sias & Cahill, 1998; Sias & Jablin, 1995) demonstrate that friends often turn to one another for support when dealing with a problematic work environment; however, at times such support leads to employees quitting their jobs, while other times, the relationships forged via such interaction essentially "chain" employees to dysfunctional work environments. Examination of actual social support conversations would provide rich insights into why and how social support functions differently across situations and dyads.

Finally, as noted above, current friendship research examining gender is limited by postpositivist conceptualizations that equate gender with biological sex, ignoring the socially constructed nature of gender and gender-specific roles. Social construction research could provide insights into the links between workplace friendship and gender by examining how employees construct and "perform" gender and gender-specific roles in their interaction with coworkers. Such analyses could reveal how men and women may vary or be similar in their performance of gender. Moreover, as noted above, women are often excluded from male-dominated friendship networks. This is likely due, in part, to the difficulties that arise in developing and maintaining cross-sex workplace friendships. Examining communication between cross-sex friends, and between the friends and other individuals in the workplace, may reveal functional and effective methods for engaging in successful cross-sex workplace relationships.

In sum, social construction theory can guide scholars toward a variety of important and useful research projects that would provide a rich body of knowledge to complement what we already know about workplace friendships.

CRITICAL PERSPECTIVE

Critical theory conceptualizes organizations and, by extension, workplace relationships, not just as socially constructed, but as socially constructed systems of power and domination. As noted in previous chapters, critical research is particularly concerned with the systems of power and domination (Mumby, 2000). As in previous chapters, the application of critical theory to workplace friendship research is organized here according to four main themes of critical research—reification, consent, technical rationality, and managerial bias (Deetz, 2005).

Studies of reification examine the ways socially constructed phenomena become naturalized and unquestioned. As noted above, informal friendship networks are important sites of power and influence and have been identified by many as an important barrier preventing women and minority employees from advancing in the corporate hierarchy, or breaking through the glass ceiling (Ibarra, 1993b; Kanter, 1977). Postpositivist research tends to treat organizational reality as static and unchanging. Thus, while many studies indicate women and minority employees tend to be marginalized from higher level social networks, the limitations of the postpositivist approach prevent researchers from examining and revealing the processes by which the social networks are formed and maintained. Critical research could provide important insights and practical knowledge by revealing the discursive processes that construct and maintain social networks and perceptions of the social network. Examination of employee interaction may reveal deeply rooted assumptions about reality that support the marginalization of women. Male employees, for example, may hold stereotypical gender role beliefs (e.g., women don't play golf, don't like sports, don't like to play poker, etc.) that prevent them from even considering inviting female employees to participate in the social activities that build friendship. Analysis of coworker interaction would provide insights into the extent to which employees consider social networks to be "real" and "natural" and, therefore, immutable.

The "voluntary" nature of workplace friendship makes the issue of consent particularly relevant. Current theory and research conceptualizes friendship as chosen rather than imposed (Sias & Cahill, 1998). However, research also indicates a variety of factors that impact friendship development such as sex, race, occupation, tasks, and proximity. Critical studies should question the extent to which workplace friendship is indeed voluntary and examine the social processes that may limit the "voluntariness" of friendship and the extent to which employees are actually able to choose which coworkers to befriend. Such studies might, for example, focus on identifying organizational practices and structures that prevent coworkers' access to others and, therefore, act as barriers to friendship development and the power imbued in friendships.

The notion of consent is also useful in understanding the processes and implications of extant research on racial homophily in workplace friendship networks. Mollica et al. (2003) found that the friendship networks of racial minority newcomers were more homogeneous than those of white majority newcomers, despite the fact that racial minorities had fewer "same-race ties" to choose from than did white students. Similarly, Mehra et al. (1998) found that members of racial minorities were more likely than majority employees to make "within-group" friendship choices. These studies suggest that employees, via their friendship choices, contribute and consent to their own marginalization and, to some extent, reinforce the barriers to their own career advancement.

The emotional component of workplace friendship makes research in the area of technical rationality particularly relevant. As noted throughout this chapter, friendships are affiliative relationships built on a foundation of emotions such as affect and liking. Emotional support is a key function of friendship. Emotions are considered as antithetical to rationality (Mumby & Putnam, 1992). In fact, Weber (1946) developed his theory of bureaucracy with the explicit goal of replacing emotion with rationality in organizational processes and functioning. To some individuals, rationality means that friendship does not belong in organizations (Sias & Cahill, 1998). Bridge and Baxter (1992) noted that the affect, support, and favoritism that characterize friendship conflict with the rationality and objectivity expected of coworkers. Critical research can lend important insights into emotion and rationality in key organizational processes such as decision making. Morgen's (1994) study of friendship and the making of personnel decisions exemplifies this approach. More research is needed, however, to uncover the communicative processes associated with emotion, rationality, and organizational decision making among friends.

Finally, the notion of friendship as "social capital" is relevant to the managerial bias noted in critical research. The *managerial bias* refers to the notion that what's good for the organization/management is good for employees. Extant workplace friendship research reveals a number of "outcomes" important to organizations such as satisfaction motivation, knowledge, innovation, and turnover. Friendship research also, however, conceptualizes the friendship as an important resource for individual employees; in particular, friendships provide access to information, power, and influence and are key to career advancement. Critical scholars could unpack the concept of "social capital" at the macrolevel by examining the extent to which the benefits of friendship accrue to the employees, the organization, or both. This could be accomplished, for example, with studies examining how organizational discourse such as popular business magazines and books effectively construct workplace friendship as an organizational and/or individual commodity.

STRUCTURATION PERSPECTIVE

The focus of structuration theory is on processes by which social structures and practices are produced and reproduced via human action. In addition, akin to critical theory, structuration theory addresses the ways in which structures become embedded and function below the level of consciousness (i.e., become reified). These foci could contribute much to our understanding of workplace friendship.

Applying the *duality of structure* to workplace friendship introduces innovative research topics. For example, structuration analysis could reveal the embedded structures that enable and constrain workplace friends and how those individuals reproduce and reinforce the very structures that constrain their interaction with one another. Similar to the social construction section above, for example, researchers could uncover the structures that constrain the development of cross-sex coworker relationships into close friendships compared to the structures that enable and constrain same-sex friendships.

Researchers could also address these issues through examination of *systems* or patterns of social relations across stretches of time and space. As discussed in earlier chapters, a structuration study would conceptualize workplace relationships as systems or patterns of social relations that stretch across time and space. This conceptualization would guide an interesting examination of workplace friendships. Sias et al. (2004), for example, note that individuals show a strong preference for the "depersonalization" tactic to disengage from a workplace friendship. Regardless of employee sex or hierarchical level, depersonalization appeared in their study to be the "default" tactic, suggesting that that the structure enabling/constraining workplace friendship disengagement may be institutionalized. A structuration study of this issue would examine the extent to which friendship disengagement functions similarly in various contexts, how individuals learned to disengage from workplace friendships, to which extent they are cognizant of their methods, and the like.

Using the concept of time–space distanciation, structuration research could also investigate the extent to which workplace friendship structures (e.g., regarding cross-sex relationships, same-sex relationships, as social capital, disengagement) are transported across time and context; that is, do workplace friendship structures span organizations? How do workplace friendship structures today compare to those in the past? How and why do such structures change over time? Interview, interaction, and archival data would all help address these questions. Interviews can obtain data from employees regarding what they perceive as appropriate friendship interaction, why such interaction is appropriate, and where they learned the structure (e.g., from prior relationships, the media, etc.). To what extent are workplace friendship structures (e.g., prototypes) transferable or context bound? What structures guide friendship in different social contexts (e.g., different countries, industries, occupations, hierarchical levels), and how are those structures created, maintained, and transformed?

Conclusion

Workplace friendships are plentiful in organizations, yet among the least researched types of workplace relationships. Scholars who have studied workplace friendships have provided a number of insights into the functions, developmental processes, and consequences of these relationships. As with other types of workplace relationships, however, our understanding is limited largely to postpositivist concerns. To broaden this body of knowledge, I have provided a research agenda for the future guided by multiple theoretical perspectives that will enhance our understanding of supervisor–subordinate relationships. Understanding organizational phenomena from multiple perspectives is of use not only to researchers, however. Different perspectives can also inform and improve practice by directing practitioners' attention to various aspects of actual workplace issues and problems involving workplace friendship, enabling a richer and more complex understanding of those issues. The following "Practicing Theory" case is designed to highlight the practical implications of multiple theoretical perspectives.

Too Much of a Good Thing?

Caroline was transferred to the tech support department of Simmons Manufacturing 9 months ago. Simmons is a large home furnishings manufacturer whose products are sold nationwide. The tech support department provides in-house support to all units of Simmons. Prior to her transfer, Caroline worked as an administrative assistant in the accounts receivable department. She was transferred to tech support and promoted to administrative specialist.

Caroline was excited about the move. She was ready for something challenging and new, and tech support had a reputation as a dynamic, fun department. Caroline quickly learned that reputation was well deserved. With the exception of Dan, the seven tech support employees were in their early to mid-20s, bright, and energetic, including her supervisor, Kevin. Dan was 41, recently divorced, with sole custody of his 8-year-old son.

Caroline noticed fairly soon that the younger employees, including Kevin, were a pretty strong and cohesive group, both at and away from work. They ate lunch together pretty much every day, often dropped by each other's desks to chat and goof around, often went out for drinks after work, and constantly shared "inside jokes" with each other. Caroline, young and single herself, was pleased to find herself included in this group pretty quickly after starting her new position. This job was definitely more fun than her old one.

Caroline noticed that while Dan got along okay with the others, he was rarely included in any social activities, never seemed to understand the inside jokes, and pretty much kept to himself. Dan typically ate lunch at his desk or with some friends he had in the sales department.

While Caroline enjoyed her relationships with the other employees, a few things were starting to make her uncomfortable. First, she was starting to become annoyed by frequent interruptions from the others. Caroline was very busy in her new job and concerned with performing well and making a good impression. It seemed, however, that someone was always dropping by her office to chat, joke around, and generally kill time. She felt she shouldn't be too worried given that her boss, Kevin, was a frequent visitor, but she also was finding that she would have to stay late or take work home in order to keep up with all the tasks she was required to do. She was unsure about how to handle this problem. She was afraid that if she asked people to leave, or to stop by her office less frequently, they would be offended and isolate her from the group. She was particularly uncomfortable saying anything to Kevin because he was her supervisor. In fact, she was beginning to question the wisdom of having Kevin in a supervisory position since it appeared to her that he did very little other than socialize.

Second, she was beginning to feel badly, and a little guilty, about how everyone treated Dan. While no one faulted Dan's performance, there seemed to be a consensus that he would not be included in socializing at, or away from, work. Caroline liked Dan and felt badly that he was being excluded by the others. While she made sure to say hi to Dan, she was concerned that if she talked with him too often, the others might begin to exclude her as well.

Discussion Questions

1. What coworker functions are being fulfilled and ignored in Caroline's department?

2. How does existing research explain the informal social network in Caroline's department?

3. The case is written from Caroline's perspective. What might the other employees say about these issues?

4. Consider this case from a critical perspective. What power and influence dynamics are at play in this department? What are the consequences of Dan being excluded from the social network?

5. Consider this case from a social construction perspective. How could understanding friendship and friendship networks as socially constructed help Caroline deal with her concerns?

6. Consider this case from a structuration perspective. What systemic workplace friendship structures are enabling/constraining the friendship network in this case? What systemic workplace friendship structures enabled/constrained Caroline's entrée into and participation in the department's friendship network?

5

Romantic Workplace Relationships

Workplace romance experiences are varied and unique—almost as varied as the people participating in such relationships. For many, like Sarah Kay and Matt Lacks, a workplace romance can grow to be a happy and lasting relationship. The couple met when both were employees at a New York area community center, and they quickly developed a romantic relationship after sharing lunch, stories, and interests with one another. They recently married (Rosenbloom, 2007). At the other extreme, a workplace romance can lead to disaster, such as the (in)famous case involving astronauts Lisa Nowak and William Oefelein. The two became romantically involved when they trained together in Houston. Oefelein eventually broke off the romance, sending Nowak into serious despair and depression. When Oefelein began dating another coworker, Colleen Shipman, Nowak became despondent and extremely jealous. She began harassing and stalking Shipman, in violation of a restraining order. The situation took a dangerous turn when Nowak, in disguise, drove 900 miles from her home in Houston to Orlando, approached Shipman in her parked car, and attempted to shoot Shipman with pepper spray. Arriving on the scene, police found a steel mallet, a knife, rubber tubing, $600 in cash, and garbage bags in the bag Nowak was carrying. Nowak was charged with attempted kidnapping and attempted murder ("NASA Astronaut," 2007). At the time of this writing, Nowak is awaiting trial.

Romantic relationships are among the most interesting, yet least understood, of all workplace relationships. As the stories above indicate, they can be incredibly rewarding and incredibly painful. Like workplace friendships (see Chapter 4), workplace romantic relationships transcend the boundary between private and public spheres. Like friendships, individuals blend their private and work lives in romantic relationships in unique ways. Like friendships, romantic relationships are voluntary and have a "personalistic" focus in which partners know and interact with one another as whole persons, not simply as work role occupants (Sias & Cahill, 1998). Romantic relationships differ from friendships in a number of important ways, however. The difference between friendship and romance represents the difference between liking and loving, affection and passion, intimacy and arousal. While friendships have an emotional component that can, but does not necessarily, threaten rationality, romantic relationships incorporate emotion at a higher and more intense level. The emotional, as well as physiological, nature of romantic relationships leads practitioners to fear the repercussions of workplace romance and the development of policies to "manage" or even forbid these relationships (Quinn, 1977).

Workplace romance does not need to be feared, however. These relationships can be quite rewarding for the individuals involved as well as the work environment in which they exist. In this chapter, I discuss existing research on romantic workplace relationships, focusing on developmental processes, the "gray area" between romance and sexual harassment, consequences and outcomes of workplace romance, and workplace romance policy and law. As in other chapters, I also develop a research agenda for the future by conceptualizing romantic relationships from a variety of theoretical perspectives and provide a case study highlighting the practical implications of current research and alternative theoretical perspectives.

Overview

While philosophers and scholars have found defining love an exercise in futility, researchers do agree on a few defining characteristics of workplace romantic relationships. At a broad level, a workplace romantic relationship is any "relationship between two members of the same organization that entails mutual attraction" (Pierce, Byrne, & Aguinis, 1996, p. 6). At a deeper level, workplace romances incorporate both emotional and physiological components, including the following:

> (a) an intense, passionate desire to be in the presence of one's romantic partner, (b) a shared, intimate exchange of personal disclosures, (c) affection and respect, (d) pleasant emotional states such as need satisfaction, happiness, and sexual gratification, and (e) physiological arousal and the desire for sexual acts such as kissing, petting, and intercourse with one's partner. (Pierce et al., 1996, p. 6)

Thus, workplace romantic relationships are emotional, physiological, and consensual. It is important to note that the consensual nature of these relationships distinguishes workplace romance from sexual harassment. Because the focus of this chapter is on consensual romantic relationships, I do not review the vast literature on sexual harassment in the workplace. However, romance and sexual harassment are not always clear-cut and can overlap. Moreover, what begins as a romance sometimes devolves into harassment. Accordingly, I begin this chapter with discussion of the "gray area" between romance and harassment before discussing research in the area of workplace romantic relationships. This research is summarized in Table 5.1.

Table 5.1   Summary of Workplace Romantic Relationship Research

The "Gray Area" Between Romance and Sexual Harassment

Social-Sexual Behaviors in the Workplace
- Flirting
- Quid pro quo
- Nonverbal (e.g., looks, glances, touch)
- Sexual language (e.g., comments, compliments, vulgarities)
- Confused communication (e.g., jokes, pet names)

Distinguishing Characteristics of Sexual Harassment Behavior
- Unwelcome
- Repetitive
- Severe

Romantic Workplace Relationship Development

Factors Influence Relationship Development
- Proximity (geographic, ongoing work requirement, occasional contact)
- Attitudinal similarity
- Employee attitudes toward workplace romance
- Job autonomy
- Organizational culture ("conservative" vs. "liberal")
- Organizational climate ("cold" vs. "hot")

Relationship Motives
- Job
- Ego
- Love

Relationship Types
- Fling
- Companionate
- Utilitarian

Communicating Romance
- Flirting
- Technology

Outcomes and Consequences

Impact on Coworkers
- Gossip
- Morale
- Jealousy
- Attributions of motives

Impact on Relationship Partners
- Attitudes and morale
    - Job satisfaction
    - Motivation

(Continued)

Table 5.1 (Continued)

– Behavior and performance
Productivity
Favoritism
Sexual harassment (after romance dissolves)

Workplace Romance Policy

Policy Characteristics
- Formality
- Organization vs. employee rights
- Unwritten rules

Employee Perceptions of Policy
- Fairness
- Appropriateness
- Severity

The "Gray Area" Between Romance and Sexual Harassment

Romantic communication and sexual harassment are both forms of *social-sexual behavior* (Pierce et al., 1996), which refers to "any non-work related behavior having a sexual component, including harassment, flirting and making sexual jokes" (Gutek, Cohen, & Konrad, 1990, p. 560). Social-sexual behavior is common in organizations. In fact, studies indicate the majority of employees report experiencing social-sexual behavior in the workplace (Burke & McKeen, 1992; Gutek et al., 1990). The intent of such behavior, however, is not always clear, and much research has focused on distinguishing between romantic communication and sexual harassment.

Some forms of sexual harassment are unmistakably clear (e.g., an explicit request for a sexual relationship in exchange for job-related rewards). Much social-sexual behavior, however, is unclear and ambiguous. What one person perceives as harmless fun another might perceive as harassing behavior. Flirting, for example, is defined by indirectness. The indirect nature of flirting renders it a "risky" behavior in that the target of the flirting may reject the overture and/or interpret the behavior as sexual harassment (Yelvington, 1996).

Markert (1999) organized various types of social-sexual behavior with respect to the extent to which the behavior is clearly sexual harassment, or more ambiguous and open to various interpretations. Relying on survey data, as well as sexual harassment case law, Markert argued that any "quid pro quo" behavior is clearly sexual harassment. *Quid pro quo* refers to requests for sexual favors in exchange for job security or enhancement, and case law identifies such behavior as sexual harassment. Moreover, 95% of the American public also interprets quid pro quo behaviors as sexual harassment (Markert, 1999). Markert notes, however, that this clarity becomes somewhat murky depending on who is involved in the event. Specifically, situations in which the initiator is male and the target is female are most likely to be perceived as sexual harassment. Those involving female initiators and male targets are slightly less likely to be interpreted as sexual harassment. Finally, same-sex quid pro quo is even less likely to be interpreted as sexual harassment.

The overtness of the social-sexual behavior also helps individuals identify the thin line between romance and sexual harassment, with more overt acts more likely to be interpreted as sexual harassment (Markert, 1999). Overt forms of behavior include explicit comments like "Let me pet your sweater" or the use of frank, vulgar, and explicitly sexual language. Like quid pro quo situations, overt sexual behavior is interpreted as sexual harassment by 95% of the American public (Barr, 1993).

Behaviors less likely to be interpreted as sexual harassment include compliments, looks and glances, pet names, and "asking out." There are gray areas within these behaviors, however, that make it more or less likely for them to be construed as harassing behaviors. Compliments, for example, tend to be acceptable unless they are overtly sexual. As Markert (1999) explains, "There is a difference between saying 'That's a nice dress, Jane' and 'Wow, Jane, that dress really turns me on'" (p. 42). Similarly, women are more likely than men to interpret looks and glances as sexually harassing. Finally, pet names vary in their appropriateness. Pet names that are not demeaning or overtly sexual tend to be perceived as appropriate. Asking a coworker out on a date is a necessary first step in developing a romantic workplace relationship. Thus, it is not typically seen as sexual harassment. Asking the same person out multiple times after being rejected, on the other hand, can be construed as harassment because the continued requests are perceived as pressure. Research suggests that women generally feel two refusals should be sufficient, and any requests after that constitute harassment (A. B. Fisher, 1993).

The murkiest area of social-sexual behaviors, according to Markert (1999), deals with "confused communication," in particular, remarks about sexual performance and sexual joking. According to research, people are split in their opinions of remarks about sexual performance. A large number of people see another's comments about their sexual life as inappropriate; many do not see such comments as sexual harassment. The line is crossed, however, when an individual makes comments about another employee's sex life. Sexual jokes are also open to multiple interpretations, but as Markert (1999) points out, "The sexual nature of the joke is not the problem. It is the 'butt' of the joke that is more problematic" (p. 48). Thus, jokes that disparage or denigrate a particular gender are more likely to be interpreted as sexual harassment.

More recently, Robinson, Franklin, Tinney, Crow, and Hartman (2005) reviewed existing case law distinctions between sexual harassment and romantic communication in the workplace. Their analysis revealed characteristics of social-sexual behavior that distinguish sexual harassment from nonharassing, romantic behavior. First, any social-sexual behavior that is *unwelcomed* by the target is sexual harassment. Moreover, to the extent that such unwelcome behavior is *severe* and *repetitive* and, consequently, constitutes a "hostile" work environment (i.e., the behavior interferes with target's work performance, harms their psychological well-being, creates an abusive work environment, and/or is such that leaving the organization would be the most constructive decision for the target), such behavior constitutes sexual harassment.

Burke and McKeen (1992) also examined various types of social-sexual behavior in the workplace. Their analyses revealed three primary categories—complimentary looks and comments, negative looks and comments, and sexual harassment. Complimentary looks and comments included comments, looks, and gestures of a sexual nature that the receiver perceived as complimentary and positive. Negative looks and comments included comments, looks, and gestures the receiver perceived as "put-downs." Sexual harassment included being touched in a sexual way, being required to "go out" with a man or suffer negative job consequences, and being required to engage in sexual relations to avoid negative job consequences. Thus, in Burke and McKeen's study, sexual harassment was distinguished from romantic behavior by sexual touch and quid pro quo requirements (e.g., sex for favors).

Solomon and Williams (1997) used an experimental design to identify variables that make it more likely that social-sexual behavior will be interpreted as sexual harassment rather than a romantic overture. Their results indicate messages that more explicitly convey sexual interest, that are initiated by supervisors, that are initiated by unattractive individuals, and that were directed toward attractive targets were more likely to be interpreted as sexual harassment than romantic overture. In addition, similar to other studies, female respondents were more likely than male respondents to interpret a social-sexual behavior as sexually harassing.

A recent survey by Kiser, Coley, Ford, and Moore (2006) found large agreement from respondents (75–100%) that the following behaviors constitute sexual harassment: sexual propositions, "brushing up," crude jokes (including those sent via e-mail), sexist comments (including those sent via e-mail), inappropriate comments, e-mailing inappropriate pictures, passing around inappropriate pictures or cartoons, and displaying inappropriate pictures or calendars. In contrast, few respondents perceived casual touching as sexual harassment.

J. W. Lee and Guerrero (2001), however, examined the interpretation of "touch" in greater detail. Their study focused on types of touch used in cross-sex workplace relationships. Acknowledging that employees must walk a "thin line" (i.e., the gray area) when initiating a workplace romance, they note that touch is a particularly ambiguous form of communication. As they explained, "Touch has the potential to be interpreted as friendly, affectionate, flirtatious, controlling, inappropriate and/or harassing in the context of cross-sex relationships between coworkers" (p. 198). To more clearly identify that "thin line," the authors examined employee perceptions of nine types of touch, ranging from shaking hands to face touching, by having participants watch a series of stimulus videos and rating the behavior they observed in the videos on a number of scales, including intimacy, positive affect, dominance, formality, composure, inappropriateness, and sexual harassment. Results reveal the complexity of the thin line between romance and harassment. Specifically, they found that face touch, and to a slightly lesser extent, placing an arm around another's waist, were the most powerful forms of touch with respect to both romance (e.g., flirting, friendliness, affection) and sexual harassment and inappropriateness. As the authors note, "In some cases, face touch may send a positive message of intimacy and attraction. However, in other cases, face touch may be perceived as a flirtatious gesture signaling unwanted love and romantic attraction. In the latter case, perceptions of inappropriateness and sexual harassment are likely" (p. 214).

An important question, then, is what factors make the latter interpretation more or less likely. J. W. Lee and Guerrero's (2001) study indicates the sex of the initiator may have some impact. Specifically, participants who watched videos in which the toucher was a male were more likely to interpret the touch as having romantic or sexual intentions such as flirting. In contrast, those who viewed videos in which the toucher was a woman were more likely to interpret the behavior as friendly, trusting, happy, and composed. Although there were no sex differences with respect to interpretations of sexual harassment, these findings suggest that men are perceived to be more sexual at work than women.

In sum, although social-sexual behavior is common in the workplace, those who engage in such behavior risk the possibility that it will be interpreted as harassing rather than romantic. The greatest risk occurs with messages that are overtly explicit, unwelcome, repeated a number of times, and initiated by males in positions of authority toward females in lower level hierarchical positions. Social-sexual behavior intended, and interpreted, as romantic rather than harassment represents the first step toward development of a romantic relationship. Developmental processes associated with workplace romance are discussed in the following section.

Workplace Romantic Relationship Development

Although men and women have likely engaged in romantic working relationships for centuries, scholars generally identify the mid-20th century as the "beginning" of workplace romance (Quinn, 1977). The increased number of women in the postwar workforce made workplace romance virtually inevitable. In the 1960s and 1970s, women's rights movements resulted in even more gender diversity in organizations, with women taking positions in all types of organizations at all levels (although, as noted in previous chapters, the number of women becomes drastically smaller moving up the organizational hierarchy). The increased presence of women led to increased interaction between men and women. This interaction occasionally leads to the development of a romantic relationship (Dillard, 1987). In fact, research indicates 75% to 85% of employees experience a romantic relationship at work, either as a participant or an observer (Pierce & Aguinis, 2003).

DEVELOPMENTAL FACTORS

Several scholars have attempted to identify various factors that impact the development of workplace romantic relationships. Much of this work conceptualizes the workplace environment as a type of "incubator" for romantic relationships. Studies, for example, highlight the role of proximity in romantic relationship development. Quinn (1977) identified three primary types of proximity that are associated with the development of romantic relationships. *Geographical proximity* refers to individuals being physically near one another via proximal work spaces or offices. *Ongoing work requirement proximity* refers to proximity resulting from employees working on joint projects, training workshops, business trips, and other requirements of the job that bring the individuals in close proximity to one another. *Occasional contact* refers to situations in which the individuals do not enjoy regular, patterned proximity via their work station locations or ongoing requirements of their job, but instead are brought into occasional contact with one another via such mechanisms as riding the elevator together or running into one another in other locations, such as a cafeteria, because they work in the same organization.

In a major review of research, Pierce et al. (1996) found a number of other empirical studies that revealed the important role of proximity in romantic relationship development. The authors point out that the repeated exposure individuals are provided by proximity enables them to gain information from one another and develop a liking and affection for one another. In particular, repeated exposure enables employees to determine whether they are similar to one another. Much research identifies *attitude similarity* as an important contributor to liking and eventually romance. Pierce et al. (1996) argue that such relationships are particularly likely to develop in organizations because organizations, via their hiring and selection processes, tend to attract and retain individuals with similar interests (e.g., occupation) and attitudes, and filter out those individuals who are dissimilar to the organization's general population. Thus, they argue, the workplace is a natural environment, or "incubator," for attraction.

The type of job an employee has can impact the likelihood that they will develop a romantic workplace relationship. Specifically, the more autonomous one's job, the more likely one is to engage in workplace romance (Haavio-Mannila, Kauppinen-Toropainen, & Kandolin, 1988; Pierce & Aguinis, 2003).

Job autonomy, defined as "'the ability to make decisions about one's own work' and the 'freedom to move in the work environment and to make contacts with coworkers'" (Pierce et al., 1996, p. 17), essentially enables employees to create proximity and opportunities for exposure that enhance relational development.

The organizational culture can also enhance or hinder romantic relationship development. Mainiero (1989) found that "conservative" organizations, for example, those that were slow paced, conventional, and traditional, were more likely to discourage workplace romances via formal or informal policies than were "liberal" organizations, for example, those that were fast paced, action oriented, and dynamic (Pierce et al., 1996). Moreover, the fast-paced, dynamic environments of "liberal" organizations "often contain an atmosphere of intense pressure and activity that stimulates sexual excitement" (Pierce et al., 1996, p. 16).

Similarly, Mano and Gabriel (2006) examined workplace romance in "hot" and "cold" organizational climates. Cold organizational climates are characterized by impersonal, formal organizational structures. Grounded in bureaucratic principles, such climates are designed to "exclude human feeling and emotion from mainstream organizational activities, focusing instead on instrumental, task-related relationships" (Mano & Gabriel, 2006, p. 10). Hot climates, in contrast, "involve an 'aestheticization' of labour that puts employees 'on display' with respect to their physical appearance." As Mano and Gabriel (2006) note, industries such as tourism and advertising tend to have a "sexual simmer" about them, sexualizing employees and the workplace itself. By gathering stories of romance from individuals in different types of organizational climates, Mano and Gabriel (2006) found that those in "hot" climates told more stories of romance, with more passion, and indicated a more hospitable environment for romance than did those in "cold" climates. Employees in cold climates, instead, told stories of the rare romance and employees' attempts to keep the relationship a secret.

Finally, studies indicate that an individual's attitude toward workplace romance is associated with the likelihood that she or he will engage in a romantic relationship at work. Haavio-Mannila et al. (1988) found that people who had positive attitudes toward flirting in the workplace were more likely to engage in a romantic workplace relationship.

In sum, a number of factors influence the initiation and development of romantic workplace relationships. Such relationships are more likely to emerge in work environments that encourage and provide multiple opportunities for interaction via physical proximity, shared tasks, and the like, and that tend to be fast paced, exciting, and high energy or "hot" climates. Individuals with positive attitudes toward romance and flirting in the workplace are also more likely to engage in romantic relationships themselves. Not all romantic relationships are alike, however, and different relationships emerge and evolve for different reasons. The following section addresses distinct types of romantic relationships, driven by varying motives on the parts of the romantic partners.

RELATIONSHIP MOTIVES AND TYPES

As with any type of relationship, all romantic workplace relationships are not alike. Researchers have identified a variety of romantic relationship types by examining the partners' motives for engaging the relationship. Quinn (1977) was the first to empirically address these issues. Via qualitative and quantitative studies, he identified three primary motives for participating in a romantic relationship. The *job motive* refers to instances in which individuals engage in a romantic relationship for purposes of job advancement and security, financial rewards such as promotions and bonuses, increased power, and easier or more efficient tasks. *Ego motives* reflect the desire for excitement, adventure, and ego gratification. *Love motives* reflect sincere affection, love, respect, and companionship. Employees motivated by love seek a long-term commitment from the romance.

According to Quinn's (1977) study, women and men differed with respect to their motives, and the varying combination of motives resulted in three different types of workplace romantic relationships. The *fling* represents a relationship in which both the male and female partners seek ego gratification and adventure (i.e., ego motives). *Companionate love* refers to relationships in which both partners engage in the romance for love motives and a sincere desire for long-term commitment. The *utilitarian* relationship refers to relationships in which the male partner seeks ego gratification and the female partner engages in the romance for job motives or a desire to improve her position and financial situation. This relationship represents the "sleeping up the ladder" stereotype that has persisted over the years.

It should be noted that Quinn's research was conducted nearly three decades ago, and these findings are quite dated. In a somewhat more recent study, Anderson and Fisher (1991) found little evidence that women entered romantic workplace relationships for job motives. Interestingly, however, Powell (2001) found that observers of workplace romantic relationships were more likely to perceive job motives in hierarchical romances (i.e., relationships between individuals at different hierarchical levels) when the lower-level participant was female instead of male. Thus, despite evidence from the participants' perspective that women are no more likely to engage in workplace romance for job motives than are men, perceptions of observers appear to retain the stereotype. Coworkers' perspectives of workplace romance are addressed in more detail later in this chapter when I discuss research on consequences of romantic relationships at work.

COMMUNICATING ROMANCE

Many scholars have examined the role of communication in romantic relationships. These studies, either explicitly or implicitly, assume a social construction notion of relationships; that is, they assume relationships are created and maintained via communication patterns. This research focuses primarily on flirting, banter, nonverbal communication, and communication technology.

Flirting refers to "indirect behaviour designed to communicate a possible sexual interest in another individual, as well as to inquire through this indirection, as to the other's possible interest" (Yelvington, 1996, p. 314). Scholars note a few defining characteristics of flirting. First, it is romantic and sexual (Yelvington, 1996). Second, it is an indirect behavior characterized by hints and innuendo. Third, because it is indirect, it also ambiguous and uncertain—the target of the flirting may interpret the message in a number of different ways (Henningsen, 2004). Fourth, despite the fact that flirting involves indirect communication, it is nonetheless directive, not ambient, in that the behavior is directed toward a specific target. Fifth, flirting is a risk-taking behavior (Yelvington, 1996). Risks of flirting include both possible misinterpretation (e.g., a romantic gesture interpreted as sexual harassment) and rejection (i.e., the romantic interest is not reciprocated). Flirting, therefore, is usually the first step in the development of a romantic relationship.

A recent study examined communication among romantic relationship partners via workplace e-mail technology (Hovick, Meyers, & Timmerman, 2003). Analyses yielded a number of interesting results. First, employees involved in ongoing workplace romantic relationships relied on e-mail more than any other communication medium, including face-to-face, to communicate with one another at work. They used e-mail primarily to ask their relationship partner work- and non-work-related questions, engage in small talk, and for flirting and expressing intimacy. In contrast, employees reported using e-mail only rarely to *initiate* a romantic relationship, to obtain information about their partner, and to engage in conflict. These results indicate that face-to-face interaction, including face-to-face flirting, may be important for initiating a romantic relationship, and e-mail may be less effective in the early stages of a romance. As the romance develops, e-mail appears to be important for maintaining the relationship.

As seen above, we have developed an understanding of why individuals engage in workplace romantic relationships. Research also provides some insight into how employees communicate interest in one another. We know little, however, about how workplace romantic relationships actually develop, are maintained, and are eventually terminated over time. These issues will be discussed in greater detail in the later section of this chapter. For now, we turn to discussion of the consequences of workplace romance.

Outcomes and Consequences of Workplace Romantic Relationships

Generally, scholars and practitioners have assumed that allowing workplace romance would be harmful to the organization. This likely stems from the classical management school of thought that emotion has no useful place in organizational processes (e.g., Fayol, 1949; Weber, 1946). While many studies have demonstrated the negative impact of romantic relationships, research also suggests such relationships can have positive impact, not only on the employees involved in the relationship, but also on the larger work environment.

IMPACT ON COWORKERS

Perhaps the greatest amount of research attention in this area has focused not on the individuals involved in the relationships, but on their coworkers. Specifically, studies have examined how coworkers interpret and make attributions about the romantic relationships of other employees. Despite efforts on the part of the romantic partners to hide their relationship, workgroup members tend to know when their coworkers are romantically involved (Quinn & Lees, 1984). The relationship then becomes a subject of gossip for the rest of the employees (Michelson & Mouly, 2000; Quinn, 1977). The tone of this gossip is, to some extent, dependent on the perceived motives of the participants in the romance. In general, situations in which the female partner is perceived to have engaged in the romance for job motives tend to generate negative gossip, while romances in which the male partner is perceived to have been motivated by love tend to generate more positive gossip (Dillard, 1987).

In addition to, and perhaps because of, employee gossip regarding the romantic relationship, these relationships can impact coworkers' morale and attitudes. In some cases, the romance can improve workgroup morale by providing an "uplifting" and happier work environment and creating an exciting "sexual electricity" (Horn & Horn, 1982; Smith, 1988). In other cases, the romance can have a negative impact on morale. Hierarchical romances, in particular, tend to have a more negative impact on the workgroup due to jealousy and suspicions of favoritism. As Pierce et al. (1996) explain, "Basically, members of the workgroup perceive organizational injustice as the result of boss–subordinate romances, thereby lowering morale at work" (p. 20). Similarly, Werbel and Hames (1996) found that employees reported negative attitudes regarding married couples in the workplace. These negative attitudes centered on disruption of group processes and concerns regarding favoritism. Their analysis revealed that men, supervisors, and employees in small firms were most likely to hold these negative attitudes.

Pierce, Broberg, McClure, and Aguinis (2004) examined how various characteristics of a *dissolved* workplace romantic relationship that led to harassment impact how others judge the harasser and make decisions about personnel actions. Results indicated several factors impact observers' decisions regarding appropriate personnel decisions, ranging from recommending no action be taken to support and counseling to disciplinary action. Specifically, situations involving a direct supervisor–subordinate reporting relationship, situations in which the accused (in this experiment, a male supervisor) was deemed responsible, and situations representing "utilitarian," rather than companionate or fling, relationships were perceived as deserving harsher personnel decisions than indirect reporting relationships, situations in which the accuser/complainant was deemed responsible, and situations involving companionate or fling relationships. The Pierce et al. (2004) experiments also examined how observers judge the morality of the sexual harassment. Observers were likely to judge the behavior as immoral when the dissolved romantic relationship was an extramarital relationship, when the behavior represented quid pro quo rather than a hostile environment or sexual harassment, and when the situation occurred in an organization with an explicit policy prohibiting workplace romantic relationships.

Jones (1999) examined coworker perceptions of hierarchical workplace romance (i.e., between a supervisor and subordinate employee). Using hypothetical scenarios, the author manipulated several variables to assess employee perceptions regarding the appropriateness of, attitudes toward, and consequences of the workplace romance. The manipulated variables included sex of the supervisor and the marital status of both parties involved in the relationship. Results indicated that respondents reacted more negatively when one or both of the partners were married. In addition, respondents were more likely to attribute blame to the supervisor rather than the subordinate employee. Finally, respondents were far more likely to attribute ego motives than love motives to the couple, especially when the supervisor was a male. Female supervisors were more likely than male supervisors to be perceived as having entered the relationship for love. Overall, however, the respondents in the Jones (1999) study were unlikely to perceive the romantic relationship as one of love, rather than ego gratification and excitement. Using a similar method, Powell (2001) examined coworker attitudes and responses toward hierarchical romance. Consistent with Jones (1999), respondents held the most negative attitudes toward relationships in which the supervisor was male and the subordinate employee was female, and were more likely to attribute a "job" motive to the female subordinate than either ego or love. These findings again confirm the persistence of the "sleeping up the ladder" stereotype.

In sum, existing research shows that a workplace romance has ramifications beyond the relationship itself. It impacts others in the workplace by generating gossip and impacting attitudes toward the relationship partners and toward the organization as whole.

IMPACT ON THE RELATIONSHIP PARTNERS

Of course, a romantic workplace relationship affects not only observers of that relationship, but also the partners directly involved in the romance. Research in this area focuses primarily on how a workplace romance impacts the partners' attitudes, performance, and careers.

Attitudes and Morale

A workplace romantic relationship can have both positive and negative impacts on the participants' attitudes and morale. Certainly the relationship creates a happier environment for the partners who look forward to being near each other at work. Thus, engaging in a romance can improve the participants' job satisfaction (Pierce et al., 1996). In addition, participating in a workplace romance can improve an employee's motivation (Dillard & Broetzman, 1989; Mainiero, 1989). This is likely because individuals engaged in a romance tend to feel better about themselves and show a willingness to work longer hours to be with their partners (Pierce et al., 1996). It also may result from a concern about coworker perceptions such that the partners wish to prove to others that their relationship will not affect their performance. Pierce et al. (1996) point out, however, that the impact on participant attitudes depends, in part, on the quality of the relationship itself. To the extent that an individual is unsatisfied or unhappy with the relationship, that relationship is likely to harm, not improve, job satisfaction and motivation. In addition, the attitudes of the partners' coworkers are also an important moderator of these links. If the coworkers engage in negative gossip and ostracize or otherwise "punish" the partners, the difficulties of working in such an environment may decrease participants' satisfaction, morale, and motivation.

Behavior and Performance

Similar to research on participants' attitudes, studies indicate that engaging in a workplace romance can have positive and negative effects on employee behavior and task performance. In one of the earliest studies on this topic, Quinn (1977) found that participating in a romantic relationship resulted in a variety behavior and performance changes for the partners, including preoccupation, becoming more productive, becoming less productive, showing favoritism to the other, and protecting one another in a variety of ways. The relationship type may moderate the link between romantic relationships and productivity. Specifically, hierarchical romances tend to impede productivity more than lateral relationships (Devine & Markiewicz, 1990). In addition, hierarchical romances are more likely to impede the productivity of others in the group given that the supervisor involved may be distracted and/or favoring his or her romantic partner. Dillard (1987) found that individuals who engaged in a romantic relationship for love motives tended to show an increase in productivity, in contrast to those motivated by job or ego, who showed no change in productivity.

All of the research discussed so far has examined the impact of "intact" romantic relationships on the participants and their coworkers. Pierce and his colleagues have pursued an interesting line of research regarding the impact of *dissolved* workplace romantic relationships, focusing on how and why dissolved workplace romances sometimes devolve into sexual harassment—issues that are reflected in the astronaut romance story at the beginning of the chapter. Pierce and Aguinis (1997) argued that although romance and sexual harassment are different phenomena, they do intersect, and scholars should avoid treating them as completely separate subjects. They developed a model explicating the links between the two. Specifically, their model identifies dissolved romantic relationships, particularly those between supervisors and their direct subordinate, as one such link. The dissolution of a romantic relationship evokes negative feelings and emotions for the former partners. In nonwork relationships, the individuals typically have the option to never see one another. Workplace relationships, and particularly those between supervisor and subordinate, require the former romantic partners to see each frequently. The negative feelings, combined with repeated exposure, make such situations particularly vulnerable to sexual harassment. As Pierce and Aguinis (1997) explain, one of the employees may sexually harass the other for reasons of revenge, in an attempt to rekindle the romance, or to avoid the negative feelings (e.g., in situations where the supervisor transfers or terminates the subordinate employee).

Empirical research provides some support for this argument. In 1998, a survey of human resource personnel revealed that 25% of sexual harassment claims resulted from the dissolution of a workplace romance (Society for Human Resource Management, 1988). Pierce, Aguinis, and Adams (2000) found that employees' motives for engaging in the romantic relationship (i.e., ego, job, or love) were associated with judgments regarding the subsequent sexual harassment. Specifically, harassers who engaged in the romantic relationship for ego purposes, while their partners were motivated by love, were judged more harshly (i.e., more responsible for their actions) than harassers who were motivated by love, while their accusers and former romantic partners engaged in the romantic relationship for job enhancement purposes.

Taken together, research suggests workplace romance can be a source of joy or misery for the relationship partners, depending on a number of factors, such as their motives for engaging in the relationship, the perceptions of their coworkers, the hierarchical relationship between the partners (i.e., peer or supervisor–subordinate), and the extent to which the relationship endures and dissolves. Because of these important consequences, many organizations develop and implement formal and informal policies governing workplace romance.

Workplace Romance Policy

As seen in the preceding section, workplace romantic relationships can have a number of important consequences for the romantic partners, their coworkers, and larger organizational processes. Because of this, many organizations implement formal and informal policies for managing workplace romance. Such policies are designed to protect the organization from many of the consequences discussed above, such as favoritism, decreased productivity, and sexual harassment claims. In this section, I discuss the types and effectiveness of such policies.

PRIVATE RIGHTS IN PUBLIC SETTINGS

Formal workplace romance policies vary from very strict comprehensive policies forbidding dating among all employees, to those forbidding romantic relationships only between supervisors and subordinates, to simple lenient policies that only request employees notify management if they become involved in a workplace romantic relationship (Wilson, Filosa, & Fennel, 2003). In addition, many organizations forego implementing a formal policy and rely, instead, on "unwritten rules" that employees are assumed to know and respect.

Much research on workplace romance policy addresses the tensions between individuals' personal rights and responsibilities in public settings such as organizations. Essentially, case law and the policies the law informs focus on delineating the point at which an organization's necessities outweigh the employee's right to engage in a workplace romance. Dworkin (1997) noted that the employer's ability to control employee behavior such as smoking and dating has increased over the years and recommended that courts (and organizations) adopt a "reasonable business necessity standard" in designing, and assessing, workplace romance policies. Along these lines, Paul and Townsend (1998) recommend organizations only get involved in workplace romantic relationships if they are shown to impair job performance.

More recently, Wilson et al. (2003) reviewed case law and concluded that "in many, if not most instances, the employer's legitimate business interests in maintaining a peaceful and productive work environment and avoiding liability outweigh an employee's right to privacy. This has proved to be especially true in the context of an employment relationship in the private sector" (p. 87). Thus, Wilson et al. (2003) recommend organizational policies that are reasonable and do not unduly intrude on the employees' private lives. They also recommend forbidding only supervisor–subordinate romantic relationships, as these are the ones most likely to motivate legal action.

PERCEPTIONS OF POLICIES

While the above studies provide analysis and description of laws and policies governing workplace romantic relationships, other scholars have examined how employees and employers feel about those laws and policies. Having a formal policy in place does not necessarily mean employees will agree with, and abide by, the policy. Researchers have examined employee attitudes toward workplace romance policies, specifically with respect to the perceived fairness and appropriateness of those policies.

Foley and Powell (1999) developed a model of how and why coworkers of employees engaged in a romantic relationship react toward management intervention in that relationship (e.g., interventions ranging in severity and intrusiveness from punitive action such as termination to no action at all). According to the model, coworkers are more likely to prefer punitive intervention when the workplace romance creates a conflict of interest, disrupts work procedures, involves a relationship in which one partner directly reports to the other, when the relationship is perceived as a "utilitarian" relationship, when one of the partners in the relationship is married, when the coworker has a negative attitude toward workplace romance in general, and when the coworkers work in a "conservative" versus "liberal" work environment. In a subsequent study testing some of the model's propositions, Powell (2001) found that employees prefer both punitive and positive (e.g., advice giving, counseling) interventions in cases involving supervisor–subordinate romances. Results of that study also indicated employee concerns that such relationships create disruption in work processes.

Finally, in an interesting critical study, Schultz (2003) argued that as a byproduct of sexual harassment lawsuits, courts have unduly encouraged the "sanitization" or "de-sexualization" of the workplace. Taking a critical stance on sexual harassment law, Schultz argued that such laws reflect the bureaucratic notion that emotion does not belong in the workplace and that rationality is the only appropriate organizational system. This "dehumanizing" of organizations created an emotionless, and therefore "sexless," workplace. Sexual harassment law is grounded in this rational approach, and many courts and, consequently, organizations have implemented "zero tolerance" policies for sexual harassment that function to drive all sexual behavior (welcome or not) out of the workplace and essentially "policing sex" in employees' private lives. Instead, Schultz argues, "We should question the idea that workplace sexual conduct always constitutes harassment, and become more open-minded about the presence and uses of sexuality at work" (p. 2168). In addition, organizations and practitioners should place their focus back on the original root of sexual harassment law—that of discrimination and gender inequities at work. As she explains,

> The most crucial step, therefore, is to create incentives for organizations to fully integrate their workforces, rather than simply desexualizing their environments, as a means of complying with sex harassment law. The theoretical justification for doing so is straightforward. In an ideal world, the goal would be to put women in a position of complete equality in fully integrated work settings, so that they would have equal power to shape the environments and cultures in which they work to their own liking. In such a world, even if some women ended up working in environments that included a lot of sexual conduct and expression, we would be comfortable concluding that the presence of such conduct was not itself a product of sex discrimination. Of course, even in such egalitarian environments, sexual conduct—like any other form of conduct—might still be used as a weapon of sex discrimination against individual women or men, so we would still need to protect

individuals from harassment directed at them because of their sex. But, by definition, we would not equate the mere presence of sexual conduct with sex discrimination. (p. 2174)

In sum, despite their ubiquitous nature, workplace romantic relationships have received relatively little research attention. Similar to workplace friendships, romantic relationships are not part of an organization's formal structure and are not formally sanctioned or mandated by management. They do, however, flourish in all types of organizations, at all hierarchical levels, and in all occupations. Moreover, they are relationships of consequence for employees and for the organizations in which the romances are embedded. Concerns about such consequences have led many organizations to implement formal policies governing workplace romance.

Extant research provides insights into the distinctions between workplace romance and sexual harassment (e.g., Markert, 1999), primary types of workplace romances (e.g., Quinn, 1977), employees' motives for engaging in workplace romance (Quinn, 1977), factors associated with the development of workplace romantic relationships (e.g., Mano & Gabriel, 2006), consequences and outcomes of workplace romance (e.g., Pierce et al., 2000), and development and responses to organizational workplace romance policies (e.g., Wilson et al., 2003).

Theoretical Perspectives on Workplace Romantic Relationships

Relative to the relationships discussed in previous chapters, our understanding of workplace romance is substantially underdeveloped. Much about these relationships is unknown. Similar to the research regarding other types of workplace relationships, workplace romantic relationship research is primarily guided by the postpositivist perspective and our knowledge. Our body of knowledge regarding these relationships can be greatly enriched by considering and studying them from multiple theoretical perspectives. The remainder of this chapter develops a research agenda for the future designed to address current voids in the literature. Table 5.2 summarizes these research directions.

POSTPOSITIVIST PERSPECTIVE

Postpositivism underlies the vast majority of workplace romantic relationship research. Most studies rely, for example, on self-report survey data to test hypotheses and examine research questions. Data obtained via these methods indicate the "reality" of workplace romance. And like research on other types of workplace relationships, the nature of the data results in analyses

Table 5.2 Theoretical Perspectives on Romantic Workplace Relationships

	Postpositivism	Social Construction	Critical Theory	Structuration Theory
Conceptualization of organizations	Real entities that exist beyond human perception "Contain" individuals Indicated by attitudes, behavior	Socially constructed Constituted in social practices Dynamic	Socially constructed Constituted in social practices Dynamic Systems of power, domination, and control	Socially constructed Constituted in social practices Dynamic Patterned social practices of organizational members across social systems
Conceptualization of communication	Occurs "inside" the relationship Indicates nature and status of the relationship	Constitutes social reality Constitutes relationships; as communication changes, so does the relationship	Constitutes social reality Constitutes relationships Essentializes and reifies organizational "realities" and relationships	Constitutes society and social systems Enables, produces, and reproduces structure Enabled and constrained by structure
Conceptualization of relationships	Real entities that exist beyond human perception "Contain" individuals Indicated by attitudes, communication behavior Predictive of outcomes (e.g., satisfaction, productivity, commitment) Influenced by physical environment	Socially constructed Exist in interaction Observable in interaction	Socially constructed Sites of power, domination, marginalization Sites of hegemonic, unobtrusive control	Socially constructed Constrained and enabled by structure

(Continued)

143

Table 5.2 (Continued)

	Postpositivism	Social Construction	Critical Theory	Structuration Theory
Research goals	Measuring indicators of relationship quality and status Predicting outcomes of relationships	Understanding social construction process Understanding relationship development dynamics	Understanding social construction of power, marginalization, reification, consent, domination, universalism of managerial interests and rationality	Understanding production, reproduction, and institutionalization of relationships
Sample research topics/questions		How do employees communicatively construct and transform the work relationship into a romantic relationship? How do employees communicatively dissolve a romantic relationship? How do coworker observers of a romantic relationship socially construct that relationship?	What discursive processes contribute to the reification of the "sleeping up the ladder" gender stereotype? How do gendered discursive processes regarding romantic workplace relationships disempower women? What discursive structures hinder the voluntary nature of workplace romantic relationships?	What structures constrain/enable workplace romantic relationships? What structures enable/constrain romantic and sexually harassing communication? What structures enable/constrain coworkers' interpretations of a romantic relationship?

	Postpositivism	Social Construction	Critical Theory	Structuration Theory
Sample research topics/questions (continued)		How do employees socially construct same-sex romantic relationships? How do coworker observers of a same-sex romantic relationship socially construct that relationship? How does a romantic relationship transform the relationships of the romantic partners with other coworkers? How do employees socially construct formal organizational policies governing workplace romance? How do employees socially construct "unwritten rules" governing workplace romance?	How does participation in a workplace romance (dis)empower employees? How does participation in romantic relationships reflect emotional versus rational reasoning processes? How does the "desexualization" of the workplace via organizational policies marginalize women?	How do "unwritten rules" (structures) guiding workplace romance become institutionalized via employee communication? What workplace romantic relationship structures span time and social context? How do workplace romantic relationship structures become institutionalized across time and space? How do the media and popular culture contribute to the institutionalization of workplace romantic relationship structures?

based primarily on correlation analyses (e.g., correlations, regressions, and analyses of variance). While such analyses identify associations between variables, they cannot provide insights into what direction and why the variables are associated.

The postpositivist naturalist principle is also illustrated in the many studies that rely on cross-sectional, rather than longitudinal, data to obtain an assessment or "snapshot" of the relationship at that single point in time. This method, at least implicitly, conceptualizes workplace romantic relationships as static and limits our understanding of relational change and dynamism. For example, many studies designed to identify the "gray area" between romantic behavior and sexual harassment rely on experimental methods in which one or more independent variables are manipulated in hypothetical scenarios and vignettes, and their association with various dependent variables are measured. Independent variables include such factors as the sex, marital status, and hierarchical rank of the vignette characters who typically exhibit, in the scenarios, a behavior such as touching, joking, or flirting. Study participants then rate that behavior as to its appropriateness, clarity, and the extent to which it is harassing versus romantic behavior. Such methods provide "indicators" of the reality of workplace romance at that particular point in time. While such insights are valuable, the discussion of literature above reveals we know almost nothing about the *dynamics* of such behavior. Flirting, for example, occurs in a dyadic conversation. In conversation, each statement made is dependent upon, and responsive to, the statement that precedes it. Analysis of romantic behavior (both verbal and nonverbal) from a more dynamic perspective could reveal insights into how partners together construct the behavior and the types of statements that lead the behavior toward or away from harassment. Reliance on postpositivism has also prevented understanding of developmental processes associated with workplace romantic relationships, beyond individuals' motives for engaging the relationship and how the work environment (e.g., proximity) impacts the likelihood of romance. We also know nothing about how and why romantic relationships deteriorate, or the ebb and flow of these relationships with respect to quality, emotion, and other relational dynamics.

In sum, existing research on workplace romantic relationships provides insights into a variety of important issues such as identifying the "gray area" between romance and sexual harassment, employee motives for engaging in workplace romance, and the various types of workplace romantic relationships. Research has also identified a number of factors that encourage the initiation of workplace romance such as physical proximity, repeated exposure, and similarity. Finally, extant work has revealed a number of positive and negative consequences of workplace romance for the relationship partners, their coworkers, and the organization in which such relationships exist. There is much we do not know about workplace romantic relationships, however, due to the fact that the substantial postpositivist bias of this research has constrained our conceptualizations and approaches to the study of these entities. As detailed below, we can greatly expand our knowledge by conceptualizing, and studying, workplace romantic relationships from other theoretical perspectives.

SOCIAL CONSTRUCTION PERSPECTIVE

Applying social construction concepts to workplace relationships directs our attention to a variety of processes and issues ignored by the postpositivist perspective. As a social reality, social construction theory conceptualizes organizations, and workplace romantic relationships, as socially constructed entities constituted in member interaction. A romantic relationship exists in the partners' communication with one another; it does not exist outside their interaction. Consequently, and again in contrast to postpositivism, employee behavior does not simply indicate the relationship; it constitutes the relationship, and therefore, the relationship is directly observable in the partners' communication.

Social construction's dynamic conceptualization of social reality turns research attention toward process-related issues such as the processes of creating, maintaining, and changing social reality. The social construction perspective could be particularly valuable in enriching workplace romantic relationship research by providing insights into the socially constructed nature of such relationships. For example, although evidence indicates factors such as physical proximity and repeated exposure affect workplace romance initiation, we know nothing about the nature of that initiation and, in particular, how employees communicatively construct, and transform, their coworker relationship into a workplace romance.

Similarly, to date, researchers have not examined how and why romantic relationships deteriorate. Research grounded in social construction theory would contribute greatly to the literature by revealing the communicative processes by which employees disengage from a workplace romance. Especially important is identifying processes that accomplish the dissolution of the romance while also enabling the former partners to continue to work together effectively. Such studies could be accomplished using methods similar to those examining workplace friendship developmental processes (e.g., Sias & Cahill, 1998; Sias et al., 2004; see also Chapter 4 of this volume). These studies used the retrospective interview technique (RIT) to obtain participants' narrative histories of their workplace relationships. The method involves asking participants to trace their relationship history as it changed at important turning points or points at which the relationship substantively transformed. The RIT could be used similarly to examine developmental processes in romantic relationships by obtaining information from employees regarding why they engaged in the romantic relationship and how they communicatively transformed the relationship from coworkers to romance. Scholars could use the same method to obtain information regarding romantic relationship deterioration. Such events are likely to be somewhat traumatic and, consequently, memorable; thus, respondents may be able to provide rich and vivid narrative accounts of those processes, in particular focusing on how they and their partner communicatively withdrew or disengaged from the romantic relationship.

As noted earlier in this chapter, much research suggests that the partners' coworkers are aware of the workplace romance and form perceptions about the relationship. These perceptions have consequences for employee morale, productivity, and how the coworkers treat the romantic partners. To date, while we know coworkers form perceptions about the romance (e.g., attribute motives to the partners, develop perceptions that the romance is hurting employee job performance, etc.), we know nothing about *how* those perceptions are formed. Research grounded in the social construction perspective could identify the social processes by which employees together socially construct perceptions of a workplace romantic relationship via conversation. Analysis of such interaction would provide useful insights into how and why employees make particular attributions regarding the motives of the romantic partners, and how they come to believe performance is impaired or improved. The joint conversation reconstruction (JCR) method described in Chapter 3 enables such data collection and analysis (see also Sias & Odden, 1996).

Although previous research indicates romantic workplace relationships impact coworkers' perceptions, morale, and productivity, no studies have examined how the romantic relationship might impact the relationships the romantic partners have with the other coworkers. Extant work (Sias & Jablin, 1995) suggests that workplace relationships do not exist in isolation from one another, but the relationship an employee has with one coworker (e.g., his or her supervisor) can affect the relationship(s) that employee has with other coworkers (e.g., peer coworkers). It is quite likely that once an individual becomes involved in a romantic relationship at work, that relationship will affect his or her relationships with coworkers. If, for example, the employee develops a romance with his or her supervisor, the employee's peers may suspect favoritism and begin to distrust and withdraw from their relationships with that employee. Social construction research would provide important insights into the processes by which these relational transformations occur.

As noted in an earlier section, many organizations implement formal policies governing workplace romance. Researchers have examined how employees respond to and interpret those policies, yet we know nothing about how employees socially construct the policies and their perceptions of the policies. Similarly, many organizations forego formal policies and rely on informal "unwritten rules." Scholars should examine the ways in which employees construct those unwritten rules and norms via their informal communication with one another.

Finally, existing research has centered on heterosexual romance in the workplace. We know virtually nothing about the processes associated with homosexual romantic relationships at work. Social construction research can make several important contributions to the literature. Given the difficulties and risks associated with "coming out" in the workplace, scholars should examine how employees socially construct same-sex romantic relationships at work. A social construction perspective would also enable study of how coworker observers of a homosexual romantic relationship socially construct that relationship with one another, to reveal their attributions and perceptions regarding the relationship.

CRITICAL PERSPECTIVE

As noted in earlier chapters, critical studies of organizations center on four main themes—reification, consent, the managerial bias, and technical rationality (Deetz, 2005). Considering these issues as they may apply to workplace romantic relationships suggests a number of interesting and important research projects.

Critical studies of reification examine the social processes and discursive practices that constitute organizational structures and processes as normal and natural, making alternative structures and processes appear abnormal and unnatural. As noted above, a variety of studies examining various workplace romance issues consistently indicate that women are perceived as more likely than men to engage in workplace romantic relationships for job-related, rather than love, motives (e.g., Powell, 2001). These results have been consistent over three decades of research and suggest a persistent reified stereotype, despite other research that indicates women are just as likely as men to be motivated by love or ego. Critical research should examine the discursive practices that construct and maintain this perception.

Similar to workplace friendships, the "voluntary" nature of workplace romantic relationships makes the issue of consent particularly relevant. Although romantic relationships are chosen, not mandated, a number of factors impact the initiation and development of these relationships, such as proximity and repeated exposure. Scholars should question the extent to which workplace romance is indeed voluntary and examine the social processes that may limit the "voluntariness" of romance and the extent to which employees are actually able to choose to engage in a workplace romance.

Relatedly, while researchers have identified individuals' motives for engaging in workplace romance, the actual functions of these relationships remain unexamined. Studies indicate, for example, that individuals sometimes initiate romantic relationships at work to improve their jobs in some way and to acquire power. Critical studies should investigate how such relationships do, or do not, imbue the partners with power, how the relationships impact the power structure of the work environment, how the power accrued to the romantic partners may constitute the disempowerment of others in the workplace, and the like. In other words, while we know some employees engage in romance to accrue power and influence, we have not interrogated issues of power in workplace romance in any deep and critical fashion.

The highly emotional component of workplace romance makes research in the area of technical rationality particularly relevant. One of the defining characteristics of a romantic workplace relationship is its emotional and passionate nature. Emotion and passion are considered as antithetical to rationality (Mumby & Putnam, 1992). This is why, of course, many organizations formulate policies forbidding romance in the workplace (Schultz, 2003). Critical research can lend important insights into emotion and rationality in key organizational processes such as the ways in which romance impacts (either positively or negatively) the rationality of employee decision making. Moreover, research should build on Schultz's (2003) argument that removal of sexuality from the workplace via workplace romance policies effectively "desexualizes" organizations by examining questions such as how the "desexualizing" occurs and which employees tend to be marginalized and disempowered by these processes.

STRUCTURATION PERSPECTIVE

Workplace romantic relationship research centered on the primary components of structuration theory would lend a number of important and interesting insights to the current body of literature. Central to structuration theory is duality of structure, or the reciprocal relationship between agency (human behavior) and structure (rules and resources that guide and constrain human behavior). Considering romantic relationships from this perspective, scholars could examine how romantic partners produce and reproduce the structures that simultaneously enable and constrain their interaction. Such research could address a number of important questions. For example, what structures guide romantic communication? What structures enable/constrain ego, job, and love romantic relationship types? Given the important impact of romantic relationships on coworkers not involved in the relationship, structuration research could uncover the structures that constrain and enable coworkers to interpret and react to a workplace romance. Along these lines, existing research indicates that many organizations rely on informal policies or "unwritten rules" regarding workplace romance. Structuration research could reveal the processes by which such rules are developed and shared via organizational members and the extent to which the "unwritten rules" become institutionalized in, and beyond, a particular organization.

Structuration theory would conceptualize workplace relationships as systems or patterns of social relations that stretch across time and space. This conceptualization could guide an interesting examination of the various romantic relationship "types" reviewed above. Such a study would address issues such as the prototypical qualities of the fling, companionate, and utilitarian romantic relationships and how these typical relationships, in the form of structures, are reproduced and maintained in everyday employee communication.

The structuration concept of time–space distanciation could enable research into the extent to which romantic relationship structures are transported across time and context, addressing questions such as how do romantic workplace relationship structures today compare to those in the past and how and why romantic relationship structures have or have not changed over time. Data regarding these issues could be obtained via interviews, as well as analysis of various texts such as books, news media, and film, particularly given the fact that workplace romance is a common theme in U.S. cinema.

Conclusion

Romantic workplace relationships are fascinating and consequential. These emotional and passionate relationships operate in environments designed to be objective and productive. This mix can be joyous and rewarding, exciting and heartbreaking. In this chapter, I summarized what research currently tells us about various types of romantic workplace relationships, how and why employees develop such relationships, and the consequences, both positive and negative, of workplace romance for the romantic partners, their coworkers, and the organization as a whole. I also forward an agenda for future research guided by alternative theoretical perspectives. These perspectives inform not only research, but also practice. Considering workplace romantic relationships from a variety of theoretical perspectives draws practitioners' attention to various aspects of actual workplace issues and problems involving workplace romance, resulting in a more complex understanding of those issues. Such understanding can help employees and managers address relationship problems in more substantive and effective ways. The following "Practicing Theory" case is designed to highlight the practical implications of multiple theoretical perspectives.

Regretting Romance

Jim has worked at Sycamore Farms, a large food distribution company, for 6 years. He is employed in the company's human resources department as a benefits counselor.

Jim has been quite happy with this job. He gets along very well with his coworkers, many of whom he considers to be good friends. He also has a great relationship with his supervisor, Elliott. Elliott has always been very supportive of Jim. They trust each other and talk frequently and openly about many issues—both work and personal. Elliott gives Jim a lot of latitude in what he does in his job and how he carries out his tasks, so Jim enjoys a lot of autonomy. Jim respects Elliott as a supervisor and as a person. He considers Elliott to be a good friend.

Things have lately become a bit difficult, however. About 10 months ago, Jim became romantically involved with one of his coworkers, Pam. Although he and Pam work in different areas (though both are placed in the human resources department), Pam's job as an employee relations counselor sometimes requires the two of them to work together on projects or specific employee issues and complaints. While working on one of these projects, they found they had much in common and became romantically attracted to one another. Jim and Pam are both single, young professionals, so they didn't see anything morally wrong with becoming romantically involved. However, Sycamore Farms has a formal policy prohibiting romantic relationships among employees. Thus, they kept their relationship a secret from others at work, including Elliott.

Jim felt quite guilty over the past several months keeping something like this from Elliott. It was hard not to share this information with his friend, but he also didn't want to put Elliott in a difficult position. Although Jim felt his secrecy was somewhat of a betrayal to Elliott, he continued his relationship with Pam and, admittedly, found the secretive nature to be part of the allure of the relationship.

After 9 months, Jim decided to break off the relationship with Pam. This was due to a number of factors, but the primary reason was that he felt Pam was getting too serious and too "clingy." He found he had very little time to spend with his other friends away from work, and very little time to himself. While he liked Pam, he didn't see much of a future for the relationship, so he thought it was important to end the romance before it went too far. Unfortunately, Pam didn't agree and is now making things very difficult for Jim. While he used to see Pam occasionally at work, now she is always coming by his office, calling him, and sending him e-mails. He has told her several times he didn't want to interact, but she always seems to find a reason to be around him. Her constant contact has become very annoying and stressful. And his efforts to avoid her have begun to affect his ability to do his job. In short, Jim feels harassed by Pam.

The irony of the situation is that at Sycamore Farms, employees who experience problems at work are supposed to report them to the employee relations department (where Pam works as a counselor). Clearly, this option is out of the question for Jim.

His only other option is to go to Elliott for help. He is concerned that informing Elliott of the situation will seriously harm their relationship, which would be devastating to Jim on both a professional and a personal level.

Discussion Questions

1. How does this case illustrate current research and theory in the area of workplace romance?

2. Consider this case from a structuration perspective. How does Jim's relationship with Elliott both enable and constrain his behavior and performance at work?

3. Consider this case from a social construction perspective. How is Pam's behavior constructing her relationship with Jim? How can Jim communicatively transform the relationship in a more effective way?

4. Consider this case from a critical perspective. What types of control are operating in this situation? How would you describe the power dynamics between Jim and Pam? How does the organization itself contribute to this situation?

5. What advice would you give to Jim for resolving this problem?

6

Customer and Client Relationships

Few stories highlight the financial importance of customer and client relationships better than that of Roy Pearson and Custom Cleaners, a small dry-cleaning establishment in New York City, owned by Jin, Soo, and Ki Chung. In a case widely reported by the media, Pearson went to pick up several items from Custom Cleaners and found a pair of pants was missing. A few days later, the Chungs promptly located the pants that matched Pearson's claim ticket. But Pearson insisted they were not his pants and refused to accept them. Instead, Pearson filed a lawsuit claiming damages of $64 million based on the fact that the cleaners' signs stating "Same Day Service" and "Satisfaction Guaranteed" were false and misleading. The $64 million figure reflected, in part, a charge of $1,500 for every day the "satisfaction guaranteed" sign remained on display at the Chungs's establishment (a period of 4 years), multiplied by each of the three members of the Chung family. In a contrasting case, it was the dry cleaners who filed the lawsuit. Todd Layne Cleaners in Manhattan filed a defamation suit against a former customer, Evan Maloney, seeking $100,000 in damages resulting from Maloney posting complaints about the cleaners on the Web such as "Todd Layne Cleaners SUCKS and is OVERPRICED" (Lattman, 2007). These two cases illustrate the importance for both parties of maintaining effective customer–client relationships and the costs of ignoring these important relationships.

In organizations of all types, employees work with customers or clients. In for-profit organizations, customers and clients are the source of revenue. In nonprofit entities such as social service, government, and charitable organizations, clients and their various needs are the reason for the organization's existence. Customer and client relationships are, accordingly, vital to an organization. They have been largely overlooked in organizational research, however, with marketing and management information systems scholars the primary ones to give these important relationships substantive attention. In this chapter, I discuss existing research in the area of customer and client relationships and, consistent with the book's theme, provide directions for future research.

I begin by outlining the unique characteristics of customer relationships and how these relationships differ from other types of workplace relationships. I then discuss four primary areas of research—relationship marketing, customer relationship management, customer relationship development, and research examining the various "outcomes" of customer relationships, followed by development of a set of research directions for the future guided by various theoretical perspectives. Finally, the practical benefit of considering organizational situations from various perspectives is addressed with a case study at the end of the chapter.

Overview

The terms *customer* and *client* have been used in various ways, but are often treated as synonymous terms. Traditionally, *customer* refers to "one who purchases a good or service" (*Merriam-Webster's*, 2003) while a *client* is someone who "engages the professional advice or services of another" (e.g., a lawyer) or one "who is served by or utilizes the services of a social agency" (Merriam-Webster, 2003). Thus, the primary traditional distinction between the two has to do with the type of exchange—product or professional service. More recently, however, as the U.S. and world economies have moved from an industrial to a service focus (see Chapter 7), customer and client have become increasingly synonymous terms. Because most research in this area has focused on customers, I rely on that term for the bulk of the chapter. I use the term client when discussing research specifically addressing organizations, consistent with the definition provided above.

In defining customer relationships, it is important to first note the difference between customer relationships and customer relations. The term *customer relations,* frequently called customer service, refers to the general ways employees interact with customers as a whole, rather than to a specific customer. Many organizations have "customer relations" or "customer service" departments that are responsible for managing customer questions and complaints, as well as training employees in effective customer service procedures. *Customer relationships,* in contrast, refer to relationships between an employee or employees and specific clients and customers. Consistent with the definition of *relationship* provided in Chapter 1 of this book, customer relationships are ongoing dyadic entities in which the partners engage in repeated and patterned interaction. These relationships carry expectations that differ from general service provider "encounters," including expectations of personalized service, information sharing and social support (Ford, 2001). This chapter discusses customer relationships, not customer relations. Customer relations and service are, however, relevant to the development and maintenance of relationships and are discussed as appropriate in the various sections below.

Customer relationships are unique from the other workplace relationships covered in this book in important ways. First, customer relationships are defined by the boundary that exists between the organization and its external environment. In contrast, workplace relationships such as supervisor–subordinate and peer coworker relationships exist largely within the workplace itself. While workplace friendships (see Chapter 4) and romantic workplace relationships (see Chapter 5) "blur" the organizational and personal spheres, customer relationships are by definition separated by that boundary. Second, while all relationships represent a type of social exchange, customer relationships are explicitly characterized by instrumental exchange such as the exchange of money from the customer for goods or services or the exchange of time and trust for services in nonprofit organizations. Thus, customer relationships are initially formed specifically for utilitarian, rather than affect-based, purposes. With these definitions in place, the following sections discuss existing theory and research in the area of customer relationships. Table 6.1 provides a brief summary of research on these various themes. We turn first to the topic of relationship marketing.

Relationship Marketing

Relationship marketing was introduced in the early 1980s and represented a paradigmatic shift in the way scholars and practitioners conceptualized customers and customer relationships. The shift resulted in large part from the increasingly global and competitive nature of the marketplace during the 1970s and 1980s (see Chapter 7 of this volume). While companies had previously focused attention primarily on attracting new customers, the competitive nature of the service-oriented economy emphasized the importance of retaining customers. Retaining customers required maintaining relationships with those customers. Thus, the "relationship marketing" concept was created.

As originally conceptualized, *relationship marketing* referred specifically to relationships between organizations and customers. This is reflected in Berry's (1983) definition of relationship marketing as "attracting, maintaining, and enhancing customer relationships" (p. 25). Since Berry introduced the relationship marketing concept in 1983, it has been interpreted in various ways and broadened to include relationships between organizations and a variety of other entities such as suppliers, employees, and other companies. This broader conceptualization is reflected in Gronroos's (1990) widely cited definition of relationship marketing as the process by which organizations "establish,

Table 6.1   Summary of Customer Relationship Research

Relationship Marketing

Systems Approach

Development
- Relational (trust, commitment, communication)
- Competence
- Technology
- Relational history

Outcomes
- Competitive advantage
- Financial performance
- Customer satisfaction
- Customer commitment

Customer Relationship Development

Relationship Types
- Bilateral, recurrent, dominant partner, discrete
- Primary, secondary, caretaker, orphan

Characteristics
- Relational norms (communication, role integrity, flexibility, adaptability, solidarity)

Developmental Factors
- Front people
    Skills/characteristics: knowledge, information, flexibility, adaptability, customer orientation, professional concern, sociality, nonimitability

- Contextual elements
    Organizational climate
    National culture

- Technology
    Customer relationship management (CRM)

Outcomes and Consequences

Financial
- Customer capital
- Profitability

Attitudinal/Behavioral
- Customer satisfaction
- Customer loyalty
- Trust
- Buffering

maintain, and enhance relationships with *customers and other partners, at a profit,* so that *objectives of the parties involved* are met. This is achieved by a *mutual exchange and fulfillment of promises*" (p. 138; emphasis added).

Gronroos's definition contains some important elements, which I have italicized. First, relationship marketing in its broadest form includes relationships not only with customers, but also with other companies, suppliers, and internal entities such as employees (i.e., "other partners"). For the purposes of this chapter, I focus only on relationship marketing as it applies to relationships with customers. Second, relationship marketing is, at its core, driven by financial and profit motives. Thus, at least initially, relationship marketing applied to for-profit organizations. Third, despite the profit motive, relationship marketing addresses the objectives of both the company (i.e., profit) and the customer (i.e., receipt of quality goods and services). Fourth, achieving such objectives requires mutual fulfillment of promises. Thus, both the company and customer bear responsibility for the quality of the relationship. Moreover, the exchange of promises requires trust—an issue addressed in much of existing relationship marketing research, as seen in later sections of this chapter.

The introduction of relationship marketing was considered by many scholars to be a "paradigm shift" in both scholarly and practical approaches to marketing (Gronroos, 1990, 1994; Gummesson, 1997). Prior to its introduction, the "marketing mix" model was the cornerstone of the field. This model, known as the "four P's of marketing," was, and in many ways still is, the basic model of marketing (Gummesson, 1997). The four "P's" of the model refer to product, price, place, and promotion, and the core of the model is the appropriate "mix" or combination of those four elements. Notably missing from the four P's is the customer and, specifically, customer relationships.

Relationship marketing is grounded largely in systems theory, arguing against relegating marketing solely to marketing departments and, instead, involving *all* parties, both internal and external to the organization, in customer relationship marketing. Salespeople, for example, are responsible not only for selling products but also for obtaining information about customer needs and requirements so that the organization can meet those needs and maintain a long-lasting relationship. Suppliers do not simply provide the company with necessary equipment and materials; they also connect the company to customers and potential customers. Human resource employees do not simply hire employees, but recruit specifically those with exemplary customer relations skills. Moreover, relationship marketing is conceptualized as a process, not an outcome, and in particular an ongoing and dynamic process of relationship development and maintenance (Gronroos, 1990). Relationship marketing, therefore, involves "suppliers or service providers interacting in a network with, among others, customers, suppliers, intermediaries, and environmental actors" (Gronroos, 1994, pp. 13–14), all of whom are involved in the customer relationship process.

Scholars studying relationship marketing consistently observe that relationship marketing theory and research has been fragmented and lacks a solid theoretical grounding (Lindgreen, 2001). However, as applied to customer relationships specifically, relationship marketing research addresses two primary issues—factors that influence the development of customer relationships and outcomes of relationship marketing.

Several researchers have examined the reasons or motivations of customers to engage in relationships with organizations. One of the primary motivating factors is trust. Customers are more likely to form and maintain lasting relationships with companies and organizational representatives they trust. As Hunt, Arnett, and Madhavaram (2006) explain, "Consumers desire relationship partners that they can trust. They do so because a trusted partner reduces the risks associated with relational exchange, because trust is associated with a partner's reliability, integrity, and competence" (p. 75). Customers are also more motivated to develop relationships with organizations with which they share values; thus, individuals may remain committed to doing business with a "green" (i.e., environmentally conscious) company (Morgan & Hunt, 1994). Once a relationship is formed, customers are motivated to maintain the relationship for a variety of reasons, including the fact that staying with the same company reduces the needs to obtain and process information. Knowledge about, and trust in, the relationship partner reduces uncertainty, and increases the efficiency of making decisions (Sheth & Parvatiyar, 1995).

According to relationship marketing theory, many factors impact the successful development of customer relationships. *Relational* factors such as trust, commitment, shared values, and communication contribute to relational success (Hunt et al., 2006; Morgan & Hunt, 1994). *Competence,* especially competence in the area of customer service, is also important to successful relationship marketing. In particular, consistent with systems theory, relationship marketing requires that customer relations competence must occur throughout the organization, not simply in separate marketing or customer service departments. This requires that all employees are oriented toward customer retention and are provided incentives for building customer relationships (Day, 2000).

Hunt et al. (2006) point out the importance of historical factors or the notion that success in the future is dependent on success in the past. As they explain, "Successful relationships take time to develop. Unlike short-term (transaction-based) exchanges, successful long-term relationships have a history. As a result, partners' behaviors, past and present, have the ability to affect future interactions" (p. 82). This emphasizes the importance of "keeping promises" and maintaining mutual satisfaction and trust.

Because relationship marketing was spurred in large part by new information technologies, globalization, and movement toward a service-based economy, it is not surprising that scholars identify *technology* as another factor important to successful relationship marketing (Panda, 2002). Specifically, technology that enables acquisition and management of large amounts information regarding customers is particularly crucial to relationship marketing. Such technology, called "customer relationship management," is discussed in greater detail in a later section.

Effective relationship marketing brings several positive outcomes for both the customer and the company. Specifically, research indicates successful relationship marketing results in greater competitive advantage for the organization and better financial performance (Hunt, 1997), and more satisfied customers (Adbul-Muhmin, 2002; Bolton, 1998), who are more committed to, and more likely to stay with, the organization over time (Bolton, 1998; Verhoef, 2003).

In sum, relationship marketing considers marketing to be an organization-wide competency, rather than the sole responsibility of a separate marketing department. In particular, all employees throughout the organization must be competent in customer service and building and maintaining customer relationships. The following sections discuss research addressing customer relationship development and the specific outcomes of those relationships for both the organization and the customer.

Customer Relationship Development

Most research on customer relationships has centered on identifying the development of such relationships, addressing the important question of how organizations can create and maintain effective and long-lasting relationships with customers. This body of work centers on two primary issues—the various types and characteristics of customer relationships and factors associated with customer relationship development.

TYPES AND CHARACTERISTICS OF CUSTOMER RELATIONSHIPS

O'Toole and Donaldson (2000) found that customer relationships could be distinguished by the strength of the relationship. *Relationship strength* refers to both strength in beliefs (e.g., trust, loyalty) and behavior (e.g., information sharing, adaptation, and flexibility). Their study revealed four primary types of customer relationships. The *bilateral* relationship is characterized by high levels of belief and behavior strength. In bilateral relationships, both customer and organization are loyal to one another, open in information sharing, and willing and able to adapt to one another's needs, and both invest significant resources in the relationships. Bilateral relationships are characterized by mutual effort and advantages. *Recurrent* relationships are less "strong" than bilateral relationships and are characterized by less loyalty and commitment.

In these relationships, partners are focused primarily on a practical, efficient relationship more than long-term relationship building. *Dominant partner* relationships are characterized by relatively low levels of relationship strength, particularly with respect to relationship beliefs. In this relationship, the "supplier" organization is dominant and less willing to adapt or be flexible in dealing with the customer. Finally *discrete* relationships are characterized by low levels of both belief and action relationship strength. As the authors note, in these situations the relationship is carried out on an "arm's-length" basis. These relationships are weak compared to the other three types, with partners feeling little loyalty and commitment and committing few resources to the relationship.

M. Paulin, Perrien, and Ferguson (1997) also examined relationship strength, conceptualizing strength with respect to relational norms of bank–client relationships. Their research indicates customer relationships are distinguished by four primary relational norms. *Role integrity* refers to the extent to which the organizational representative (in this case, the account manager) is perceived as knowledgeable, competent, empathetic, and courteous. *Communication* refers to the extent to which the partners engage in mutual feedback and timely, accurate, and frequent information sharing. *Flexibility* refers to the extent to which the relationship partners are willing to adapt the contract to their various needs and are responsive to changes in the relationship, and their ability to resolve conflict in the relationship. Finally, *solidarity* refers to the degree of commitment, mutual trust, and perceived benefits partners perceived of the relationship. M. Paulin et al.'s (1997) study indicated that relationships characterized by high perceived levels of adherence to these relational norms were more effective (as measured by the client's intent to stay with the bank) than those with lower levels of perceived adherence. They also, however, found significant differences in the perceptions of account managers and clients, with account managers perceiving higher levels of the relational norms than did the clients. In a subsequent study, P. Paulin, Perrien, Ferguson, Salazar, and Seruya (1998) found similar differences, and also found relational norms were positively associated not only with the client's intent to stay with the bank, but also with effectiveness of the banking service.

Frankwick, Porter, and Crosby (2001) classified customer relationships into four main types—primary, secondary, caretaker, and orphan. *Primary* relationships are characterized by a great deal of contact between salespeople and their customers, such as keeping customers informed about organizational or product changes, frequently checking in with customers as to their satisfaction, and tailoring their sales suggestions to the unique needs of the customer. *Secondary* and *caretaker* relationships are characterized by significantly less positive contact, as well as service failures. *Orphan* status is reserved for relationships in which there was little communication, but no service failure (in contrast to secondary and caretaker status).

DEVELOPMENTAL FACTORS

Given their importance to organizational success and survival, many scholars have examined the factors associated with the development of effective customer relationships. This research centers on organizational roles and organizational practices that impact customer relationships.

Front People

Although the literature tends to refer to the relationship between the customer and organization, in practice, the customer relationship exists between a customer and one or more organizational employees. These employees, referred to often as "front people" or "boundary spanners," are crucial to effective development and maintenance of customer relationships. In many organizations, the front people are sales representatives and account managers. In nonprofit or social organizations, front people might be caregivers or counselors. Regardless of their official titles, these employees are usually the first and most consistent organizational participants in the customer relationship. Not surprisingly, then, much research has focused on the role of "front people" in customer relationship development, centering primarily on identifying the skills, competencies, and personality traits necessary for effective customer relationship building.

McGivern (1983) was among the first to devote substantial attention to customer relationship development. His research demonstrated that successful consultant–client relationships are both mutual and balanced with respect to the fulfillment of expectations and obligations of both client (e.g., assistance in identifying problems and implementing consultant suggestions to resolve problems) and consultant (e.g., achieving a satisfactory resolution of the problems). Three primary factors contribute to the development of such relationships. These include trust, high levels of quality interaction (including mutual information sharing), and the consultant's willingness to adapt to the client's needs (what McGivern refers to as use of "contingent methods"). Similarly, Ford (2001) found that customers expect to engage in social conversations with service providers with whom they perceive a relationship (rather than just an encounter) and they expect such service providers to spend time with them discussing both social and task issues.

As Fojt (1995) noted a decade ago, customers value two primary characteristics of salespeople they deal with directly—the salesperson's knowledge and information they share with the customer and the nature of their relationship with the salesperson. To maintain effective customer relationships with customers, salespeople must understand the customer's needs and values, and be able to adapt to the needs and values of various customers (Fojt, 1995).

Thus, the flexibility and adaptability dimensions noted by M. Paulin et al. (1997) are particularly important for front people.

M. R. Williams (1998) found that a salesperson's "customer orientation" was positively associated with customer relationship development (as indicated by measures of satisfaction, trust, and commitment to the relationship). Customer orientation refers to the customer's perception that the salesperson willingly shares information, is flexible in dealing with the customer, is willing to explore various solutions to problems, and is adaptable to the customer's needs. Similarly, as noted above, Frankwick et al. (2001) found information sharing and adaptability (in the form of tailoring suggestions to unique customer needs) crucial in developing and maintaining high-quality "primary" customer relationships. In addition, Koermer, Ford, and Brant (2000) found that service provider "sociality" (e.g., engaging in courteous communication and communicating a personal connection through self-disclosure, teasing, etc.) was positively associated with customer satisfaction, which in turn, was positively associated with customer loyalty.

The impact of front people on customer relationships is not constant over time, however. Jap (2001) investigated links between sales representatives and customer perceptions of the organizational-customer relationship over the stages of the relationship life cycle. Results of that study indicated that sales reps had their greatest impact on relationship quality during the "buildup" stage. This phase is characterized by a great deal of mutual information sharing and uncertainty reduction. As the author explains, "The salesrep's honest communications, extrarole efforts and demonstrations of benevolence toward the customer can have tremendous value in cultivating customer satisfaction with the relationship and products" (p. 104). The sales rep continues to be important to the customer relationship during the following "maturity" phase, albeit to a lesser degree. This may be due to the relationship partners becoming accustomed to the relationship. It also may result from the customer experiencing uncertainties in the relationship. The "decline" phase, as noted earlier, marks a point at which one or both of the parties begin to disengage from the relationship (for example, a bank customer closes her account, or a consumer stops shopping at a particular store). The sales rep is important in managing "an orderly termination process" and maintaining good will with the customer. In sum, Jap's (2001) study indicates the links between "front people" and the customer relationship are dynamic and complex.

The important role of front people in customer relationship development highlights the potential damage created by turnover of these boundary spanners. Lovett, Harrison, and Virick (1997) noted that when a boundary spanner, such as a sales rep or other front person, leaves an organization, their turnover impacts customers with whom the boundary spanner has formed a relationship. The customer may follow the employee to their new organization, meaning a loss to the original organization. The customer may seek alternative service providers. Or the customer may remain with the organization and form a relationship with a new boundary spanner. Lovett et al. (1997) developed a model explaining factors associated with these various potential outcomes. Their model centers on the concept of *nonimitability,* or customer perceptions that they cannot replicate the customer relationship with another front person or organization. The model further distinguishes between nonimitability of the relationship with the boundary spanner specifically and nonimitability of the relationship with the larger organization. The greater the nonimitability of the relationship with the boundary spanner, the more likely the customer is to terminate the links to the organization and follow the boundary spanner to the new organization. The greater the nonimitability of the organization, the less likely boundary spanner turnover will impact the customer. Nonimitability results from a variety of factors, including trust, the perceptions of "social obligations" to the boundary spanner or organization, and the extent to which the boundary spanner learned about the customer and tailored or "customized" service to the customer's unique needs. While the model has yet to be empirically tested, it provides many directions for future research and highlights the previously overlooked links between employee and customer turnover.

Relatedly, Mills and Moshavi (1999) developed a model of client relationships highlighting the role of "professional concern" in relationship development and maintenance. Professional concern requires the front person to have authority to act on the customer's behalf, an objective attitude (which enables flexibility and adaptability), and social affiliation (interpersonal skills such as courtesy, pleasantness, and tactfulness). A final dimension of professional concern recognizes the client's role in the relationship. This dimension, "client role accountability," refers to the responsibility of the client to uphold his or her end of the bargain (e.g., a patient following his doctor's instructions, a client providing quality information to her consultant). The authors propose that professional concern strengthens the customer relationships and leads to improved quality of service and satisfaction. Specifically, professional concern helps mitigate two potential problems in client relationships—information asymmetry and uncertainty.

Metcalf, Frear, and Krishnan (1992) proposed and tested a model of customer relationships centering on the concepts of information and social exchange. *Information exchange* refers, of course, to the mutual exchange of information between the two parties in the relationship. *Social exchange* refers to the interpersonal relationship between the two parties and specifically the degree of mutual trust between the relationship partners. Their study revealed that social exchange was positively related to the exchange of quality information and the extent of cooperation and adaptation between buyers and customers.

Although the bulk of research on "front people" and customer relationships has centered on customers in for-profit organizations, some scholars have examined these issues in nonprofit or service organizations such as government agencies, nursing homes, and elderly care. Chaston and Baker (1998) examined relationships between small business owners/managers and government-funded support and advisory agencies. Specifically, they identified factors that influence the development and quality of such relationships. Their results indicated that, similar to the studies discussed above with for-profit organizations, factors such as mutual trust, commitment, frequent communication, and knowledge of, and adaptability to, client needs were most important to these client relationships.

Grosenick and Hatmaker (2000) found several characteristics to be important for substance abuse counselors in building trusting relationships with clients, including the counselor's knowledge and experience, availability, supportiveness, and nonthreatening behavior. Similarly, Piercy (2000) found supportiveness to be associated with the development of close relationships (e.g., friendships and "family-like" relationships) among home health caregivers and their elderly patients. Her study also revealed the importance of consistency in building these client relationships; that is, maintaining contact with the same caregiver over time, rather than sending different caregivers, contributed to relationship development. In addition, her results indicated that relationships were more likely to grow closer when the caregiver and client were of the same gender.

In a rare critical study of client relationships, Vaughn and Stamp (2003) examined the power structures that characterize relationships between clients and counselors at a battered women's shelter. Interviews from shelter workers revealed four primary power structure properties of client–counselor relationships. The *circumstantial dichotomy* refers to different financial and emotional situations of shelter workers and clients. These different circumstances served to empower the shelter worker and disempower the clients who tended to be both financially dependent upon the shelter and emotionally depressed, and therefore disadvantaged in that they might feel "intimated or demeaned by the dichotomy" (p. 159). *Contrasting experiences* refers to the fact that none of the shelter workers in this particular sample had experienced domestic abuse themselves. The shelter workers all claimed to be knowledgeable about domestic abuse from the education and training they received, while the clients experienced the phenomenon firsthand. As the authors pointed out, "It may be inconsistent and inherently contradictory that the client would take the subservient role of a student in a subject matter about which she is an expert" (p. 160). The power structure of these client relationships was also characterized by *asymmetrical roles* in that, despite the fact that the shelter workers all were concerned with developing "symmetrical friendships" with the clients, they also were required to enforce rules, policies, and discipline to keep order in the shelter, requiring them to exhibit power in the relationship. Finally, shelter workers were dominant partners in the client relationship via *resource control,* including control over the admittance of clients to the shelter and the distribution of resources among shelter residents. This study highlights the unique nature of such client relationships from other types of client and customer relationships. Clients of social agencies appear to possess significantly less power and influence than, say, a client in a consulting firm due to their high level of dependence on the social service agency.

In sum, extant research indicates front people (e.g., sales reps, account managers, substance abuse counselors, and health care providers) are crucial to effective customer relationship development. In particular, front persons' knowledge about the customer and the product or service, as well as concern for mutual benefits from the relationship, are key competencies. In addition, skills such as information sharing, flexibility, and adaptability contribute to positive customer relationships. Front people are not solely responsible for customer relationships, however. The following sections discuss other factors associated with customer relationship development.

Organizational Factors

Various organizational factors, other than "front people," impact customer relationship development. Martin and Bush (2003) revealed the importance of *organization climate* to customer relationship development. In particular, climates that foster employee security, open communication, and decentralized decision making are associated with healthier customer relationships. Relatedly, sales managers' leadership is linked to customer relationship development. Martin and Bush (2003) found that when managers "empower" their sales people (i.e., "front people") via transformational leadership techniques that encourage employee understanding of and sharing in organizational goals and values, those employees have a greater understanding of the organizational climate and are better equipped to make decisions that address customers' unique situations and needs and, therefore, foster positive customer relationships. Macaulay and Cook (1993) similarly highlight the important role of managers in helping front people learn the skills necessary for customer relationship development.

National culture can also impact customer relationship development due to different cultural approaches to relationships. So and Speece (2000) found account managers in U.S. and Hong Kong banks perceived of and enacted relationship marketing in different ways. *Guanxi* or "personal connection" is a deeply rooted value in Chinese culture, in contrast to the more individualistic U.S. culture. Thus, U.S. account managers were more likely to explicitly recognize and implement elements of "relationship marketing" in their customer relationships, while in the Hong Kong banks, customer relationships underlied all elements of the enterprise. As the authors explained,

> Account managers in Asian banks seem to view relationship marketing more strongly in the context of traditional guanxi connections, characterized and maintained by social relationships rather than the business relationship. Relative to the account managers in Western banks, those in Asian banks consider social activities more important, and business activities less important. The exploratory factor analysis also suggests that those in Asian banks may not perceive social activities as an entirely separate dimension from various business activities. Account managers in Western banks distinguish dimensions of business activities more clearly, with social elements as separate, not intermixed. (p. 325)

Power distance (i.e., respect for authority, the expectation and acceptance of the unequal distribution of power, and the centralization and formalization of authority) also impacts customer relationship development. Dash, Bruning, and Guin (2006) studied customer relationship dynamics in Canadian and Indian banks and found that power distance moderated customer perceptions of interdependence (i.e., reciprocal, rather than asymmetrical, dependence between customer and salesperson) and the quality of customer relationships. Specifically, with banks in Canada (a low power distance culture), customers were more likely to tolerate and experience interdependent relationships than bank customers in India (a high power distance culture).

Customer Relationships and Technology

As noted above, one of the most important elements in developing and maintaining effective customer relationships is knowing the customer's needs and unique situation and being able to adapt the product or service to that customer. Being knowledgeable, of course, means being informed. Much research in the area of customer relationships, therefore, focuses on obtaining and managing customer and client information. A key mechanism in this process is information technology.

Customer Relationship Management

Most research examining customer relationship information technology and management falls under the heading *customer relationship management.* Customer relationship management (CRM) refers to the systematic gathering, storing, and analysis of information about customers. This is typically accomplished with a variety of information technologies.

Scholars began addressing CRM in the 1980s as relationship marketing became an integral part of the business landscape (Berry, 1983). At a broad

level, CRM initially referred to the establishment, development, maintenance, and optimization of long-term, mutually valuable relationships
between consumers and the organizations (Panda, 2002). Thus, CRM is similar to relationship marketing. As early scholars in the area noted, information technology is fundamental to CRM (Axson, 1992). Over time, the term
CRM has come to represent the strategies and technologies organizations use
to obtain and manage demographic and psychographic information about
customers in support of an overall relationship marketing plan. In particular, data collection, data analysis, and database management technologies are
crucial for managing vast amounts of customer information with the goal of
managing and maintaining long-term customer relationships (Axson, 1992;
Crosby & Johnson, 2000).

Much scholarship has centered on developing customer relationship models. Park and Kim (2003) delineate four primary types of customer information necessary for effective customer relationship management. *Of-the-customer*
information refers to information about a customer such as personal data and
information about their transactions (e.g., sales volumes, purchasing patterns,
etc.). *For-the-customer* information refers to information provided to the
customer by the company regarding products, services, and the organization
itself. This information is typically disseminated via direct mail or Web pages.
By-the-customer information refers to feedback from the customer such as
complaints, suggestions, and other information. This information is particularly important to customer relationships in that it helps the organization
develop new products and services and ensure the company is meeting the
unique needs of the customer.

Different types of information are important at different stages of customer relationship development (Park & Kim, 2003). Of-the-customer information is useful during the initiation of a customer relationship so the company
can become knowledgeable about the customer. This enables the company to
produce for-the-customer information during the later stages of development
that is tailored specifically to that customer. At that point, customers provide
by-the-customer information in the form of feedback that enables the company
to adapt their products or services to the customer's needs and desires. Park and
Kim's (2003) research demonstrated the importance of multichannel customer
information systems (CIS) that enable effective of-the-customer, for-the-
customer, and by-the-customer information exchange.

While Park and Kim (2003) proposed a model of CRM and customer relationship development, Stefanou, Sarmaniotis, and Stafyla (2003) modeled the
stages through which an organization develops CRM strategies and capabili-
ties. During the first stage, the *preliminary, non-IT-assisted* phase, companies
do not use, or use in a very limited way, information technology for the purpose of customer relationship management. Customer information at this

point is limited to manually obtained information regarding customer satisfaction or complaints (e.g., customer comment cards). During the second, *IT-assisted* CRM stage, companies begin using information technology such as spreadsheets and statistical software to analyze customer information that is obtained manually. At this point, organizations also develop Web pages to disseminate information to customers. During the third, *IT-automated* CRM stage, organizations use multiple technologies to emphasize customer interaction (e.g., the Internet, telephone/computer integration). These technologies enable companies to track customer buying patterns and develop customer profiles. At this point, the organizations have an active Web presence and engage in e-commerce (e.g., online orders). At the fourth stage, the *integrated CRM* (i-CRM) stage, organizations have sophisticated CRM technologies that enable "highly integrated back-office, front-office and Internet functions" (Stefanou et al., 2003, p. 624). These systems include "personalization" software that helps organizations develop and maintain "customer-centric knowledge." In particular, these sophisticated integrated systems provide access to this information to "every decision maker inside the organization" (Stefanou et al., 2003, p. 624), in the true spirit of relationship marketing discussed earlier.

Cohn (2002) developed a model of CRM focused more on organizational structure than on the technology itself. Arguing that CRM is a "postmodern organizational model," Cohn notes that including the customer in central organizational processes removes the traditional boundary between organization and environment of the "modern" era. His model of CRM centers on the structural concepts of formalization, centralization, complexity, and integration. The model proposes that organizations "formalize" CRM practices such as the technologies and practices that enable the collection and analysis of customer information. Decision making becomes more "decentralized" in this CRM model, encouraging the empowerment of all parties, internal and external, to make decisions that best serve the customer and maintain the customer relationship. This requires a "customer-centric" culture in which all employees understand and value the importance of the customer and make decisions consistent with that understanding and value. Finally, the Cohn (2002) CRM model sees functional integration as key to effective CRM. Specifically, "Integration denotes that departments and customers are talking to each other and that products and services are coordinated" (p. 98).

Outcomes and Consequences of Customer Relationships

Given the enormous human and financial resources organizations are placing in developing and maintaining effective customer relationships, it is not surprising that much research has been directed toward assessing the efficacy of those efforts. These studies examine the "outcomes" of relationship marketing and CRM strategies.

Researchers interested in the outcomes of the effectiveness of customer relationships and relationship marketing efforts tend to focus on financial or attitudinal metrics. Studies of financial outcomes center on how customer relationships affect the organization's "bottom line." Chang and Tseng (2005) developed a measure of "customer capital" that links effectiveness to "relationship equity" or the "tendency of the customer to stick with the brand, above and beyond the customer's objective and subjective assessments of the brand" (p. 256). Their study indicated relationship marketing activities were positively associated with relationship equity, which, in turn, impacted customer capital or the intent of continued purchasing from the company.

Reichheld (2006) recently developed the "net promoter score" to assess the dollar value of customer relationships. The score is based on customer satisfaction measures. In his study, Reicheld linked customer satisfaction to financial outcomes including customer retention rates, spending, profit margins, cost efficiencies, and word-of-mouth referrals. Similarly, Croteau and Li (2003) found positive relationships between the use of CRM technology and customer retention rates, customer satisfaction, and customer profitability.

Studies of attitudinal and behavioral outcomes of customer relationships are more common. These center primarily on the links between customer relationships and customer/client satisfaction, customer loyalty and trust, and the "buffering" function of customer relationships. Several studies demonstrate links between effective customer relationships and customer satisfaction. Specifically, these studies analyze the association between specific relationship marketing practices (e.g., empowerment of front people, professional orientation, communication skills, client role orientation) and customer or client satisfaction with the product, service, and organization (Beard, 1996; Covin & Fisher, 1991; Gainey & Klaas, 2003; Koermer et al., 2000; Sparks, Bradley, & Callan, 1997). Others have examined links between customer relationships and customer trust and loyalty. Garbarino and Johnson (1999, 2001) found that strong customer relationship bonds were characterized by high levels of trust and commitment, which in turn were linked to greater customer satisfaction and greater intent to continue the company's services.

Finally, research demonstrates interesting "buffering" functions of customer/client relationships. Halpern (1994) found that friendships impacted pricing expectations in business transactions, finding that, "Remarkably, without discussion, friends agree on prices for commodities, whereas strangers do not" (p. 647). Other studies indicate that customer/client relationships can "buffer" the organization from customer losses resulting from performance or ethical lapses. Hess, Ganesan, and Klein (2003) examined links between customer relationships and customer reactions to a service failure from the company. Results indicated that customers in stronger relationships (i.e., greater expectation of continuing the relationship) were more satisfied with service after the "recovery" and were more likely to attribute the failure to an unstable and unpredictable cause than those in weaker customer relationships. In a similar vein, Ingram, Skinner, and Taylor (2005) found that highly committed customers were more likely to forgive companies for ethical lapses than customers with low levels of commitment. Importantly, however, the researchers noted that perceptions of the amount of harm mediate that relationship, such that as the perceived harm increases, so does customer dissatisfaction with the company. Taken together, these studies indicate that customer relationship can buffer and protect organizations from occasional performance or ethical lapses and other activities (such as price negotiation).

Theoretical Perspectives on Customer and Client Relationships

Customer and client relationships have received a great deal of research attention, particularly from marketing and management scholars. This body of work provides important and useful insights into the importance of customer relationships and influences on their development. Virtually all of the existing research, however, is grounded in postpositivism. Thus, while we know much about customer relationships, our knowledge is bounded by postpositivist assumptions and conceptualizations, and our understanding of customer relationships is, as a result, quite limited. The remainder of this chapter develops a research agenda for the future designed to address current voids in the literature. Table 6.2 summarizes the various theoretical perspectives discussed in Chapter 1 and the future research topics these perspectives inform.

POSTPOSITIVIST PERSPECTIVE

A review of the postpositivist assumptions and goals summarized in Table 6.2 indicates that virtually all research in the area of customer relationships is grounded postpositivism. The vast majority of existing studies rely on self-report survey data to test hypotheses and examine research questions. The data obtained via these methods indicate the "reality" of the customer relationship. These data are analyzed primarily with correlation analyses such as correlations, regressions, and analyses of variance, which provide indications of associations between variables, but provide no insights into the nature of those associations.

Table 6.2   Theoretical Perspectives on Customer/Client Relationships

	Postpositivism	Social Construction	Critical Theory	Structuration Theory
Conceptualization of organizations	Real entities that exist beyond human perception "Contain" individuals Indicated by attitudes, behavior	Socially constructed Constituted in social practices Dynamic	Socially constructed Constituted in social practices Dynamic Systems of power, domination, and control	Socially constructed Constituted in social practices Dynamic Patterned social practices of organizational members across social systems
Conceptualization of communication	Occurs "inside" the relationship Indicates nature and status of the relationship	Constitutes social reality Constitutes relationships; as communication changes, so does the relationship	Constitutes social reality Constitutes relationships Essentializes and reifies organizational "realities" and relationships	Constitutes society and social systems Enables, produces, and reproduces structure Enabled and constrained by structure
Conceptualization of relationships	Real entities that exist beyond human perception "Contain" individuals Indicated by attitudes, communication behavior Predictive of outcomes (e.g., satisfaction, productivity, commitment) Influenced by physical environment	Socially constructed Exist in interaction Observable in interaction	Socially constructed Sites of power, domination, marginalization Sites of hegemonic, unobtrusive control	Socially constructed Constrained and enabled by structure

(Continued)

Table 6.2 (Continued)

	Postpositivism	Social Construction	Critical Theory	Structuration Theory
Research goals	Measuring indicators of relationship quality and status Predicting outcomes of relationships	Understanding social construction process Understanding relationship development dynamics	Understanding social construction of power, marginalization, reification, consent, domination, universalism of managerial interests and rationality	Understanding production, reproduction, and institutionalization of relationships
Sample research topics/questions		What communication characteristics distinguish different types of customer relationships? How do customer relationships develop (e.g., how is a bilateral relationship transformed to a recurrent relationship)? How and why do customer and client relationships deteriorate?	What ideological assumptions about customers are enacted in customer relationships? How do customer relationship partners enact power, influence, and resistance in their conversations with one another? How and why do customers consent to surveillance via CRM?	What structures enable and constrain customer relationships? How are these prototypes (i.e, structures) maintained, reproduced in customer–organizational representative interaction? How are these structures transported across time and context? How are customer relationships structured over time?

	Postpositivism	Social Construction	Critical Theory	Structuration Theory
Sample research topics/questions (continued)		How do customers/clients and organizational representatives communicatively disengage from a customer/client relationship? What communication patterns and practices constitute "customer orientation" and "professional concern"? What communication patterns and practices constitute a nonimitable customer relationship? How do front people socially construct nonimitability with customers and with management? What communication patterns and practices constitute social exchange and information exchange in customer/client relationships?	How do customer relationship partners negotiate tensions between instrumentality and affiliation in their interaction with one another? How do customer relationships function as social capital for organizations? What societal discursive formations reify customer relationships as social capital serving the interests of the organization?	What structures guide customer relationship interaction in different social contexts (e.g., different countries, industries, occupations, hierarchical levels), and how are those structures created, maintained, and transformed? How have customer relationship structures been transformed over time?

The postpositivist naturalist principle is also illustrated in the many studies that rely on cross-sectional, rather than longitudinal, data to obtain an assessment or "snapshot" of the relationship at that single point in time. This method, at least implicitly, conceptualizes customer relationships as static and limits our understanding of relational change and dynamism. For example, many studies categorize customer relationships into "types" such as bilateral, recurrent, and dominant partner relationship types. While the relationships examined may represent those types at the particular time of the study, the cross-sectional design of the research serves to "freeze" those relationships, implicitly assuming their permanence. Moreover, the design, and naturalist principle on which it is based, precludes examination and understanding of the processes that contribute to and maintain customer relationships.

In sum, existing research on customer/client relationships provides insights into a variety of important issues such as identifying various types of customer relationships, and the competencies, personality traits, and skills required for developing and maintaining effective customer relationships and a number of outcomes of customer relationships. There is much we do not know about customer relationships, however, due to the fact that the substantial postpositivist bias of this research has constrained conceptualizations and approaches to the study of these entities. As detailed below, we can greatly expand our knowledge by conceptualizing, and studying, customer relationships from other theoretical perspectives.

SOCIAL CONSTRUCTION PERSPECTIVE

Social construction theory conceptualizes organizations, and workplace relationships, as socially constructed entities, constituted in human interaction. Similarly, customer relationships are socially constructed entities constituted by the interaction of the relationship partners. Thus, a customer relationship does not exist outside the partners engaged in that relationship; it exists *in* their communication. These assumptions direct research attention to issues of process—the process of creating, maintaining, and transforming "reality." This different theoretical lens has much to offer to our understanding of customer relationships. For example, existing research identifies various types of customer relationships, but we know nothing about the communication characteristics that distinguish those relationship types. Social construction research would yield insights, for example, into what a bilateral relationship "sounds like" and how it is communicatively distinct from a recurrent relationship. Moreover, social construction scholars could examine the communicative processes by which customer relationships develop and transform over time. Such studies, for instance, would reveal the process by which a recurrent customer relationship may become a bilateral customer relationship over time. Social construction research would also reveal the processes by which customer relationships deteriorate over time. Similarly, scholars note that effective customer relationships are characterized by trust, support, customer orientation, and "professional concern," yet we have little understanding of the communicative nature of such practices. Social construction research would be helpful in revealing the communication patterns and practices that constitute such relational characteristics.

Social construction research would also provide important insights into how employees construct different realities about customer relationships. Lovett (1997), for example, noted that to the extent the relationship a particular front person develops with a customer is "nonimitable," the loss of that front person can be harmful to the company. Social construction research could uncover the communication characteristics of nonimitable and highly valuable customer relationships. Moreover, social construction scholars could identify how front people socially construct themselves to their supervisors and to the customer as irreplaceable or nonimitable. In addition, some scholars and practitioners have suggested the value of mentoring for developing "star performers" such as non-imitable front people (DeLong & Vijayaraghavan, 2003). Research grounded in social construction theory would provide valuable insights into the communicative nature of such mentoring. Finally, extant models of customer relationships center on the concepts of information (i.e., the exchange of information between the relationship partners) and social exchange (i.e., the degree of mutual trust between the partners). Social construction research would provide deeper insights in the communicative nature of such exchanges.

In sum, examination of customer relationships from a social construction perspective would guide scholars toward the study of a variety of customer relationship dynamics that have been largely overlooked to date. Critical theory, grounded in large part in social construction concepts, would provide further insights. This is discussed in the following section.

CRITICAL PERSPECTIVE

Grounded in social constructionism, critical theory assumes a socially constructed reality. Moreover, critical theory acknowledges reality, and, by extension, organizations and organizational relationships, as socially constructed systems of power and domination. Similar to earlier chapters, I organize the discussion of critical theory as it applies to customer relationships using the four primary themes detailed in Chapter 1—reification, managerial bias, consent, and technical rationality (Deetz, 2005). Studies of reification address the ways socially constructed phenomena become discursively naturalized and, consequently, unquestioned. A number of interesting insights into customer relationships would be provided by critical studies. For example, such work could reveal hegemonic assumptions regarding customer relationships that impact organizational functioning (for example, the assumption that "the customer is always right") and the discursive processes that serve to maintain and reify such assumptions. A number of different types of data could be used to examine such a question. Studies of micropractices would focus on analyzing customer–organizational representative interaction to identify assumptions regarding customers and the customer relationship enacted in everyday interaction. Critical research could also examine macrolevel discursive formations regarding customers and customer relationships through examination of popular press business magazines, books, and textbooks.

The issue of power is particularly interesting and complex in the context of customer and client relationships (e.g., Vaughn & Stamp, 2003). Customers are powerful partners in these relationships due to the fact that they provide revenue for the organization. The organization, more specifically, organizational representatives (e.g., front people and other boundary spanners), are powerful in their impact on the customer in the form of providing and controlling products or services. Critical research is needed to reveal and unpack the various ways both partners in the customer relationship communicatively enact power and influence, and to interrogate tensions regarding power and influence that may characterize such relationships. Analysis of in-depth interviews with customers and with organizational representatives could be used to obtain data reflecting the partners' perceptions, understandings and assumptions regarding their relative power and influence in the relationship. Critical incident interviews, in particular, could lend insights into communicative strategies the partners use to enact power in specific situations.

The notion of consent is also potentially useful for understanding customer relationships, particularly with respect to customer relationship management technologies. While such technologies provide an important information-gathering function for organizations that assists with relationship marketing activities, a critical perspective is necessary for problematizing the surveillance function of such technologies. Critical scholars could lend important insights into the use of CRM for surveillance and, in particular, the ways in which customers consent to being surveilled for the profit goals of the organization. Such issues could be addressed via a number of methods, including critical examination of CRM technologies and mechanisms specifically, as well as interviews with customers regarding their perceptions and understanding of CRM practices and their participation in those practices.

Critical studies of the spirit of technical rationality in the context of customer relationships would also make important contributions to our understanding of these partnerships. Unlike the other types of workplace relationships discussed in this book, customer relationships are explicitly defined as utilitarian, rather than affiliative. Their utilitarian nature implies a privileging of technical, rather than emotional, rationality. Yet as noted in the preceding, customer relationships can evolve to incorporate affiliative elements such as friendship (O'Toole & Donaldson, 2000) that may threaten that technical rationality. Critical scholars should address these issues and tensions and uncover the communicative processes associated with emotion, rationality, and decision making among customers and organizational representatives.

The notion of customer relationships as "social capital" is relevant to the managerial bias noted in critical research. The managerial bias refers to the notion that what's good for the organization/management is good for employees. By extension, the managerial bias also refers to the notion that what's good for the organization is good for customers and clients. Critical scholars could unpack the concept of social capital at the macrolevel by examining the extent to which the benefits of customer relationships accrue to the organization, the customer, or both. Critical research could also examine the ways in which technology empowers, rather than commodifies or controls, customers. Such dynamics are indicated in the case discussed at the beginning of the chapter in which a dissatisfied customer posted his complaints about a dry cleaning firm on the Web, harming the firm's business.

STRUCTURATION PERSPECTIVE

As detailed in Chapter 1, the duality of structure, or the reciprocal relationship between agency (human behavior) and structure (rules and resources that guide and constrain human behavior), is central to structuration theory. Rather than privileging structure over agency, or agency over structure, structuration theory posits that agency and structure exert simultaneous and reciprocal influence. Applying the duality of structure to customer relationships turns research focus in several interesting directions. Structuration research would be particularly useful for revealing the embedded structures that enable and constrain customer relationships and how customer and organizational representatives reproduce and reinforce (and potentially reify) the very structures that constrain their interaction with one another. The duality of structure could help researchers uncover the structures that constrain the development of customer relationships at various levels.

Structuration theory addresses how structures develop into systems, or patterns of social relations across stretches of time and space, and would conceptualize customer relationships as systems or patterns of social relations that stretch across time and space. Such a conceptualization suggests interesting examinations of customer relationships. Hunt et al. (2006) suggest that a customer relationship's history impacts its future, in particular with respect to the building and maintenance of trust. Structuration research could examine the structuring of customer relationships over time, specifically focusing on identifying the structures enacted and reproduced in the interaction between the partners, as well as the ways in which such structures both enable and constrain partners' actions.

The structuration concept of time–space distanciation refers to processes by which structures transcend time and contexts. Structuration research along these lines could investigate the extent to which customer relationship structures are transported and/or transformed across time and context. Such research would provide information regarding customer relationship structures that span organizations, industries, and cultural contexts. These studies would lend insights into how customer relationship structures today compare to those in the past and how and why such structures have changed over time. Data addressing such issues could be obtained via interviews, taped or reconstructed interaction, and archival texts. Interviews can obtain data from customers and organizational representatives regarding what they perceive as appropriate customer interaction, why such interaction is appropriate, and where they learned the structure (e.g., from prior relationships, the media, etc.), as well as the extent to which customer relationship structures are transferable or context bound. Interview and interaction data would reveal structures that guide customer relationships in different social contexts (e.g., different countries, industries, occupations) and how those structures are created, maintained, and transformed. Finally, textual data (e.g., popular press books, textbooks, films, and novels) from various eras could lend insights into customer relationship structures (re)produced in different eras and how and when those systems were transformed at a broad, societal level.

Conclusion

In this chapter, I turned attention to the boundary between organizations and the external environment and, in particular, the relationships that span that boundary—customer/client relationships. In addition to spanning the organization–society boundary, these relationships are also unique due to their explicit, at least initially, utilitarian focus. A great deal of research has identified various types of customer relationships, strategies organizations use to develop and maintain these relationships, the important role of the technology of customer relationship management, and a variety of financial and attitudinal outcomes of customer relationships. A research agenda grounded in alternative perspectives will both broaden and deepen our body of knowledge in this area in important and innovative ways. The "Practicing Theory" case below helps demonstrate how these alternative perspectives guide more complex understanding and approaches to real-world customer relationship concerns and problems.

Losing Trust in the National Trust Bank

Jill Martin was an account manager for a branch of the National Trust Bank located in a large metropolitan area in the southeastern United States. In that job, she managed the accounts of several large businesses in the area. Her job required her to maintain contact with clients, advise them regarding their banking services and needs, and assist clients with any problems or concerns that arose with their accounts.

Jill was well liked and respected by her clients. They saw Jill as highly knowledgeable, not only about the bank and its services, but also about the clients' unique situations and needs, and about U.S. economics and financial principles and strategies in general. Jill always responded quickly and earnestly to client queries and requests. More importantly, clients trusted Jill and perceived her as being concerned with the clients' needs, not just the bank's.

Jill had worked for National Trust for 23 years. What she enjoyed most about her job was the interpersonal contact she had with her clients, many of whom she considered friends. She enjoyed their company and often spent time with them, for example over lunch, during which the bank and banking services were never even discussed. She felt these activities were important to maintaining trusting and close relationships with her clients.

Like many other financial institutions, the National Trust Bank had begun to increasingly rely on technology to conduct its business. Jill generally saw such technologies as useful; and no one enjoyed using a Blackberry as much as Jill! She became very frustrated, however, with the actions taken by the bank's marketing and information technology units. These units were given the charge of developing a customer relationship management (CRM) program designed to assist the bank and its account managers with the development and maintenance of effective client relationships. Key to this program was the use of technology to gather and analyze information about clients and provide information to clients via the Web, e-mail, text-messaging, and direct mailings.

Jill initially was intrigued by these notions and thought they could be helpful to her as she interacted with her client organizations. She found, however, that the CRM folks more often went around her in dealing with clients. More than once, a client called Jill either angry or confused, or both, after receiving an e-mail, text message, or postcard, suggesting a new financial product from the bank or asking for "updated" information regarding the clients' organizations and financial strategies. Jill was usually unable to answer her clients' questions about these contacts and generally told the client to simply ignore the communications from anyone else at the bank. She worried that this made her look incompetent and unknowl-edgeable to her clients, and it made the bank appear very unorganized. Her com-plaints to upper management were met with concern, but the problems continued. When she complained to the managers in the CRM program, she was told that there were still a "few bugs" to work out with the system, but that they were work-ing on it and things should run more smoothly soon.

After 3 months of frustration, Jill was fed up. She reasoned that perhaps she was too old and set in her ways to deal with these technological advances. She discussed the problem with one of her clients (the CFO of a large consumer elec-tronics retailer) over lunch. To her surprise, her client called her 2 days later and offered her a job as his senior financial adviser. Jill jumped at the chance and took the job. And several of Jill's other clients left the National Trust and turned their accounts over to other banks in the area.

Discussion Questions

1. How does existing research on relationship marketing and CRM explain what went wrong at the National Trust Bank? What principles of rela-tionship marketing did the bank violate?

2. What principles and communicative practices enabled Jill's success at developing and maintaining effective customer relationships? How were those impacted by the new CRM program?

3. Consider this case from a social construction perspective. How did Jill socially construct CRM with her clients? What did she think the CRM pro-gram was communicating about her and the bank?

4. Consider this case from a critical perspective. Whose interests were served by the CRM program? How did clients view their relationship with the bank versus their relationship with Jill? How did the clients consent to and/or resist the CRM program?

5. Consider this case from a structuration perspective. What structures enabled and constrained Jill's interaction with clients? What structures enabled and constrained Jill's reaction to the CRM program?

6. How could the bank have handled implementation of the CRM program more effectively? What can the bank's management do now to salvage the CRM system and prevent the loss of more clients?

7

Workplace Relationships and Society

When the Boston area experienced its second major snowstorm of the winter in January 2008, many workers who had attempted, and failed, to get to work during the first snowstorm decided to forego the commute and, instead, work from home (Abel & Bray, 2008). This option was possible only because of technologies such as the Web, e-mail, and texting. Such technologies effectively remove, or at least blur, the boundary between work and home, and between organizations and society. Such developments have advantages and disadvantages. Ben was an employee who stayed home during that January snowstorm. He enjoyed not having to dress for work and being able to play with his kids. His wife noted, however, that Ben staying home "throws a wrench in our schedule" (Abel & Bray, 2008). David also appreciated not having to navigate the treacherous commute, but found he had to deal with a "different set of distractions," including "the noises of my son, whatever it is he's doing" (Abel & Bray, 2008). Although these employees' forays into telecommuting were brief and isolated, their experiences highlight a number of important ways in which the links between organizations and society have transformed substantially over the past two decades. As shown in this chapter, these transformations have many important implications for workplace relationships.

Until now, the chapters in this book have implicitly treated organizations as relatively isolated and self-contained phenomena. Although each chapter addresses the embeddedness of workplace relationships in the larger organization, the embeddedness of the organization in a larger environment and society has been ignored. In this chapter, I discuss the link between organizations and society, focusing particular attention on how workplace relationships impact, and are impacted by, the world beyond the organization.

I first discuss broad international organizational trends such as technological innovation and globalization. I then turn the focus to the changing nature of work and organization at the national level, including the "new social contract," work–family issues, and increasing movements toward workplace spirituality. Finally, as in the preceding chapters, I develop a research agenda for the future guided by multiple theoretical perspectives and provide a case study to illustrate the practical benefit of approaching situations from various perspectives.

Overview

Early theories of organizations and management largely ignored the situated nature of organizations and, instead, focused on internal components and processes such as division of labor, formal structure, and span of control (Fayol, 1949; Weber, 1946), as well as employee morale, employee motivation, and performance (e.g., Likert, 1961). The lack of attention to, or even recognition of, an organization's external environment reveals implicit assumptions of a stable, predictable, and relatively placid environment, and in fact, the organizational environments of those decades appear remarkably stable, predictable, and placid when compared to today.

Many adjectives can be used to describe 21st-century society, but stable, predictable, and placid are not among them. Today's world is characterized by constant and rapid change, uncertainty and surprise, turbulence, and instability. As McLagan and Christo (1995) foresaw a decade ago, "Communication and information technology, globalization of markets, technology in the workplace, the rise of the customer as boss, increased workforce diversity, and the emergence of democracy as the major political framework worldwide, are changing the rules" (p. 10). In addition to, or perhaps because of, these changes, organizations and employees are developing new relationships toward one another and new approaches toward work and life.

The link between organizations and society is reciprocal, of course, not unidirectional. While society impacts organizations, organizations also impact society. Sheep (2006) reminds us that the "world can be increasingly described as a 'society of organizations' . . . [and] it is incumbent upon organizational researchers to account for the role of organizations in determining the well-being of societies and the individuals that comprise them" (p. 357). As Deetz (1992) noted, organizations do not necessarily enhance the "well-being" of society. They have, however, increased the bureaucratization and "corporatization" of society.

The external environment was not explicitly and substantively considered by organizational scholars until the late 1960s when theorists appropriated biological principles of living systems (Bertalanffy, 1962) and applied those principles to organizational systems (Katz & Kahn, 1966). Systems theory has subsequently provided the theoretical framework for much organizational research on a wide variety of topics, including, of course, relationships (e.g., Sias & Jablin, 1995). Systems theory places an organization's external environment at the center of organizational functioning and recognizes the interdependent relationship between an organization and its environment—the organization relies on the environment for "inputs" such as materials, customers, and employees, and as an outlet for "outputs" in the form of products and services. At the same time, the environment depends on the organization for products and services and as a site for employment and vendor support. In particular, systems theory addresses an organization's "relevant environment," which refers to persons and entities directly linked to the organization, such as customers, competitors, suppliers, and potential employees.

Certainly, members of an organization's relevant environment are important and consequential elements of society. However, organizations are embedded in society at large, and elements of that society, whether directly "relevant" or not, impact, and are impacted by, the organization. For example, a major cultural event occurred on October 3, 1995, an event that had, and continues to have, a great deal of cultural and societal resonance. That morning, a jury returned their verdict on the O. J. Simpson murder trial—the verdict of "not guilty." The trial dealt with what was largely considered at the time to be the "crime of the century," trying a major sports and entertainment celebrity for the brutal double murder of his ex-wife, Nicole Simpson, and her friend, Ronald Goldman. Simpson's celebrity status gave an air of spectacle to the trial, which was broadcast in its entirety on television. The case was also largely considered to be a statement on the role of race and celebrity in society. The time of the verdict was announced to the public the day prior, and people in the United States and, not surprisingly, people around the world were very eager to learn the jury's pronouncement. Most did not foresee, however, the announcement's impact on business. Businesses around the world reported that from 1:00 to 1:05 p.m. (Eastern Standard Time) on the afternoon of October 3rd, business came to a virtual standstill ("The Verdict," October 1995). AT&T Corporation reported a 60% drop in phone traffic during that period. At the Boston Stock Exchange and the Chicago Board of Trade, trading came to a virtual standstill while traders watched the verdict on nearby TV screens, preventing billions of dollars worth of trading. While the Simpson jury in Orange County, California, would not likely be considered part of the Chicago Board of Trade's "relevant environment," for those 5 minutes it was the board's most consequential environmental element.

Clearly, organizations affect and are affected by societal conditions. Because organizations are essentially systems of relationships, these societal conditions have consequences for workplace relationships. Two of the most important and most widespread current societal conditions are technology and globalization. Technology and globalization are, of course, related to one another and together have spurred the other trends discussed in this chapter. I, therefore, begin with a discussion of technology and globalization and their links to workplace relationships. Table 7.1 provides a brief summary of research on these various themes.

Technology, Globalization, and Workplace Relationships

Two major, and related, elements transformed organizations, and subsequently, organizational relationships, in lasting and fundamental ways—technology and globalization. These elements have transformed not only the ways organizations function, but also links between individuals and organizations, and, of course, links between those organizational members in the form of workplace relationships.

Table 7.1   Summary of Workplace Relationships and Society Research

Technology, Globalization, and Workplace Relationships

Computer-Mediated Communication
- Telecommuting and distributed work
- E-mentoring
- Technology and social groups

Surveillance Technology
- Impact on employee relationships

Globalization
- Diversity and workplace relationships

Workplace Relationships and the Life-World

New Social Contract
- Decreased loyalty and commitment
- Contingent workforce

Spirituality in the Workplace
- Response to new social contract
- Emphasis on meaningful relationships at work
- Elements of workplace spirituality (connection, caring, community)
- Linked to job satisfaction, job involvement, self-esteem

Work–Family Balance
- Depleting and enriching effects of work–family relationships
- Supervisor supportiveness
- Social construction of family, parenthood, and relationship development
- Workplace relationships and social support

TECHNOLOGY

The Industrial Revolution in the early 20th century resulted from techno-logical innovations such as the assembly line and mass production. These new technologies revolutionized the ways U.S. companies did business. As a result, the United States transformed from an agrarian and craft-trade society to an industrial society. Small companies formerly owned and operated by families and highly skilled craftspeople gave way to large companies steeped in the principles of bureaucracy and administrative management and comprised of a large number of employees recognized for their role in the organization (and on the assembly line), not for their family relations, personality, or unique skills and background (Bluestone & Harrison, 1982).

The Information Age that began in the late 20th century and continues today also results from technological innovations and has similarly revolution-ized the way America and the rest of the world does business. This time, however, it is information technology, not production technology, that has funda-mentally altered the world's organizational landscape. Introduction of personal computers, group decision support software (GDSS), e-mail, the World Wide Web, and video-conferencing have transformed the U.S. and world economies from product based to service based. These information technologies enable people to obtain, share, and analyze vast amounts of information quickly and across any distance. As a consequence, new communication technologies have compressed time and space to the point of virtual irrelevancy. To a large extent, anyone can communicate at any time with anyone else anywhere. Information technology has enabled the information society. Information and knowledge, rather than the physical ability prized in the industrial era, have become coin of the realm in this new environment, and "knowledge workers" are among the most sought-after employees (Eisenberg & Goodall, 2004).

The new technologies have transformed not only industry but also orga-nizing processes within those industries. As Kiesler (1986) noted, new com-munication technologies have "unintended social effects that change the way social and work activities are organized" (p. 46). The effects of communication technology on organizing processes are somewhat paradoxical in that such technologies both connect *and* separate people and organizations. As men-tioned above, technologies such as e-mail, teleconferencing, and the Web con-nect people at unprecedented levels, providing access to information and communication. Thus, for example, employees previously isolated from com-munication networks due to being located away from headquarters or main company locations can now become active members of the network via tech-nology. At the same time, the qualities of computer-mediated communication, such as lack of nonverbal cues, social context, and emotion, can create distance between employees. Kiesler (1986) argued these distancing characteristics can lead users to become more self-centered. As she explained, "When communi-cation lacks dynamic personal information, people focus their attention on the message rather than on each other. Communicators feel a greater sense of anonymity and detect less individuality in others than they do on the phone or face-to-face. They feel less empathy, less guilt, less concern over how they compare with others and are less influenced by norms" (p. 48). Clearly, such effects are consequential for workplace relationships. Kiesler made these statements in 1986, and two decades of subsequent research on the social effects of technology provide mixed support for those predictions. This research has focused primarily on how new technologies impact supervisor–subordinate relationships and peer relationships.

Communication technologies have enabled organizations to organize in a variety of new and innovative ways, including "distributed work" or telecommuting, in which organizational members operate in different physical locations (e.g., from home, from a satellite or annex location), staying connected with other members via computer-mediated communication (CMC) technologies. A number of early studies indicated telecommuting can negatively impact coworker relationships, due largely to decrease in informal communication and contact among the employees (Huws, Korte, & Robinson, 1990; Olson, 1987).

Reinsch (1997) used survey and interview data to examine how telecommuters responded to such arrangements and how telecommuting affected the employees' relationships with their supervisors (i.e., the quality of their leader–member exchange [LMX] relationships; see Chapter 2 for details on LMX). Reinsch noted that the traditional arrangement of a "central office" in which employees and their supervisors work in the same physical location rested on the assumption that members would informally communicate with each other as needed to complete their tasks and maintain their working relationships. The extent to which informal communication is hindered, or perhaps enhanced, by CMC is an important question. Telecommuters in Reinsch's study reported positive effects of telecommuting on their LMX relationships, but only for those in the early stages of the telecommuting experience. Respondents who had telecommuted for a year or more were more likely to report a decrease in the quality of their LMX relationships. As Reinsch explains, employees chosen for telecommuting (at least at the time of the study) typically are competent employees with good relationships with their supervisors. These relationships enjoy a "honeymoon period" at the onset of telecommuting, characterized by the excitement and novelty of doing work in a different way. The disconnection, and decrease in informal interaction, created by telecommuting, however, eventually may diminish the quality of the LMX relationship. As noted in Chapter 2, high-quality LMX relationships are characterized by a high level of personal interaction, trust, and emotional support—qualities not easily supported via CMC.

Scholars have also addressed the qualities and effectiveness of "virtual mentoring" or "e-mentoring" (Ensher & Murphy, 2007). *Virtual mentoring* refers to "a computer-mediated relationship between a senior individual who is the mentor with a lesser skilled protégé with the goal of developing the protégé in a way that helps him or her succeed" (Boyle Single, & Muller, 2001, p. 107). The virtual nature of e-mentoring makes such relationships fundamentally distinct from traditional, face-to-face mentoring relationships. These distinctions provide both benefits and challenges. Among the benefits noted by Bierema and Hill (2005) are the fact that mentoring can happen anytime and in any place, making professional development more accessible for employees. They also argue that the written nature of e-mail can lead to more thoughtful, systematic mentoring. Moreover, protégés have a written text to which they can refer when they want to refresh their memories. As noted in Chapters 2 and 3, many employees, such as women and minority employees, lack access to powerful mentors due to their traditionally marginalized status in organizations. Virtual mentoring can provide easier, more convenient, and more egalitarian access to mentors than face-to-face mentoring, which requires mentors and protégés to be physically co-located.

Bierema and Hill (2005) also note a number of disadvantages and challenges associated with virtual mentoring. Among these challenges is the fact that the "digital divide" may inhibit access for those employees who need mentoring the most. The digital divide refers to the fact that not all employees have access to communication technologies and/or the training and skills needed to effectively use those technologies. Thus, while virtual mentoring can increase access to mentors, those employees on the wrong side of the digital divide are not privy to that access. Privacy concerns also present challenges to virtual mentoring. Mentoring relationships are characterized by trust, candid advice, and, at times, emotional support (Kram & Isabella, 1985). Employees may be wary of communicating in an open way about sensitive issues via a medium that leaves a text record. Moreover, the decreased social presence of CMC makes such interaction difficult, making maintaining quality mentoring relationships difficult.

CMC is an important tool for work teams and virtual groups. Such technologies enable employees to connect to one another across any distance and at any time. Organizations are becoming increasingly reliant on virtual teams and groups to be competitive in the global economy (discussed at length in a later section of this chapter). Such technologies have important implications for social groups/networks in organizations. As noted in Chapter 4, informal social networks such as friendship networks provide members access to information, power, and influence. Being part of, or isolated from, the social network is of great consequence (Sias, in press).

Little research has focused on the link between technology and social networks, but a recent study by Ahuja, Galletta, and Carley (2003) suggests that technology has not diminished the importance of being socially connected at work. The researchers analyzed e-mail messages exchanged among members of an intact virtual research and development group from two points over a 4-year period. Specifically, they examined the impact of individual characteristics and social network involvement (i.e., centrality or the extent to which an individual is highly connected and active in the group's social network) on team member performance. Their results indicated that, like face-to-face groups, being an active member of the social network is linked to higher levels of performance. In fact, their analyses suggest that while individual characteristics such as organizational role and status impact one's social network centrality, centrality was more important than individual characteristics in impacting individual job performance in these virtual groups. Thus, social networking is as important in virtual groups as it is in face-to-face contexts.

While the above addresses the ways relationships impact technology use and performance, scholars have also addressed the ways technology use impacts employee relationships. Friedman and Currall (2003) developed a model explaining how communicating regarding an issue of conflict via e-mail, rather than face-to-face, can exacerbate rather than resolve the conflict, leading to relationship damage. They note several structural features of e-mail that inhibit effective conflict management and that can harm relationships among employees. These features include the relative lack of feedback available via e-mail that can inhibit individuals' ability to repair and self-correct their messages. The asynchronous nature of e-mail may prevent individuals from self-correcting in a timely way so as to "preempt" disagreement when an individual senses the other has misunderstood the message. The limited feedback available via e-mail can also inhibit relational development because, as noted in other chapters, obtaining knowledge about others is an important developmental mechanism and feedback during conversation is important to obtaining such knowledge. Finally, the "reviewability and revisability" of e-mail messages can impact interaction dynamics in that individuals may perceive greater intent behind a particular message since, unlike face-to-face interaction in which one can easily commit a "slip of the tongue," people assume any e-mail message sent was done so thoughtfully and intentionally. The occasional misstatements and "slips of the tongue" people actually do commit via e-mail are less forgivable than those in face-to-face conversation and, consequentially, potentially more damaging to the relationship. No empirical work has tested this model, and examinations of its various propositions would provide important insights into the links between CMC and coworker relationships.

Recent empirical work provides a more optimistic view of CMC and coworker relationships, highlighting the ways individuals use the technology is more important than the technology itself. Timmerman and Scott (2006) examined how the communication practices of virtual groups are associated with the relationships among virtual group members, using data obtained from members of 98 different virtual teams. Results showed positive relationships between responsiveness, thoroughness, and channel selection and team trust, cohesiveness, identification, and communication satisfaction. These results suggest that computer-mediated communication does not necessarily decrease connection among employees; rather, competent virtual communication practices can actually enhance connectedness.

Although the majority of scholarly work addressing technology and workplace relationships has focused on CMC, other types of technology have the potential to impact relationships. Botan (1996) examined links between employee surveillance technologies (e.g., telephone monitoring, video cameras, accounting technologies that track transactions, etc.) and employee perceptions of uncertainty, self-esteem, and social isolation. Of particular relevance to this chapter, results of that study indicated that individual perceptions of being "surveilled" by such technologies were negatively linked to communication with other employees. In other words, individuals who perceived they were being electronically monitored reported being less engaged in workplace communication and, consequently, more isolated from the social network.

In sum, although scant, existing research indicates links between new technologies and workplace relationships. Those links are complex and bidirectional, and studies indicate that, as with any other tool, communication technology is less important than the ways human beings actually use that technology. These issues will be addressed in the latter part of this chapter developing research programs for the future. For now, we turn to another issue closely linked with technology—globalization.

GLOBALIZATION

One of the most important impacts of the communication technologies developed in the late 20th century is globalization. New communication and information technologies did more than simply connect geographically dispersed workers; they connected the world in ways previously unimaginable. With e-mail, the World Wide Web, teleconferencing, cell phones, and text messaging, anyone can talk to anyone anywhere at any time; anyone can instantly obtain information on virtually any topic at any time. Information technology enabled, and is responsible for, globalization and, in particular, globalization of business and industry (Korac-Kakabadse & Kouzmin, 1999).

Globalization is fundamentally about connectedness. Its relevance to relationships is, therefore, substantial. Specifically, *globalization* refers to "the interconnected nature of the global economy, the interpenetration of global and domestic organizations, and communication technologies that blur temporal and spatial boundaries" (Stohl, 2001, p. 325). Globalization refers not only to connections between nation states, industries, economies, and organizations, but also to connections between the people who comprise those larger entities. In the global economy, international and multinational organizations compete, collaborate, and are connected in unprecedented numbers. In the global economy, the majority of the U.S. workforce is employed in international and multinational organizations, and the majority of products and services in the U.S.

economy are provided by global organizations. Buying "American" is becoming increasingly difficult because there are few completely "American" companies today. Even commonly perceived "American" companies such as the Ford Motor Company are more global than local. The Ford Fusion car, for example, is built in Mexico. The Chrysler PT Cruiser is comprised primarily (65%) of parts built in Mexico. Similarly, Japanese cars are not very "Japanese." Eighty percent of the Toyota Camry is made in the United States ("Selling It," April 2007). Clearly, today's employees work in a context much more racially, nationally, and culturally diverse than ever before. Such diversity can both enhance and inhibit their workplace relationships. While many scholars have studied globalization from economic, political, and social perspectives, very little work has addressed links between globalization and workplace relationships. This work centers largely on issues of diversity and workplace relationships.

DIVERSITY AND WORKPLACE RELATIONSHIPS

As noted in earlier chapters, a theme that runs consistently through research on all types of workplace relationships is the homophily principle, or the notion that individuals are attracted to, and form relationships with, people like themselves (Sherif, 1958; Turner & Oakes, 1986). Individuals tend to form closer relationships with people they perceive to be similar. Diversity, therefore, can make forming and maintaining workplace relationships difficult. Moreover, employees in international and multinational organizations also face challenges with different language, cultural values, and cultural norms.

Scholars have examined the impact of diversity on workplace relationships, focusing primarily on supervisor–subordinate relationships. This body of work represents two primary approaches to globalization. Research taking the divergence approach centers on identifying cultural differences and how cultural differences impact organizing processes. Research from the convergence approach centers on how organizations in the global economy have become more similar than different. Such studies examine structural adaptation of multinational organizations (Stohl, 2005).

Research on cultural divergence focuses on identifying cultural differences among nations, conducting cross-cultural comparisons, and examining how organizational members (typically expatriate managers) work with or "lead" culturally different employees. This line of research is grounded in the notion that organizations cannot simply impose the home country's culturally grounded organizational processes and structures on employees in different national subsidiaries. Instead, effective managers must gain an understanding of the host culture and manage employees in ways consistent with that culture (Kim, 1999). Among the most important cultural elements are varying understandings, values, and approaches toward interpersonal relationships (Bright, 2005; Korac-Kakabadse & Kouzmin, 1999).

Much of the early work in this area was grounded in Hofstede's typology of culture dimensions and Hall's (1966) examination of culture. In a large multinational study, Hofstede (1984) identified four primary dimensions that differentiate national cultures from one another—*power distance* (the extent to which authority and status distinctions are accepted and institutionalized), *uncertainty avoidance* (the extent to which cultural members are able to deal with ambiguous and uncertain circumstances), *individualism/collectivism* (the extent to which cultural members value belonging to a group and behave in ways that benefit the collective over the individual), and *masculinity* (the extent to which the culture differentiates sex roles and values masculine characteristics such as assertiveness and achievement). At the time of his study, Hofstede found national cultures differed from one another on these dimensions with, for example, U.S. culture identified as high in individuality and masculinity, while Asian cultures tended to rate high in power distance and collectivism.

According to Hall, cultures also differ in the extent to which they approach life in a monochronic or polychronic way. *Monochronic* cultures approach situations in a linear, rational manner; value timeliness; and use cause–effect reasoning to solve problems. People in monochronic cultures tend to develop short-term relationships with one another. North American and Germanic cultures tend to approach life monochronically. Members of *polychronic* cultures, in contrast, place greater value on developing and maintaining long-term relationships, are less concerned with time and scheduling and more concerned with relationships, and deal with many situations at once, rather than taking a linear approach to situations. According to Hall and Hall (1990), people from Arab and Asian nations, as well as Mediterranean areas, tend to approach life polychronically.

Michael (1997) used both Hofstede's and Hall's typologies to develop a model of effective expatriate management. Expatriate managers are individuals from the home country (e.g., an American manager of IBM) who take a management position in one of the company's international subsidiary branches. Many organizations send expatriate managers to lead operations in a subsidiary without considering the host country's culture. According to Michael (1997), expatriate managers need to display different approaches to relationships depending on the nature of the host culture. Those in collectivist, feminine, and polychromic cultures, for example, should engage in more mentoring, team building, and networking behaviors with their subordinate employees than those in individualist, masculine, and monochronic cultures.

An empirical study of expatriate managers sent to Chinese subsidiaries revealed how cultural differences impacted the supervisor–subordinate relationship (Sergeant & Frenkel, 1998). In particular, the high power distance that characterized the Chinese culture proved to be a barrier to open, frank, and clear leader–employee communication. As one of the study's participants explained, "You must understand the anxiety to please, and you need to understand that you cannot be too confrontational. The locals will rarely disagree with you and will constantly defer to your opinion" (p. 26). This study suggests that the characteristics of a high-quality LMX relationship (see Chapter 2) may not apply to high power distance cultures such as China. Managers attempting to develop such relationships by encouraging and expecting open, frequent discussion and role negotiation may become frustrated and may harm, rather than improve, their relationships with subordinate employees.

Stage's (1999) study of American subsidiaries in Thailand went beyond simply identifying cultural differences between American and Thai employees, and also examined how organizational members negotiated these differences in the context of their interpersonal relationships. Differing cultural approaches to relationships created a variety of tensions for Thai employees. Consistent with the homophily principle, expatriate and Thai employees tended to develop friendships within their own cultural groups, demonstrating the desire for independence from culturally different coworkers. At the same time, the Thai employees recognized their interdependent relationships with the American employees with respect to completing their tasks. Different approaches to interpersonal relationships hindered Thai employees' ability to form relationships with the expatriates. For example, Thai employees took a long-term view of their jobs and of interpersonal relationships, while they perceived the expatriates to take more short-term views. The high power distance of the Thai culture also made forming relationships with expatriate managers difficult.

Far fewer scholars of diversity and workplace relationships have been guided by the convergence perspectives. These projects examine how organizations become more similar to one another, rather than focusing on cultural differences. They also examine how multinational and international organizations become "transnational," developing, in essence, a "third culture" or "global culture" that results from the merging and negotiation of the relevant national cultures. McBride (1992) uses a "microworld" approach in her discussion of a global organization simulation called "Foodcorp." This simulation demonstrates how global managers, rather than imposing a culture on subsidiaries, or adapting to local subsidiary culture, instead develop a "microculture" with its own unique "ecology" of relationships, attitudes, beliefs, and behaviors. Organizational "microcultures" transcend traditional notions of space and boundaries (i.e., the Thai subsidiary, the German subsidiary, the U.S. subsidiary) and instead represent a global "space." This is consistent with the view of others who argue that globalization necessarily alters our traditional notions of space, emphasizing instead social networks (Sheppard, 2002). As Massey (1994) explained, "Instead, then, of thinking of places as areas with boundaries around, they can be imagined as articulated moments in networks of social relations and understandings, but where a large proportion of those relations, experiences and understandings are constructed on a far larger scale" (pp. 154–155). "Third cultures" and "microcultures," then, are constituted in, and defined by, social relationships.

Workplace Relationships and the Life-World

The preceding sections discussed how societal developments and trends have impacted organizations and the workplace relationships that comprise those organizations. As noted in the introduction, however, links between society and organizations are not unidirectional. And in fact, the boundaries between organizations and society, the boundaries between work and personal spheres, are more porous and permeable than clear and defined. In this section, I discuss reciprocal links between organizations, in particular, workplace relationships and the "life-world," or the larger sphere of lived experience, focusing on areas of overlap between work and personal issues such as family and spirituality. I begin by placing these issues in the context of the "new social contract" that links workers and organizations in today's global information age.

THE NEW SOCIAL CONTRACT

Scholars argue that technology and globalization have fundamentally altered the relationship between organizations and employees, in essence, creating a new "social contract" defining how individuals and organizations relate to one another (Tsui & Wu, 2005). Work in the mid-20th century was characterized largely by careers, rather than jobs. People took positions in an organization with the expectation that they would carry out their careers in that organization. Loyalty and commitment characterized the employee organization relationship. Employees expected loyalty and support from their company, and organizations expected commitment from their employees.

This traditional social contract is no longer the norm. Motivated by the hypercompetitive nature of the technological and global economy, the information age ushered in a new social contract characterized not by relational loyalty, but by contractual economic exchange. Under these conditions, downsizing, merging, and other cost-saving measures made long-term employment more tenuous than ever. As Tsui and Wu (2005) explain, corporate downsizing at all ranks across all industries broke the

> traditional deal of a lifelong job with mutual loyalty between the employer and the employee. Replacing this tradition is the so-called "new employment relationship" [Stewart, 1998]. Instead of loyalty (i.e., job security), the employer offers the employee a challenging job, a fixed compensation package and the promise of opportunities to learn valuable skills [Roehling, Cavanaugh, Moynihan, & Boswell, 2000]. The employee, in turn, pays back the employer through job performance without making a strong commitment to the organization. In other words, the bond between the employer and employee has shifted from a long-term relationship involving loyalty and commitment to a contract-like economic exchange. (pp. 115–116)

The new social contract's emphasis on economics over relational loyalty has had an important impact on the nature of the workforce. Cost-saving efforts have led to an increase in the number of temporary, contract, and freelance employees for whom the company does not need to pay benefits. Workers, feeling less loyalty to companies, are leaving positions sooner, and many work as independent contractors to increase their autonomy and mobility. The "contingent workforce" has become an important economic power (Conrad & Poole, 1997).

The new social contract clearly has implications for traditional workplace relationships. As noted in previous chapters, close and high-quality relationships take time to develop—time less available to temporary or independent contractors. Moreover, increased reliance on CMC has decreased opportunities for employees to interact face-to-face and, as discussed earlier in this chapter, this can affect employee relationships in a number of ways.

Research examining links between the new social contract and workplace relationships is quite sparse, however. Schweiger, Ivancevich, and Power (1987) found downsizing impacted employee morale in a number of ways, including disappointment at the loss of workplace friends who were fired. This disappointment, in turn, impacted the relationships between remaining employees and their managers, who were blamed for the layoffs and firings. Employers often overlook the relational costs that come with cost-saving downsizing. Cooke (2006) found increased reliance on outsourcing and independent contractors has changed the traditional supervisory job from primarily in-house tasks to increased focus on boundary-spanning activities, including managing relationships between the organization, unit, and outsource personnel.

SPIRITUALITY IN THE WORKPLACE

The weakened attachment between individuals and organizations is perhaps partly responsible for the increased focus employees are putting into finding meaning in their lives. One primary "meaning-centered" societal movement is that of *workplace spirituality*. Although derived from religious writings and philosophies, workplace spirituality does not refer to a religious movement, but rather to a broader focus on human experience, growth, and advancement. In the competitive global market characterized by downsizing, reengineering, and tenuous links between individuals and organizations, many organizations, and organizational employees, are seeking wisdom, gratification, and connection via mental growth, belonging, challenge, trust, ethics, and "doing good" (Burack, 1999; Shaw, 1997).

According to Burack (1999), workplace spirituality generally refers to three primary concepts: (1) spiritual growth and advancement of the human experience via mental growth (e.g., problem solving and learning), (2) gratification of individual needs such as "belonging" and achievement (via work–family connections and in the workplace setting), and (3) leadership that involves sensitivity to and interest in the employees. Ashar and Lane-Maher (2004) note three primary definitions of spirituality in the workplace. The first is individually oriented and refers to a "personal search for meaning and connectedness" (p. 252). The second definition provides a more practical and applied characterization, referring to the outcomes and applications of personal spirituality. Such outcomes and applications include ethics, integrity, relationships characterized by caring and kindness, and the like. The second definition includes doing meaningful work and experiencing interconnectedness with others. The third definition refers to spirituality at the organizational level, where organizational spirituality is found in organizational policies and behaviors that incorporate and support "virtues, ethics, values, emotions, and intuition" (p. 253).

Relationships such as friendships and involvement in the social network are key to achieving a sense of belonging. Leadership that centers on the employee requires, to a large extent, high-quality LMX relationships (see Chapter 2 of this volume). Despite clear connections between workplace spirituality and workplace relationships, however, little research has actually addressed the two concepts together. Ashar and Lane-Maher (2004) interviewed law enforcement executives about how they defined success. Contrary to their expectations that success would be defined using economic and political (e.g., power and status) benchmarks, their participants instead defined "success" as connection, balance, and wholeness. In particular, the executives defined a successful person as "a common, functional individual who aspires [sic] a sense of accomplishment and who cherishes relationships, care, and connectedness. It is an individual who tends to the inner self and to his or her family." The participants' emphasis on relationships was so strong, in fact, that the authors dubbed today's societal state the "relationship age."

Much existing work contrasts workplace spirituality with bureaucratic organizing principles, via the approaches' different perspectives on relationships (Casey, 2004). The bulk of this work is theoretical and provides propositions regarding links between workplace spirituality, workplace relationships, and various outcomes such as organizational commitment and performance (e.g., Jurkiewicz & Giacalone, 2004). Though few in number, recent empirical studies provide some support for these notions.

Burack (1999) examined three large organizations that have incorporated "spirituality" in their organizational policies. Hewlett-Packard's "HP Way" emphasizes "cooperative relationships and achieving and sustaining leadership in creative products and manufacture" (p. 284). Tom's of Maine bases their organizing principles on the Buddhist notion of the "middle way," which emphasizes balance. Toward that end, the company's "soul" derives from core values and beliefs that emphasize "doing good" economically, socially, and environmentally and that conceptualize mind and spirit as interconnected and related to market share, and a belief that the corporation's identity is defined by the quality of relationships among the company's constituencies (including employees, customers, and other stakeholders). Ford Motor Company incorporated spirituality in their organizational policies as they attempted to recover from downsizing in the early 1980s. Key to their success were "trustful" relationships between managements and workers. These examples demonstrate the fundamental links between workplace spirituality and the quality of workplace relationships such as supervisor–subordinate, peer, friendship, and customer relationships.

Sass (2000) examined the organizational culture of a nursing home and discovered a large organizational emphasis on spirituality characterized by "organizational practices that are based on relationships rather than on rational-legal bureaucracy" (p. 205). The organization's "relationship-based organizing" process emphasized warm, caring, and quality relationships between employees, and between employees and clients/patients. The largely informal, family-like culture supported this organizing system and constituted the organization's "spirituality."

Milliman, Czaplewski, and Ferguson (2003) examined links between workplace spirituality and employee attitudes such as organization commitment, intention to quit, intrinsic work satisfaction, job involvement, and organization-based self-esteem. Of particular relevance to this chapter, they examined the spiritual dimension of "community," or the extent to which "people see themselves as connected to each other and that there is some type of relationship between one's inner self and the inner self of other people" (p. 429). This dimension of spirituality specifically refers to connections among employees in organizational groups and teams. Results indicated an employee's sense of "community" was positively related to commitment, satisfaction, job involvement, and organization-based self esteem, and negatively related to intent to quit. Thus, workplace relationships as they contribute to a spiritual sense of community are linked to healthy and organizationally productive employee attitudes. Finally, in a recent study grounded in an interpretive, social construction approach, Considine (2007) examined how care providers in a variety of "caregiving" professions (e.g., counseling, teaching, social work, etc.) communicated "care" to clients.

In sum, as societal movements toward globalization and technology have weakened the link between individuals and organizations, these movements have led individuals to seek meaning in a variety of ways, including in human relationships in public and private life. The following section addresses similar issues by centering on how individuals attempt to balance work and family.

WORK–FAMILY BALANCE

Balancing work and family has always been a concern for individuals. The challenges of balancing have become increasingly difficult in the 21st century, however. Part of this challenge arises from communication technologies that make employees accessible to organizations virtually 24 hours a day, 7 days a week, increasing the potential for intrusion in family life. Moreover, the lack of job security, increased expectations for productivity and performance, and fears of being downsized contribute to employees' putting work before family when forced to choose.

Not surprisingly, then, many scholars have turned their research attention toward work–family issues. This research explicitly acknowledges two issues: (1) Individuals actively engage in both work and personal spheres, and (2) the spheres are not separate but instead overlap and impact one another. Although early management approaches structured organizations and organizational processes with the explicit intent of removing emotion and personal issues from the workplace (Weber, 1946), employees do not leave their personal lives at the office door when they go to work. Rather, events and issues in our personal lives impact our work and vice versa. More relevant to this chapter, our personal lives impact our workplace relationships and our workplace relationships can impact our personal lives.

Research on work–family issues is fairly recent, with empirical attention beginning largely within the past decade. It is not surprising that much of this work is at least implicitly grounded in the critical perspective, given critical theory's focus on individual over managerial interests (Mumby, 2001). Nonetheless, work–family research does generally address how an individual's ability to balance work and family contributes to the organization's productivity and bottom-line concerns. Rothbard (2001), for example, studied the extent to which engaging in work and family roles has a "depleting" or "enriching" effect on the individual's effectiveness in those roles. She examined the effects from two directions—work depleting/enriching family and family depleting/ enriching work. Results of the study provide a number of interesting insights into work–family challenges. First, there was more evidence of enrichment than depletion. In particular, results indicated depletion only in the work–family direction and only for women. That is, women were more likely than men to have their work roles negatively impact their family roles. Rothbard (2001) suggests that "women may be more likely than men to ruminate on work events, causing them to become self-focused and decreasing their family engagement" (p. 677). Moreover, women tend to have more "synergistic mental models of work and family roles than men" (p. 677). Thus, Rothbard's results indicate women are more likely to take their work problems home with them and to have those problems detract from their family lives. The study also indicated enrichment in both directions. Again, however, gender differences moderated these links. Specifically, work enriched family engagement for men only, while family enriched work engagement for women only. The author suggests these gender differences may be due to cultural norms regarding gender and work that involve more permeable boundaries between work and family for women than for men, and that make it culturally unacceptable for family experiences to affect work for men. In sum, this study indicates the links between work and family are strong and complex. Given such links, it is not surprising that empirical research focused on work–family balance has grown significantly over the past decade. Only a small portion of such research, however, links work–family issues with workplace *relationships*. I discuss such research in the following sections.

Research indicates that the supervisor–subordinate relationship is a central element in work–family conflict and balance. Specifically, supportive supervisors (e.g., a high-quality LMX relationship) help employees manage stress that results from work–family conflict (Cramer & Pearce, 1990; Warren & Johnson, 1995). Building on this line of work, Kirby (2000) examined how supervisors and employees talk about work–family benefits and how that talk impacted employee decisions about whether or not to take advantage of those policies. Her research, grounded in social construction theory, indicated that employees received a number of "mixed messages" from their supervisors. For example, a supervisor might praise an employee for working extra hours while at the same time encouraging employees to spend time with their families. Mixed messages had both negative and positive effects on employees, however. They, of course, contributed to conflict and stress as the employees were unsure about appropriate work–family boundaries and the extent to which their supervisors were actually supportive of using the benefits. On the other hand, mixed messages often provided enough ambiguity around work–family benefits that employees perceived greater freedom in their decisions about whether or not, and in what ways, they would use the benefits.

Scholars have examined a number of ways work and family are socially constructed in the context of workplace relationships. Farley-Lucas (2000) examined the discursive construction of "motherhood" and in particular the ways working women socially construct their "motherhood" at work. Analysis of interviews with working women revealed three central discursive themes. "Children in the workplace" refers to women bringing their children to work with them either physically, technologically (via e-mail, cell phones), or symbolically (e.g., photos). "Speaking of motherhood" refers to the ways in which talking about one's children functioned as a way of "bringing children to work." Such talk served to "bond" employee/parents together, contributing to the development of multiplex workplace relationships. It also served, however, to marginalize employees who did not have children, creating a clear boundary between the two groups of employees. "Supervising motherhood" concerns the ways women interacted with, and interpreted messages from, their supervisors as they made decisions about whether or not to talk about their motherhood at work. Analysis indicated supervisors "set the tone" for the extent to which motherhood talk was appropriate and acceptable. This study demonstrates that the work–family connection both impacts workplace relationships (e.g., via the development of "cliques" comprised of working parents and the marginalization of those without children) and is impacted by workplace relationships (e.g., the supervisor–subordinate relationship and interaction).

Research also indicates workplace relationships provide important support for employees with children. Hochschild (1997) reported that many employees consider workplace relationships to be "havens" from family problems and stress. Medved (2004) found employees relied heavily on one another for help and support as they attempted to balance work and family. Supportive supervisors, for example, might arrange an employee's schedule to better fit his or her family's needs. Coworkers might take another employee's shift or help that employee with their tasks when family emergencies or other needs arise. These studies indicate the important of having quality workplace relationships characterized by both instrumental and emotional support in balancing work and family.

Research in the area of work–family balance focuses almost exclusively on how *coworkers* perceive and deal with work–family conflict and balance. A recent study took a different approach and examined how *married couples* (rather than coworkers) perceive work–family conflicts. Streich, Casper, and Salvaggio (2008) examined the extent to which couples shared similar perceptions of the extent to which work interfered with their family life. Survey data obtained from 224 dual-earner couples indicated the couples agreed more than they disagreed regarding the extent to which work interfered with their family. In particular, they tended to agree more regarding how the wife's work interfered with family matters than with respect to the husband's work.

In sum, research on workplace relationships and society coincided with fundamental changes in societal and global conditions. As information and communication technologies evolved, enabling industries and businesses to operate globally, the organizational landscape in both the United States and around the world changed dramatically. New technologies have led to an increasing number of "distributed workers," "telecommuters," and "virtual organizations." Globalization results in increased, and increasingly complex, diverse workforces. Technological innovation and globalization, together, contribute to increased downsizing, reengineering, and corporate mergers, leading to a new social contract in which the relationship between employee and employer is based on economic exchange, rather than loyalty and commitment. To cope with this new arrangement, employees and organizations are attempting to derive meaningful experiences by incorporating spirituality at work and by explicitly addressing, and implementing, policies that blend rather than separate work and family.

Scholars have responded to these fundamental societal shifts by developing theory and conducting research in these areas. Very little research attention has been given to societal conditions and *workplace relationships*, however. This is unfortunate because workplace relationships are clearly relevant and important as we move farther into the technological, global, and, as Ashar and Lane-Maher (2004) refer to it, "relationship age." Consequently, the nexus between workplace relationships and society has great potential for important and fruitful scholarly contributions.

Theoretical Perspectives on Relationships and Society

In general, and similar to the other relationships discussed in this book, research on workplace relationships and society has been guided by the postpositivist perspective, focusing on identifying links between a variety of relatively static and "objective" factors such as sex, nationality, geographic location, productivity, performance, satisfaction, and the like. In the following sections, I discuss the postpositivist approach to research on workplace relationships and societal conditions. I then turn discussion to development of a research agenda for the future guided by social construction, critical, and structuration theoretical perspectives. Table 7.2 provides a summary of the key assumptions and goals of the various theoretical perspectives.

POSTPOSITIVIST PERSPECTIVE

Postpositivism underlies the majority of research examining workplace relationships and society. Studies of new technologies and relationships, for example, tend to focus on the physical impact of technology on employees (e.g., creating geographical distance between coworkers). These studies rely on self-report survey data regarding employee attitudes and communication frequency with coworkers and supervisors. Reports of traditional employees and telecommuters are then compared to identify differences. These data indicate the "reality" of virtual workplace relationships.

Studies of relationships and globalization similarly rely on self-report survey data. These studies are largely grounded in the naturalist principle in a number of ways. First, research tends to rely on cross-sectional, rather than longitudinal, data to obtain an assessment or "snapshot" of the relationship at that single point in time. This method, at least implicitly, conceptualizes workplace relationships, as well as culture and nationality, as static and limits our understanding of relational and cultural change and dynamism. Second, most existing studies assess culture with a single item self-report (e.g., "American" or "Thai"). Such methods provide useful information regarding links between culture and workplace relationship at a fairly broad, and somewhat superficial, level. The dynamic nature of culture, however, is ignored.

Research in the area of workplace spirituality has been less reliant on postpositivist approaches. In fact, much of that research has been grounded in

Table 7.2 Sample Research Topics for Workplace Relationships and Society

	Postpositivism	Social Construction	Critical Theory	Structuration Theory
Conceptualization of organizations	Real entities that exist beyond human perception "Contain" individuals Indicated by attitudes, behavior	Socially constructed Constituted in social practices Dynamic	Socially constructed Constituted in social practices Dynamic Systems of power, domination, and control	Socially constructed Constituted in social practices Dynamic Patterned social practices of organizational members across social systems
Conceptualization of communication	Occurs "inside" the relationship Indicates nature and status of the relationship	Constitutes social reality Constitutes relationships; as communication changes, so does the relationship	Constitutes social reality Constitutes relationships Essentializes and reifies organizational "realities" and relationships	Constitutes society and social systems Enables, produces, and reproduces structure Enabled and constrained by structure
Conceptualization of relationships	Real entities that exist beyond human perception "Contain" individuals Indicated by attitudes, communication behavior Predictive of outcomes (e.g., satisfaction, productivity, commitment) Influenced by physical environment	Socially constructed Exist in interaction Observable in interaction	Socially constructed Sites of power, domination, marginalization Sites of hegemonic, unobtrusive control	Socially constructed Constrained and enabled by structure

(Continued)

Table 7.2 (Continued)

	Postpositivism	Social Construction	Critical Theory	Structuration Theory
Research goals	Measuring indicators of relationship quality and status Predicting outcomes of relationships	Understanding social construction process Understanding relationship development dynamics	Understanding social construction of power, marginalization, reification, consent, domination, universalism of managerial interests and rationality	Understanding production, reproduction, and institutionalization of relationships
Sample research topics/questions		How do employees socially construct new technologies and technology use? How do coworkers socially construct and maintain virtual relationships? How do employees terminate virtual friendships? How do supervisors and employees construct high-quality LMX relationships via technology?	How does the "digital divide" impact employee access to and use of new communication technologies? How does CMC impact social networks in the workplace? Who is marginalized and how are they marginalized? How do organizations use technology as a tool for "managing" workplace relationships (e.g., surveillance and employee monitoring technology)?	How is the digital divide structured and reproduced? What structures guide employee technology use and abuse? What structures guide virtual workplace relationships (e.g., social vs. system integration)? How are traditional management structures reproduced and/or transformed in virtual environments?

	Postpositivism	Social Construction	Critical Theory	Structuration Theory
Sample research topics/questions (continued)		How does surveillance and monitoring technology impact workplace relationship development? How do employees socially construct intercultural workplace relationships? How do global employees construct "third culture" workplace relationships? How do contingent employees construct workplace relationships? How do traditional and contingent employees construct relationships with one another? How do supervisors and contingent employees socially construct LMX relationships?	How and why do employees consent to technological monitoring and control? How is dominance constituted in workplace relationships embedded in global organizations? How do global employees appropriate dominant relationship norms and processes? How do "parent" employees marginalize single or childless coworkers? How do social/friendship networks disempower single and childless employees? How do single and childless employees develop social networks? How are employees discursively made to form "spiritual" workplace relationships?	How are "global" workplace relationship structures reproduced across time and space (e.g., convergence)? What structures do employees use to reproduce their spiritual approaches to workplace relationships? How have religious and historical-cultural spiritual principles been structured in workplace spirituality? How do workplace relationships (re)produce such structural practices? How have structures enabling/constraining work-family balance changed over time?

(Continued)

Table 7.2 (Continued)

	Postpositivism	Social Construction	Critical Theory	Structuration Theory
Sample research topics/questions (continued)		How do employees communicate "spirituality"? What are the characteristics of "spiritual" workplace relationships? How do employees socially construct "connection"? How do employees disengage from "spiritual" relationships such as friendships? How do individuals communicatively construct work–family balance? How do employees communicatively blend family and work roles?	How is employee consent to workplace spirituality manufactured by management and organizational policy? How does workplace spirituality commodify workplace relationships as social capital contributing to managerial interests? How do spiritual emotions guide reasoning and decision making? How does spirituality replace or complement the technical rationality that underlies the modern corporation?	

social construction theory, as discussed in the following section. Nonetheless, postpositivist assumptions underlie some studies. Models of links between workplace spirituality, relationships, and various organizational outcomes (e.g., Gull & Doh, 2004; Jurkiewica & Giacalone, 2004), for instance, rely on the naturalist principle by conceptualizing organizations and workplace relationships as containers separate from people and in which people behave, in this case, spiritually. The relatively few and recent empirical studies of workplace spirituality and outcomes such as employee attitudes and performance share these postpositivist assumptions. These studies provide valuable insights into the extent to which employees share spiritual approaches to relationships and to work and the extent to which such behavior is associated with individual and organizational performance. Again, however, reliance on survey methods provides no insight into the causal nature of those links.

Research on work–family issues has been similarly less reliant on postpositivist approaches, instead relying more on social construction and critical theory. Some scholars have, however, studied work–family issues with postpositivist approaches. Rothbard (2001), for example, used a survey method to determine the extent to which engagement in work and family roles enriched or depleted individuals' performance in those roles. Her study, bifurcating individuals and organizations, provides insights into how an individual's involvement in various relationships (e.g., work and family) impacts attitudes, motivation, and perceived performance in those roles. The survey method provides knowledge of the widespread and normative nature of those relationships, as well as differences among men and women with respect to enrichment and depletion of the two life spheres.

While postpositivist research has provided many insights into issues regarding workplace relationships and society, there is much we do not know about workplace relationships and society. As detailed below, we can greatly expand our knowledge by conceptualizing, and studying, workplace relationships from other theoretical perspectives.

SOCIAL CONSTRUCTION PERSPECTIVE

The assumptions and conceptualizations of social construction theory suggest a variety of interesting and innovative research directions for scholars examining workplace relationships and society. As noted in the discussion of existing research, new technologies and globalization have transformed the worldwide organizational landscape and, along with that, have transformed workplace relationships of all kinds, including supervisor–subordinate, peer coworker, and friendship relationships. Social construction research focuses on the communicative processes by which individuals develop, maintain, and transform such relationships (see Chapters 2–5 of this volume). Research to date consistently identifies physical proximity, similarity, and increasingly broad and intimate communication as central relational process mechanisms. Such mechanisms are unlikely to function similarly in virtual and/or global/multicultural workplace relationships. The defining characteristic of a virtual relationship, for example, is the *lack* of physical proximity. Research examining virtual workplace relationships must rely on different developmental models for such relationships. Social construction approaches would be fruitful in guiding the development of such models. Having individuals recount their relationship histories via methods such as the retrospective interviewing technique (see Chapter 5 of this volume) could reveal the factors and virtual communication practices that enable distant coworkers to develop supervisor–subordinate relationships of varying quality, peer relationships of varying types (e.g., information, collegial, and special peers), and friendships with one another. Moreover, because virtual coworkers rely on CMC, social construction scholars have access to rich and insightful interaction data. With such data, scholars could conduct longitudinal examination of virtual coworker interaction to identify the ways in which such communication changes and flows as the relationships grow closer and grow farther apart. Such studies might reveal that physical proximity is replaced by other factors, such as shared projects or online socializing, for virtual coworkers. They would also likely reveal factors unique to virtual workplace relationship development.

Social construction studies of global and multicultural workplace relationships could use similar methods to examine how coworkers develop relationships with one another when they are dissimilar, at least with respect to culture and nationality. Such research would provide important insights into how coworkers from different cultures develop and negotiate relationships and, perhaps, construct a "third culture" unique to the negotiation of their two national cultures.

Social construction theory also suggests a variety of fruitful research directions for the "life-world" issues addressed in the discussion of existing research. Under the "new social contract," for example, employees can expect to work with a particular coworker for a limited length of time, rather than a career. The new environment has increased the number of "contingent" workers in the U.S. workforce (e.g., temporary, contract, and freelance employees). Given the importance of time and commitment to relationship development (see Chapters 2–5), the development of relationships among contingent workers, and between permanent and contingent employees, is an important area for future research. Such studies might address issues such as how employees construct workplace relationships in the context of the new social contract, and how the limited time horizon impacts the communicative accomplishment of relational development. Given that employees would generally expect the relationship to terminate naturally (i.e., with turnover), social construction research would be useful in understanding how contingent coworkers accomplish relationship disengagement. Again, retrospective interview techniques would enable examination of these questions. Moreover, because many contingent workers rely heavily on CMC, analysis of coworker interaction is another method available.

Our understanding of spirituality in the workplace would also profit from research grounded in social construction theory. In particular, although we know connection, love, and trust are defining characteristics of workplace spirituality, we do not know how such characteristics are communicated. Similar to Considine's (2007) study of the communication of "caring," social construction research could reveal the communicative nature of other elements of spirituality, such as connection, love, and trust via analysis of coworker interaction or via critical incident interviews in which employees report memorable conversations and turning points in their relationships with respect to "spiritual" components. Along these lines, Frye, Kisselburgh, and Butts (2007) call for research examining how spiritual "followership" is socially constructed in the context of leader–follower relationships. Such research would examine issues such as how employees empowered by spiritual approaches to organizing, and by leaders enacting workplace spirituality principles, communicatively negotiate the paradoxes and tensions involved with employee empowerment and followership.

Another important avenue of research in the area of workplace spirituality has to do with relational deterioration. The very act of diminishing connection, trust, and caring with a coworker would appear to violate the "spirit" of spirituality. Social construction research would reveal the extent to which workplace relationship deterioration occurs in the context of a spiritual workplace and how individuals communicatively disengage from workplace relationships consistent with "spiritual" communication or in violation of same.

Finally, as pointed out earlier, much existing research in the area of work–family balance and conflict has actually been guided by social construction theory. Extant studies have revealed how individuals socially construct "parenthood" and "motherhood," how supervisors and employees socially construct norms regarding use or nonuse of organizational work–family benefits, and how coworkers socially construct "parent networks" in and out of the workplace. Social construction research could provide additional insights into these issues, however. For example, much of the existing research has focused on an individual's communication at work. We know comparatively little about how individuals socially construct work–family balance and conflict at home. As discussed earlier, Streich et al. (2008) found that couples tended to share similar perceptions of the extent to which their work interfered with the family. These shared perceptions likely are formed in the couples' communication with one another. Moreover, the Streich et al. (2008) study found more agreement regarding the extent to which the wife's work, rather than the husband's work, interfered with the family. This could indicate that the couples discuss the impact of the wife's work on the family more often, or perhaps more negatively, than they discuss the impact of the husband's work. Social construction research could lend many valuable insights into these dynamics, examining questions such as how employees communicate with family members, how they socially construct work–family connections and tensions with their family members, and how individuals communicatively "blend" their work and family roles. Again, such insights could be gained via analysis of family interaction or via critical incident interviewing in which participants recall important or memorable family conversations regarding work–family issues.

CRITICAL PERSPECTIVE

Although grounded in the notion of a socially constructed reality, critical theory goes beyond that assumption and conceptualizes reality as socially constructed systems of power and domination. By extension, critical approaches to organizations conceptualize organizations and workplace relationships as socially constructed systems of domination, power, and marginalization. As in the previous chapters, I apply critical theory to the topic of workplace relationships and society according to the four primary themes of critical research discussed in Chapter 1: reification, managerial bias, consent, and instrumental reasoning (Deetz, 2005).

Studies of reification, or the processes by which social phenomena (such as relationships) become "naturalized" or "real" via social construction, could make a number of important contributions to research in the area of workplace relationships and society. With respect to technology, scholars should examine the ways in which new technologies reinforce or liberate reified relationship structures. As noted in earlier chapters, the glass ceiling continues to marginalize women and minority employees from top level managerial positions of power. The lack of access to, and marginalization from, informal social networks (e.g., friendship networks) contributes to the glass ceiling effect (Kanter, 1977). Research in the area of e-mentoring suggests technology can provide access to mentoring to those who previously lacked such access. It also indicates, however, that the "digital divide" precludes access to mentoring for those who likely need it most. Critical scholars should examine the socially constructed nature of the digital divide by addressing issues such as how access to, and training in, new technologies are socially constructed. How does management make decisions about technology access, and how are those decisions communicated? How, and whom, do such actions preclude from using new technologies? How do these marginalized employees develop social networks, and how do the social networks developed and maintained via CMC empower those included and disempower those excluded? In other words, research grounded in critical theory would lend insights into how technology reifies and/or transforms social networks in organizations.

Reification studies would also contribute to our understanding of workplace relationships and globalization. Particularly interesting would be research that addresses the reified nature of culture and relationships. As noted by many researchers, national cultures vary on a number of dimensions such as power distance, collectivism, and approaches to relationships (Hofstede, 1984). The values and assumptions that guide these differences are deeply rooted and seen as "natural" in each culture. Researchers studying "cultural convergence" should examine the ways in which reified approaches to workplace relationships are reinforced or perhaps transformed in global and multinational organizations. Moreover, given research that indicates the increasing "Westernization" and "Americanization" of global organizations; critical scholars would be well qualified to examine the discursive construction of "Americanization" in workplace relationships.

Research in the area of workplace spirituality would also benefit from critical study. For example, many organizations are implementing "spirituality" into their formal structures and policies. Critical scholars should seek insights into the discursive processes by which employees are made to form "spiritual" relationships at work characterized by connection, caring, and love. To what extent do employees consent to such relationships, and how is such consent manufactured by management and organizational policy? Moreover, critical studies should question the extent to which workplace spirituality commodifies workplace relationships as a type of social capital contributing to managerial interests and the organizational "bottom line." Frye et al. (2007), for example, call for research examining how employees/followers participate in workplace spirituality practices to benefit dominant ideologies in the organization.

As mentioned above, much research in the area of relationships and work–family conflict is grounded in social construction theory. Critical research could build on this body of work by examining how employees, via their discussion of work–family issues, discursively marginalize those employees without children. How are the roles of childless and single employees socially constructed? Existing research indicates employees with children tend to form strong social networks at work with one another. How are childless and single employees discursively marginalized and disempowered by being prevented access to such networks? How do childless and single employees develop their own social networks in the workplace, and in what ways are other employees marginalized from those networks?

The emotional component of workplace spirituality and work–family conflict makes research in the area of technical rationality particularly relevant. Family relationships are based on high levels of intimacy and emotion. In contrast, work relationships are expected to operate according to rationality and instrumental reasoning. The tensions between the emotionality of family relationships and rational expectations of workplace roles have been ignored in research to date. Critical theorists should interrogate these tensions, examining the nature of the tensions and how employees negotiate the tensions as they attempt to balance work and family. Similarly, workplace spirituality principles are based on emotional concepts and processes such as caring, connection, and even love. How do spiritual emotions guide reasoning and decision making? How does spirituality replace or complement the technical rationality that underlies the modern corporation? Such issues would be fruitfully addressed through a critical lens.

STRUCTURATION PERSPECTIVE

Structuration theory is particularly applicable to studies of workplace relationships and society because it specifically addresses how social systems are constructed, maintained, and reproduced across time and contexts. Many important insights into relationships and society would be obtained with structuration research. In the area of technology, for example, while only a decade or so ago, many employees were unsure of and unskilled at using communication technology at work, technologies such as the Web, e-mail, and text-messaging have become increasingly commonplace. Employees develop understandings of how to use technologies and have even developed unique languages used in texting and e-mailing. Structuration theory could guide studies centering on revealing the structures that guide such mediated communication between coworkers, and provide insights into how these structures developed and have been institutionalized across contexts. Relatedly, the duality of structure is a useful concept for developing a deeper and richer understanding of the new social contract and its impact on workplace relationships Research along these lines could help uncover the structures that enable and constrain relationships among "contingent" workers, and among contingent and permanent employees.

Structuration theory also addresses the construction of *systems* or patterns of social relations across stretches of time and space. Accordingly, a structuration study would conceptualize workplace relationships as systems or patterns of social relations that stretch across time and space. Such an approach would be very useful for examining issues associated with globalization and relationships. As noted earlier, existing globalization research is largely guided by a "divergence" perspective, and little empirical research has examined cultural "convergence." Structuration theory is particularly well suited for studies of workplace relationships and cultural convergence, addressing issues such as how various relationship structures (e.g., supervisor–subordinate, peer, etc.) are transported across cultural contexts and spaces. Such research would provide knowledge and deeper understanding of how employees, via their relationships with one another, construct and reproduce "third cultures" or "transcultures" unique to their organizational environment. Structuration research centered on the institutionalization of structures across time and space would be particularly helpful in understanding the social processes via which the new social contract has replaced the old.

Using the concept of time–space distanciation, structuration research could provide interesting insights into workplace spirituality. As mentioned earlier, much of workplace spirituality is grounded in ancient and modern religions. Structuration research could unpack the religious and other historical-cultural roots of workplace spirituality and reveal the social processes via which such roots have developed into current workplace spirituality practices. Moreover, such research could delineate the role of workplace relationships in (re)producing those structural practices.

Finally, structuration theory would be useful in developing a more complex understanding of work–family balance issues. For example, the increased attention to work–family balance by both scholars and practitioners suggests a societal shift toward inclusion of family concerns in the workplace, rather than explicit separation of work and personal spheres that characterized organizations a few decades earlier. Structuration research could reveal how structures that enable and constrain work–family balance have changed over time.

Conclusion

Organizations are embedded in the larger society. Links between organizations and society are characterized by interdependence and dynamism. Thus, society impacts organizational processes, and organizational processes impact society. As this chapter demonstrates, broad societal trends such as globalization and technological advancement have important implications for links between organizations and society, employees and organizations, and of primary relevance to this book, society and workplace relationships. While research linking workplace relationships and society is relatively limited, the potential for building useful bodies of knowledge guided by multiple perspectives is very promising. Acknowledging and understanding these issues from multiple perspectives can also enable practitioners to analyze and address workplace problems and concerns in a more complex and rich manner. The following "Practicing Theory" case is designed to illustrate the practical implications of multiple perspectives.

Spirited Away

Linda has worked at Donaldson Industries, Inc., for the past 12 years. Donaldson Industries is a paper products company that manufactures and distributes a wide range of paper products throughout the western United States. For the past 5 years, Linda has been manager of the accounts receivable department at Donaldson's. In that position, she supervises a staff of 15 employees.

Linda has a solid reputation as a highly competent manager. She is also known as a somewhat authoritarian manager. She prides herself on "running a tight ship." Her employees consider her to be fair, but somewhat cold and distant. This is consistent with Linda's view that supervisors should maintain a professional distance from their employees in order to remain objective in the best interests of the organization.

Donaldson's chief operations officer, Dan Martinez, and director of human resources, Emily Stearns, organized a large 2-day retreat of department managers a month ago to introduce a new organizational training program the company is implementing throughout the organization. Linda attended that retreat, along with all other managers in the company.

The new program emphasizes "spirituality in the workplace." According to Dan and Emily, workplace spirituality is the latest corporate trend designed to improve both employee morale and performance. They were extremely excited about the program and received approval from the company president to mandate implementation of workplace spirituality training through the entire company. Managers at this retreat participated in 2-day training session, which they were then directed to conduct in their own departments. While Emily offered the assistance of human resource staff, she and Dan encouraged the managers to implement the training on their own as their "authentic" participation would highlight the managers' "authentic" commitment to the principles of workplace spirituality. Linda went through the activities with a great deal of discomfort and skepticism.

Spirituality, according to Dan and Emily, was focused on helping employees achieve balance in their lives, to feel better about themselves, and feel more connected and committed to the organization. This was accomplished through various principles, including creativity, communication, respect, vision, partnership, flexibility, self-understanding, and fun. Linda and the other managers went through a series of exercises and activities designed to emphasize these principles and teach them skills for enacting the principles. They were then directed to return to their departments and run their employees through the same activities.

Linda left the training meeting bewildered. She did not really understand the concept of workplace spirituality and how it applied to the workplace. She also felt it was crucial to maintain a boundary between work and personal lives, and to minimize chaos and maintain order. Given Dan and Emily's enthusiasm, and their mandate, however, Linda felt she had no choice but to implement the training.

She began, as instructed, by organizing a meeting in which employees are asked and encouraged to reflect on and discuss a number of issues related to personal–work balance. All staff members attended the meeting. Linda began the discussion by introducing the concept of "spirituality in the workplace." She then asked the staff a series of questions and invited them to both write their thoughts in a notebook and discuss them with the others during the meeting. Among the questions guiding the discussion were:

What gives meaning and purpose to my life?

How do I engage in quiet reflection about my life and what is meaningful to me?

What values drive or guide my life?

What qualities do I admire most in other people?

What moves me in the deepest part of my heart?

How can I achieve a more enriching and balanced life?

How do my spouse, significant other, and children see me?

How can I create more caring and connected relationships with others at work and home?

How creative and fun am I?

Not surprisingly, the discussion was awkward and uncomfortable. The employees were confused and cynical. They noted to one another (but not to Linda) after the meeting that Linda never showed any interest in their personal lives before. They couldn't just open up to her upon request. She must be convinced that doing this will improve the department's bottom line, since that's all she's ever really cared about.

After the meeting, Linda announced the next two elements of the spirituality program. First, she was scheduling a second daylong meeting in which employees would participate in a series of exercises and activities designed to help them enact the principles of workplace spirituality. Second, she was organizing weekly lunches in which all employees would participate. There would be no agenda for these lunches, just an opportunity for employees to interact and get to know each other better.

The staff attended the second training session. They also dutifully attended the lunches (though they felt they were superfluous since many of them usually ate lunch together anyway).

The employees remained skeptical and engaged in "workplace spirituality" in a pretty superficial way. They even started joking about it, approaching each other with sarcastic comments like, "I really care about you," "Have you been moved to the depths of your heart today?" and "Don't bother me now, I'm engaging in quiet reflection about the meaning of my life." These comments, of course, were always made out of earshot of Linda.

Interestingly, however, Linda responded to the workplace spirituality program quite differently. She was actually enjoying it. No one was more surprised than Linda herself at how much she was enjoying learning new things about her staff and how much she liked attending the weekly lunches. She found herself becoming more interested in the employees and actually liking and caring about them more than she ever had considered before. She began to feel a greater connection to the company and to her employees that she found rewarding. She also learned, however, that these feelings and insights were making decisions about things like task assignments, evaluations, and so on, more complex and difficult. However, she felt her decisions were actually better now than they had been before.

Discussion Questions

1. How did the organization's approach to implementing spirituality in the workplace impact the effectiveness of the program?

2. How do the principles of workplace spirituality fit into the "culture" of the accounts receivable department?

3. Consider this case from a social construction perspective. How did Dan and Emily socially construct the workplace spirituality program for the managers? How have Linda and the staff members from her department socially constructed the program? What are the consequences and implications of these dynamics? How does social construction theory explain Linda's transformation?

4. Consider this case from a critical perspective. What motivated Donaldson Industries to implement a workplace spirituality program? Whose interests are being served by the program as it's been implemented in the organization? What would a critical theorist say about the methods by which Donaldson Industries is implementing workplace spirituality? How are the employees consenting to and/or resisting the program?

5. Consider this case from a structuration perspective. What structures constrain and enable Linda's and her employees' enactments of the principles of workplace spirituality? What structures may inhibit or encourage workplace spirituality in the accounts receivable department? What does the case indicate about employees' "spiritual" behavior prior to and after the training sessions? How does structuration theory explain Linda's transformation?

Afterword

As I write the afterword to this book, I revisit the goals laid out in the preface. My first goal was to provide a summary of existing research on workplace relationships. In particular, I wanted to create a comprehensive volume inclusive of all types of workplace relationships. Thus, Chapters 2 through 5 cover the primary types of relationships internal to the organization—supervisor–subordinate, peer coworker, friendship, and romantic relationships. The last two chapters span the organization/society boundary by examining customer/client relationships and the very strong and permeable links between workplace relationships and society.

The summary of research provided in this book reveals important strengths and weaknesses. One strength stems from the fact that research on workplace relationships spans a variety of disciplines. Organizational communication, management, marketing, psychology, and sociology scholars all have taken workplace relationships as an important topic of research. The unique insights provided by the different disciplines provide a well-rounded understanding of workplace relationships. Notably missing, however, is significant interdisciplinary crossover within research programs. Published studies tend to cite research in their specific disciplines, while ignoring related research in other disciplines. While this is somewhat natural, it also creates some redundancy in research programs, as well as limits the scope of research programs. I hope providing an interdisciplinary summary of research will provide new insights and knowledge to workplace relationships scholars and open a space for increased interdisciplinary conversation and research.

Related to the above, although workplace relationships have been studied from many different disciplinary perspectives, scholars across disciplines have relied primary on a postpositivist approach. As each of the chapters makes clear, we have developed an important, substantial body of knowledge using postpositivist theories and methods. As each of the chapters also makes clear, however, we could greatly enrich this body of knowledge by studying workplace relationships from alternative theoretical perspectives. A second goal for this book was to develop an innovative research agenda for the future grounded in social construction, critical, and structuration theories. This agenda is laid out in each chapter, and my hope is that readers will pursue these research programs with enthusiasm.

Finally, I have learned that considering any situation from multiple perspectives is incredibly useful for developing a thorough understanding of that situation. Like the soccer game described in Chapter 1, multiple perspectives compel one to consider aspects of a situation she or he may have never thought to consider otherwise. Social construction theory, for example, draws our attention to processes, rather than outcomes. Critical theory directs our attention to individual concerns and experiences, rather than organizational goals and outcomes. Structuration theory enables attention to the processes that create and maintain deeply rooted systemic structures that maintain workplace relationship dynamics. Considering workplace relationship problems or situations in organizational settings from different perspectives helps practitioners develop a better understanding of those problems, and more creative and substantive solutions to those problems. Toward this end, my third goal in this book was to highlight the practical implications of a multiple-perspective approach to workplace relationships, and the "Practicing Theory" cases provided in each chapter were designed with that goal in mind.

As I stated in the preface, if the book comes close to accomplishing my three goals, I will be satisfied.

References

Abel, D., & Bray, H. (2008, January 15). Many workers make it a telecommute. *Boston Globe*. Retrieved March 14, 2008, from http://www.boston.com/business/articlse/2008/01/15/many-workers

Achim, W., & Gemunden, H. G. (2000). Bridging the gap between suppliers and customers through relationship promoters: Theoretical considerations and empirical results. *Journal of Business & Industrial Marketing, 15*, 86–105.

Aeppel, T. (1998, January 14). Losing faith: Personnel disorders sap a factory owner of his early idealism. *Wall Street Journal*, p. 14.

Ahuja, M. K., Galletta, D. F., & Carley, K. M. (2003). Individual centrality and performance in virtual R&D groups: An empirical study. *Management Science, 49*, 21–38.

Albert, M., Cagan, L., Chomsky, N., Hahnel, R., King, M., Sargent, L., et al. (1986). *Liberating theory*. Boston, MA: South End Press.

Albrecht, T. L., & Adelman, M. B. (1987). *Communicating social support*. Newbury Park, CA: Sage.

Allen, B. J. (2005). Social constructionism. In S. May & D. K. Mumby (Eds.), *Engaging organizational communication theory and research: Multiple perspectives* (pp. 35–54). Thousand Oaks, CA: Sage.

Allinson, C. W., Armstrong, S. J., & Hayes, J. (2001). The effects of cognitive style on leader–member exchange: A study of manager–subordinate dyads. *Journal of Occupational and Organizational Psychology, 2*, 201–220.

Anderson, C. J., & Fisher, C. (1991). Male–female relationships in the workplace: Perceived motivations in office romance. *Sex Roles, 25*, 163.

Ashar, H., & Lane-Maher, M. (2004). Success and spirituality in the new business paradigm. *Journal of Management Inquiry, 13*, 249–260.

Ashcraft, K. (2005). Feminist organizational communication studies: Engaging gender in public and private. In S. May & D. K. Mumby (Eds.), *Engaging organizational communication theory and research: Multiple perspectives* (pp. 141–170). Thousand Oaks, CA: Sage.

Ashcraft, K. L. (2000). Empowering "professional" relationships. *Management Communication Quarterly, 13*, 347–392.

Ashford, S. J. (1993). The feedback environment: An exploratory study of cue use. *Journal of Organizational Behavior, 14*, 201–225.

Ashforth, B. E., & Mael, F. A. (1998). The power of resistance: Sustaining valued identities. In R. M. Kramer & M. A. Neale (Eds.), *Power and influence in organizations* (pp. 89–119). Thousand Oaks, CA: Sage.

Atwater, L. A., Waldman, D., Atwater, D., & Cartier, P. (2000). An upward feedback field experiment: Supervisors' cynicism, follow-up and commitment to subordinates. *Personnel Psychology, 53,* 275–297.

Axson, D. A. J. (1992). A return to managing customer relationships. *International Journal of Bank Marketing, 10,* 30–36.

Baert, P. (1998). *Social theory in the twentieth century.* New York: New York University Press.

Baldwin, T. T., Bedell, M. D., & Johnson, J. L. (1997). The social fabric of a team-based M.B.A. program: Network effects on student satisfaction and performance. *Academy of Management Journal, 40,* 1369–1397.

Banks, S., & Riley, P. (1991). Structuration theory as an ontology for communication research. *Communication Yearbook, 16,* 167–196.

Barker, J. R. (1993). Tightening the iron cage: Concertive control in self-managing teams. *Administrative Science Quarterly, 38,* 408–437.

Barr, P. A. (1993). Perception of sexual harassment. *Sociological Inquiry, 63,* 460–470.

Bass, B. M. (1985). *Leadership and performance: Beyond expectations.* New York: Free Press.

Bauer, T. N., & Green, S. G. (1996). Development of leader–member exchange: A longitudinal test. *Academy of Management Journal, 39,* 1538–1567.

Beard, F. (1996). Marketing client role ambiguity as a source of dissatisfaction in client–ad agency relationships. *Journal of Advertising Research, 36,* 9–20.

Belliveau, M. A., O Reilly, C. A., III, & Wade, J. B. (1996). Social capital at the top: Effects of social similarity and status on CEO compensation. *Academy of Management Journal, 39,* 1568–1593.

Benedict, M. E., & Levine, E. L. (1988). Delay and distortion: Tacit influence on performance appraisal effectiveness. *Journal of Applied Psychology, 73,* 507–514.

Bennis, W., & Nanus, B. (1985). *Leaders: The strategies for taking charge.* New York: Harper & Row.

Berends, H., Boersma, K., & Weggeman, M. (2003). The structuration of organizational learning. *Human Relations, 56*(9), 1035–1056.

Berger, C., & Calabrese, R. (1975). Some explorations in initial interaction and beyond: Toward a developmental theory of interpersonal communication. *Human Communication Research, 1,* 99–112.

Berger, P. L., & Luckmann, T. (1966). *The social construction of reality: A treatise in the sociology of knowledge.* New York: Doubleday and Company.

Berry, L. L. (1983). Relationship marketing. In L. L. Berry, G. L. Shostack, & G. D. Upah (Eds.), *Emerging perspectives on service marketing* (pp. 25–28). Chicago: American Marketing Association.

Bertalanffy, L. von. (1962). General systems theory. *General systems, 7,* 1–12.

Bierema, L. L., & Hill, J. R. (2005). Virtual mentoring and HRD. *Advances in Developing Human Resources, 7,* 556–568.

Bies, R. J., & Tripp, T. M. (1998). Two faces of the powerless: Coping with tyranny in organizations. In R. M. Kramer & M. A. Neale (Eds.), *Power and influence in organizations* (pp. 203–219). Thousand Oaks, CA: Sage.

Bingham, S. G. (1994). Introduction: Framing sexual harassment—Defining a discursive focus of study. In S. G. Bingham (Ed.), *Conceptualizing sexual harassment as discursive practice* (pp. 17–30). Westport, CT: Praeger.

Blau, G. (1981). An empirical investigation of job stress, social support, service length, and job strain. *Organizational Behavior and Human Performance, 27,* 279–302.

Bluestone, B., & Harrison, B. (1982). *The deindustrialization of America: Plant closings, community abandonment, and the dismantling of basic industry.* New York: Basic Books.

Bolino, M. C., Varela, J. A., Bande, B., & Turnley, W. H. (2006). The impact of impression-management tactics on supervisor ratings of organizational citizenship behavior. *Journal of Organizational Behavior, 27,* 281–297.

Bolton, R. N. (1998). A dynamic model of the duration of the customer's relationship with a continuous service provider: The role of satisfaction. *Marketing Science, 17,* 45–56.

Botan, C. (1996). Communication work and electronic surveillance: A model for predicting panoptic effects. *Communication Monographs, 63,* 292–313.

Bottger, P. C., & Chew, I. K. H. (1986). The job characteristics model and growth satisfaction: Main effects of assimilation of work experience and context satisfaction. *Human Relations, 39,* 575–595.

Boyd, N. G., & Taylor, R. R. (1998). A developmental approach to the examination of friendship in leader–follower relationships. *Leadership Quarterly, 9,* 1–25.

Boyle Single, P., & Muller, C. B. (2001). When email and mentoring unite: The implementation of a nationwide mentoring program. In L. K. Stromei (Ed.), *Creating mentoring and coaching programs* (pp. 107–122). Alexandria, VA: American Society for Training and Development.

Bozionelos, N. (2003). Intra-organizational network resources: Relation to career success and personality. *International Journal of Organizational Analysis, 11,* 41–66.

Brandes, P., Dharwadkar, R., & Wheatley, K. (2004). Social exchanges within organizations and work outcomes: The importance of local and global relationships. *Group & Organization Management, 29,* 276–301.

Brass, D. J., & Burkhardt, M. A. (1993). Potential power and power use: An investigation of structure and behavior. *Academy of Management Journal, 36,* 441–471.

Bridge, K., & Baxter, L. A. (1992). Blended relationships: Friends as work associates. *Western Journal of Communication, 56,* 200–225.

Bright, M. I. (2005). Can Japanese mentoring enhance understanding of Western mentoring? *Employee Relations, 27,* 325–339.

Bullis, C., & Bach, B. W. (1989). Are mentoring relationships helping organizations: An exploration of developing mentor–mentee organizational identification using turning point analysis. *Communication Quarterly, 37,* 199–213.

Burack, E. H. (1999). Spirituality in the workplace. *Journal of Organizational Change Management, 12,* 280–291.

Burke, R. J., & McKeen, C. A. (1992). Social-sexual behaviours at work: Experiences of managerial. *Women in Management Review, 7,* 22–31.

Burke, R. J., Rothstein, M. G, & Bristor, J. M. (1995). Interpersonal networks of managerial and professional women. *Women in Management Review, 10,* 21–28.

Burleson, B. R., Applegate, J. L., & Delia, J. G. (1995). The socialization of person-centered communication: Parents' contributions to their children's social-cognitive and communication skills. In M. A. Fitzpatrick & A. L. Vangelisti (Eds.), *Explaining family interactions* (pp. 34–75). Newbury Park, CA: Sage.

Burns, J. M. (1978). *Leadership.* New York: Harper & Row.

Cahill, D. J., & Sias, P. M. (1997). The perceived social costs and importance of seeking emotional support in the workplace: Gender differences and similarities. *Communication Research Reports, 14,* 231–240.

Carless, S. A. (1998). Gender differences in transformational leadership: An examination of supervisor, leader, and subordinate perspectives. *Sex Roles, 39,* 887–888.

Casey, C. (2004). Bureaucracy re-enchanted? Spirit, experts and authority in organizations. *Organization, 11,* 59–79.

Chang, A., & Tseng, C. N. (2005). Building customer capital through relationship marketing activities: The case of Taiwanese multilevel marketing companies. *Journal of Intellectual Capital, 6,* 253–266.

Chaston, I., & Baker, S. (1998). Relationship influencers: Determination of affect in the provision of advisory services to SME sector firms. *Journal of European Industrial Training, 22,* 249–256.

Cheney, G. (1995). Democracy in the workplace: Theory and practice from the perspective of communication. *Journal of Applied Communication Research, 23,* 167–200.

Clair, R. P. (1993). The use of framing devices to sequester organizational narratives: Hegemony and harassment. *Communication Monographs, 60,* 113–136.

Clair, R. P. (1998). *Organizing silence: A world of possibilities.* Albany: State University of New York Press.

Clegg, S. (1994). Power relations and the constitution of the resistant subject. In J. M. Jermier, D. Knights, & W. R. Nord (Eds.), *Resistance and power in organizations* (pp. 274–325). London: Routledge.

Cogliser, C. C., & Schriesheim, C. A. (2000). Exploring work unit context and leader–member exchange: A multi-level perspective. *Journal of Organizational Behavior, 21,* 487–511.

Cohn, J. G. (2002). Emerging organizational models: Customer relationship management. *Futurics, 26,* 94–100.

Combs, G. M. (2003). The duality of race and gender for managerial African American women: Implications of informal social networks on career advancement. *Human Resource Development Review, 2,* 385–405.

Comer, D. R. (1991). Organizational newcomers' acquisition of information from peers. *Management Communication Quarterly, 5,* 64–89.

Conrad, C., & Poole, M. S. (Eds.). (1997). Communication in the age of the disposable worker [Special issue]. *Communication Research, 24.*

Considine, J. (2007). The dilemmas of spirituality in the caring professions: Care-provider spiritual orientation and the communication of care. *Communication Studies, 58,* 227–242.

Cooke, F. L. (2006). Outsourcing of public services and implications for managerial knowledge and careers. *Journal of Management Development, 25,* 269–284.

Corman, S. R. (2005). Postpositivism. In S. May & D. K. Mumby (Eds.), *Engaging organizational communication theory and research: Multiple perspectives* (pp. 15–34). Thousand Oaks, CA: Sage.

Covin, T. J., & Fisher, T. V. (1991). Consultant and client must work together. *Journal of Management Consulting, 6,* 11.

Cox, S. A. (1999). Group communication and employee turnover: How coworkers encourage peers to voluntarily exit. *Southern Communication Journal, 64,* 181–192.

Craig, R. T. (1999). Communication theory as a field. *Communication Theory, 9,* 119–161.

Craig, R. T., & Muller, H. L. (Eds.). (2007). *Theorizing communication: Readings across traditions.* Los Angeles: Sage.

Cramer, K, & Pearce J. (1990). Work and family policies become productivity tools. *Management Review, 79,* 42–44.

Crosby, L. A., & Johnson, S. L. (2000). Customer relationship management. *Marketing Management, 9,* 4–6.

Croteau, A., & Li, P. (2003). Critical success factors of CRM technological initiatives. *Canadian Journal of Administrative Sciences, 20,* 21–34.

Dash, S., Bruning, E., & Guin, K. K. (2006). The moderating effect of power distance on perceived interdependence and relationship quality in commercial banking: A cross-cultural comparison. *International Journal of Bank Marketing, 24,* 307–326.

Day, G. S. (2000). Managing marketing relationships. *Journal of the Academy of Marketing Science, 28,* 24–30.

Day, N. E., & Schoenrade, P. (1997). Staying in the closet versus coming out: Relationships between communication about sexual orientation and work attitudes. *Personnel Psychology, 50,* 147–163.

Deetz, S. (2005). Critical theory. In S. May & D. K. Mumby (Eds.), *Engaging organizational communication theory and research: Multiple perspectives* (pp. 85–112). Thousand Oaks, CA: Sage.

Deetz, S. A. (1992). *Democracy in an age of corporate colonization: Developments in communication and the politics of everyday life.* Albany: State University of New York Press.

Deetz, S. A. (2001). Conceptual foundations. In F. M. Jablin & L. L. Putnam (Eds.), *The new handbook of organizational communication: Advances in theory, research, and methods* (pp. 3–46). Thousand Oaks, CA: Sage.

DeLong, T. J., & Vijayaraghavan, V. (2003). Let's hear it for B players. *Harvard Business Review, 81,* 96–103.

Deluga, R. J. (1994). Supervisor trust building, leader–member exchange and organizational citizenship behaviour. *Journal of Occupational and Organizational Psychology, 4,* 315–327.

Deluga, R. J. (1998). Leader–member exchange quality and effectiveness ratings. *Group & Organization Management, 23,* 189–216.

Deluga, R. P., & Perry, J. T. (1994). The role of subordinate performance and ingratiation in leader–member exchanges. *Group & Organization Studies, 19,* 67–87.

Devine, I., & Markiewicz, D. (1990). Cross-sex relationships at work and the impact of gender stereotypes. *Journal of Business Ethics, 9,* 333–338.

Dillard, J. P. (1987). Close relationships at work: Perceptions of the motives and performance of relational participants. *Journal of Social and Personal Relationships, 4,* 179–193.

Dillard, J. P., & Broetzmann, S. M. (1989). Romantic relationships at work: Perceived changes in job-related behaviors as a function of participants' motive, partners' motive, and gender. *Journal of Applied Social Psychology, 19,* 93–110.

Djurkovic, N., McCormack, D., & Casimir, G. (2005). The behavioral reactions of victims to different types of workplace bullying. *International Journal of Organization Theory and Behavior, 8,* 439–461.

Dow, S. (1983). Trust differences between men and women in superior–subordinate relationships. *Group & Organization Studies, 8,* 319–337.

Duck, S., & Pittman, G. (1997). Social and personal relationships. In M. L. Knapp & G. R. Miller (Eds.), *Handbook of interpersonal communication* (2nd ed., pp. 676–695). Thousand Oaks, CA: Sage.

Duffy, M. K., Ganster, D. C., Shaw, J. D., Johnson, J. L., & Pagon, M. (2006). The social context of undermining behavior at work. *Organizational Behavior and Human Decision Processes, 101,* 105–126.

Dunegan, K. J., Uhl-Bien, M., & Duchon, D. (2002). LMX and subordinate performance: The moderating effects of task characteristics. *Journal of Business and Psychology, 17,* 275–285.

Dworkin, T. M. (1997). It's my life—Leave me alone: Off-the-job employee associational privacy rights. *American Business Law Journal, 35,* 47–103.

Eagly, A. H., & Johnson, B. T. (1990). Gender and leadership style: A meta-analysis. *Psychological Bulletin, 111,* 3–22.

Eagly, A. H., Karau, S., & Makhijani, M. (1995). Gender and the effectiveness of leaders: A meta-analysis. *Psychological Bulletin, 117,* 125–145.

Einarsen, S. (2000). Bullying and harassment at work: A review of the Scandinavian approach. *Aggression and Violent Behaviour, 5,* 379–410.

Eisenberg, E. M., & Goodall, H. J. (2004). *Organizational communication: Balancing creativity and constraint* (4th ed.). Boston: St. Martin's Press.

Elangovan, A. R, & Shapiro, D. L. (1998). Betrayal of trust in organizations. *Academy of Management Review, 23*(3), 547–566.

Elsesser, K., & Peplau, L. A. (2006). The glass partition: Obstacles to cross-sex friendships at work. *Human Relations, 59,* 1077–1100.

Ely, R. J. (1994). The effects of organizational demographics and social identity on relationships among professional women. *Administrative Science Quarterly, 39,* 203–239.

Embrick, D. G., Walther, C. S., & Wickens, C. M. (2007). Working class masculinity: Keeping gay men and lesbians out of the workplace. *Sex Roles, 56,* 757–766.

Engle, E. M., & Lord, R. G. (1997). Implicit theories, self-schemas, and leader–member exchange. *Academy of Management Journal, 40,* 988–1011.

Ensher, E. A., & Murphy, S. E. (2007). E-mentoring: Next generation research strategies and suggestions. In B. R. Ragins & K. E. Kram (Eds.), *The handbook of mentoring at work: Theory, research and practice* (pp. 299–322). Thousand Oaks, CA: Sage.

Fairhurst, G. T. (1993). The leader–member exchange patterns of women leaders in industry: A discourse analysis. *Communication Monographs, 60,* 321–351.

Fairhurst, G. T., & Chandler, T. A. (1989). Social structure in leader–member interaction. *Communication Monographs, 56,* 215.

Farley-Lucas, B. (2000). Communicating the (in)visibility of motherhood: Family talk and the ties to motherhood with/in the workplace. *Electronic Journal of Communication/La Revue Electronique de Communication, 10.* Retrieved March 21, 2008, from http://www.cios.org/www/ejcrec2.htm

Farmer, S. M., & Aguinis, H. (2005). Accounting for subordinate perceptions of supervisor power: An identity-dependence model. *Journal of Applied Psychology, 90,* 1.

Fayol, H. (1949). *General and industrial management* (C. Storrs, Trans.). London: Pitman.

Fedor, D. B. (1991). Recipient responses to performance feedback: A proposed model and its implications. In G. R. Ferris & K. M. Rowland (Eds.), *Research in personnel and human resources management* (Vol. 9, pp. 73–120). Greenwich, CT: JAI.

Fedor, D. B., Rensvold, R. B., & Adams, S. M. (1992). An investigation of factors expected to affect feedback seeking: A longitudinal field study. *Personnel Psychology, 45,* 779–805.

Fehr, B. (1996). *Friendship processes.* Thousand Oaks, CA: Sage.

Ferris, G. R., Hall, A. T., Royle, T. M., & Martocchio, J. J. (2004). Theoretical developments in the field of human resource management: Issues and challenges for the future. *Organizational Analysis, 12,* 231–258.

Ferris, G. R., & Judge, T. A. (1991). Personnel/human resources management: A political influence perspective. *Journal of Management, 17,* 447–488.

Fine, G. A. (1986). Friendships in the work place. In V. J. Derlega & B. A. Winstead (Eds.), *Friendship and social interaction* (pp. 185–206). New York: Springer-Verlag.

Finkelstein, L. M., Protolipac, D. S., & Kulas, J. T. (2000). The role of subordinate authoritarianism in cross-level extra-role relationship. *Journal of Psychology, 135,* 435–442.

Fisher, A. B. (1993). Sexual harassment: What to do. *Fortune, 23,* 84–87.

Fisher, C. D. (1979). Transmission of positive and negative feedback to subordinates: A laboratory investigation. *Journal of Applied Psychology, 64,* 533–540.

Fix, B., & Sias, P. M. (2006). Person-centered communication, leader-member exchange, and job satisfaction. *Communication Research Reports, 23,* 35–44.

Floyd, S. W., & Woolridge, B. (1999). Knowledge creation and social networks in corporate entrepreneurship: The renewal of organizational capability. *Entrepreneurship Theory and Practice, 23,* 123–143.

Fojt, M. (1995). Becoming a customer-driven organization. *Journal of Services Marketing, 9,* 7–9.

Foley, S., Linnehan, F., Greenhaus, J. H., & Weer, C. H. (2006). The impact of gender similarity, racial similarity and work culture on family supportive supervision. *Group & Organization Management, 31,* 420–441.

Foley, S., & Powell, G. N. (1999). Not all is fair in love and work: Coworkers' preferences for and responses to managerial interventions regarding workplace romances. *Journal of Organizational Behavior, 20,* 1043–1056.

Ford., W. S. Z. (2001). Customer expectations for interactions with service providers: Relationship versus encounter orientation and personalized service communication. *Journal of Applied Communication Research, 29,* 1–29.

Francis, D. H., & Sandberg, W. R. (2000). Friendship within entrepreneurial teams and its association with team and venture performance. *Entrepreneurship Theory and Practice, 25,* 5–25.

Frankwick, G. L., Porter, S. S., & Crosby, L. A. (2001). Dynamics of relationship selling: A longitudinal examination of changes in salesperson–customer relationship status. *Journal of Personal Selling & Sales Management, 21,* 135–146.

French, J. R., & Raven, B. (1959). The bases of social power. In D. Cartwright (Ed.), *Studies in social power* (pp. 150–167). Ann Arbor: University of Michigan Press.

Friedman, R. A., & Currall, S. C. (2003). Conflict escalation: Dispute exacerbating elements of e-mail communication. *Human Relations, 56,* 1325–1347.

Fritz, J. H. (1997). Men's and women's organizational peer relationships: A comparison. *Journal of Business Communication, 34,* 27–46.

Fritz, J. H. (2002). How do I dislike thee? Let me count the ways. *Management Communication Quarterly, 15,* 410–438.

Frost, P. J. (2004). Handling toxic emotions: New challenges for leaders and their organizations. *Organizational Dynamics, 33,* 111–127.

Frye, J., Kisselburgh, L. G., & Butts, D. (2007). Embracing spiritual followership. *Communication Studies, 58,* 243–260.

Gagnon, M. A., & Michael, J. H. (2004). Outcomes of perceived supervisor support for wood production employees. *Forest Products Journal, 54,* 172–177.

Gainey, T. W., & Klaas, B. S. (2003). The outsourcing of training and development: Factors impacting client satisfaction. *Journal of Management, 29,* 207–230.

Gallagher, E., & Sias, P. M. (in press). The new employee as a source of uncertainty: Veteran employee information seeking about new hires. *Western Journal of Communication.*

Garbarino, E., & Johnson, M. S. (1999). The different roles of satisfaction, trust, and commitment in customer relationships. *Journal of Marketing, 63,* 70–87.

Garbarino, E., & Johnson, M. S. (2001). Effects of consumer goals on attribute weighting, overall satisfaction, and product usage. *Psychology & Marketing, 18,* 929–949.

Ghiselli, E. E. (1963). Intelligence and managerial success. *Psychological Reports, 12,* 898.

Gibbons, D. E. (2004). Friendship and advice networks in the context of changing professional values. *Administrative Science Quarterly, 49,* 238–262.

Gibson, C. B. (1995). An investigation of gender differences in leadership across four countries. *Journal of International Business Studies, 26,* 255–280.

Giddens, A. (1979). *Central problems in social theory.* London: Macmillan.

Giddens, A. (1984). *The constitution of society.* Berkeley: University of California Press.

Girardi, P., Monaco, E., Prestigiacomo, C., & Talamo, A. (2007). Personality and psychopathological profiles in individuals exposed to mobbing. *Violence and Victims, 22,* 172–188.

Glomb, T. M., & Welsh, E. T. (2005). Can opposites attract? Personality heterogeneity in supervisor–subordinate dyads as a predictor of subordinate outcomes. *Journal of Applied Psychology, 90,* 749–757.

Gluckman, M. (1963). Gossip and scandal. *Current Anthropology, 4,* 307–316.

Goffman, E. (1959). *The presentation of self in everyday life.* Garden City, NY: Doubleday.

Graen, G., & Cashman, J. F. (1975). A role-making model of leadership in formal organizations: A developmental approach. In J. G. Hunt & L. L. Hunt (Eds.), *Leadership frontiers* (pp. 143–165). Kent, OH: Kent State University Press.

Graen, G. B., Liden, R., & Hoel, W. (1982). Role of leadership in the employee withdrawal process. *Journal of Applied Psychology, 67,* 868–872.

Graen, G. B., & Scandura, T. (1987). Toward a psychology of dyadic organizing. In B. Staw & L. L. Cummings (Eds.), *Research in organizational behavior* (Vol. 9, pp. 175–208). Greenwich, CT: JAI.

Graen, G. B., & Uhl-Bien, M. (1995). Relationship-based approach to leadership: Development of a leader–member exchange (LMX) theory of leadership over 25 years—Applying a multi-level multi-domain perspective. *Leadership Quarterly, 6,* 219–247.

Graves, L. M., & Elsass, P. M. (2005). Sex and sex dissimilarity effects in ongoing teams: Some surprising findings. *Human Relations, 58,* 191–221.

Gronroos, C. (1990). *Service management and marketing: Managing the moments of truth in service competition.* Lexington, MA: Free Press/Lexington Books.

Gronroos, C. (1994). From marketing mix to relationship marketing: Towards a paradigm shift in marketing. *Management Decision, 32,* 4–22.

Grosenick, J. K., & Hatmaker, C. M. (2000). Perceptions of staff attributes in substance abuse treatment. *Journal of Substance Abuse Treatment, 19,* 273–284.

Gull, G. A., & Doh, J. (2004). The "transmutation" of the organization: Toward a more spiritual workplace. *Journal of Management Inquiry, 13,* 128–139.

Gummesson, E. (1997). Relationship marketing as a paradigm shift: Some conclusions from the 30R approach. *Management Decision, 35,* 267–272.

Gutek, B. A., Cohen, A. G., & Konrad, A. M. (1990). Predicting social-sexual behavior at work: A contact hypothesis. *Academy of Management Journal, 33,* 560–577.

Haavio-Mannila, E., Kauppinen-Toropainen, K., & Kandolin, I. (1988). The effect of sex composition of the workplace on friendship, romance, and sex at work. In B. A. Gutek, A. H. Stromberg, & L. Larwood (Eds.), *Women and work: An annual review* (Vol. 3, pp. 123–137). Newbury Park, CA: Sage.

Hackman, M. Z., & Johnson, C. E. (2003). *Leadership: A communication perspective* (4th ed.). Prospect Heights, IL: Waveland Press.

Hafen, S. (2004). Organizational gossip: A revolving door of regulation and resistance. *Southern Communication Journal, 69,* 223–240.

Hall, E. T. (1966). *The hidden dimension.* New York: Doubleday.

Hall, E. T., & Hall, M. R. (1990). *Understanding cultural differences.* Yarmouth, ME: Intercultural Press.

Halpern, J. J. (1994). The effect of friendship on decisions: Field studies of real estate transactions. *Human Relations, 49,* 1519–1547.

Harris, K. J., & Kacmar, K. M. (2006). Too much of a good thing: The curvilinear effect of leader–member exchange on stress. *Journal of Social Psychology, 146,* 65–84.

Hearn, J., & Parkin, P. W. (1987). *"Sex" at "work": The power and paradox of organization sexuality.* Wheatsheaf, NY: St. Martin's.

Hemphill, J. K. (1955). Leadership behavior associated with the administrative reputations of college departments. *Journal of Educational Psychology, 46,* 385–401.

Herold, D. M., Liden, R. C., & Leatherwood, M. L. (1987). Using multiple attributes to assess source of performance feedback. *Academy of Management Journal, 30,* 826–835.

Hersey, P., & Blanchard, K. H. (1982). *Management of organizational behavior* (4th edition). Englewood Cliffs, NJ: Prentice-Hall.

Hess, R. L., Jr., Ganesan, S., & Klein, N. M. (2003). Service failure and recovery: The impact of relationship factors on customer satisfaction. *Academy of Marketing Science Journal, 31,* 127–146.

Higgins, C., Judge, T. A., & Ferris, G. R. (2003). Influence tactics and work outcomes: A meta-analysis. *Journal of Organization Behavior, 24,* 89–106.

Higgins, M. C., & Kram, K. K. (2001). Reconceptualizing mentoring at work: A developmental network perspective. *Academy of Management Review, 26,* 264–288.

Hill, S. E. K., Bahnuik, M. H., Dobos, J., & Rouner, D. (1989). Mentoring and other communication support in the academic setting. *Group & Organization Studies, 14,* 355–369.

Hinds, P. J., & Bailey, D. E. (2003). Out of sight, out of sync: Understanding conflict in distributed teams. *Organization Science, 14,* 615–632.

Ho, V. T., & Levesque, L. L. (2005). With a little help from my friends (and substitutes): Social referents and influence in psychological contract fulfillment. *Organization Science, 16,* 275–289.

Ho, V. T., Rousseau, D. M., & Levesque, L. L. (2006). Social networks and the psychological contract: Structural holes, cohesive ties, and beliefs regarding employer obligations. *Human Relations, 59,* 459–481.

Hochschild, A. (1983). *The managed heart.* Berkeley: University of California Press.

Hochschild, A. (1997). *The time bind: When work becomes home and home becomes work.* New York: Metropolitan Books.

Hodson, R. (1996). Dignity in the workplace under participative management: Alienation and freedom revisited. *American Sociological Review, 61,* 719–739.

Hodson, R., Roscigno, V. J., & Lopez, S. H. (2006). Chaos and the abuse of power. *Work and Occupations, 33,* 382–416.

Hofstede, G. (1984). *Culture's consequences: International differences in work-related values.* Beverly Hills, CA: Sage.

Hopkins, K. M. (1997). Supervisor intervention with troubled workers: A social identity perspective. *Human Relations, 50,* 1215–1238.

Horn, P., & Horn, J. (1982). *Sex in the office.* Reading, MA: Addison-Wesley.

Hornstein, H. A. (1996). *Brutal bosses and their prey: How to identify and overcome abuse in the workplace.* New York: Riverhead Books.

House, J. S. (1981). *Work stress and social support.* Boston, MA: Addison-Wesley.

House, R. J. (1971). Path–goal theory of leader effectiveness. *Journal of Contemporary Business, 3,* 81–97.

Hovick, S. R. A., Meyers, R. A., & Timmerman, C. E. (2003). E-mail communication in workplace romantic relationships. *Communication Studies, 54,* 468–482.

Huang, A. J. (2002). E-mail communication and supervisor–subordinate exchange quality: An empirical study. *Human Systems Management, 21,* 193–204.

Hultin, M., & Szulkin, R. (2003). Mechanisms of inequality: Unequal access to organizational power and the gender wage gap. *European Sociological Review, 19,* 143–159.

Hunt, S. D. (1997). Competing through relationships: Grounding relationship marketing in resource-advantage theory. *Journal of Marketing Management, 13,* 431–445.

Hunt, S. D., Arnett, D. B., & Madhavaram, S. (2006). The explanatory foundations of relationship marketing theory. *Journal of Business & Industrial Marketing, 21,* 72–87.

Hurley, A. E. (1996). Challenges in cross-gender mentoring relationships: Psychological intimacy, myths, rumours, innuendoes and sexual harassment. *Leadership & Organization Development Journal, 17,* 42–49.

Huws, U., Korte, W., & Robinson, S. (1990). *Telecommuting: Towards the elusive office.* Chichester, UK: Wiley.

Ibarra, H. (1993a). Network centrality, power, and innovation involvement: Determinants of technical and administrative roles. *Academy of Management Journal, 36,* 471–502.

Ibarra, H. (1993b). Personal networks of women and minorities in management: A conceptual framework. *Academy of Management Review, 18,* 56–88.

Ibarra, H. (1995). Race, opportunity, and diversity of social circles in managerial networks. *Academy of Management Journal, 38,* 673–704.

Ingram, R., Skinner, S. J., & Taylor, V. A. (2005). Consumers' evaluation of unethical marketing behaviors: The role of customer commitment. *Journal of Business Ethics, 62,* 237–252.

Jablin, F. M. (1979). Superior–subordinate communication: The state of the art. *Psychological Bulletin, 86,* 1201–1222.

Jablin, F. M. (1987). Organizational entry, assimilation, and exit. In F. M. Jablin, L. L. Putnam, K. H. Roberts, & L. W. Porter (Eds.), *Handbook of organizational communication: An interdisciplinary perspective* (pp. 679–740). Newbury Park, CA: Sage.

Jablin, F. M. (2001). Organizational entry, assimilation, and disengagement/exit. In F. M. Jablin & L. L. Putnam (Eds.), *The new handbook of organizational communication: Advances in theory, research, and methods* (pp. 732–818). Thousand Oaks, CA: Sage.

Jap, S. D. (2001). The strategic role of the salesforce in developing customer satisfaction across the relationship lifecycle. *Journal of Personal Selling & Sales Management, 21,* 95–108.

Jones, G. E. (1999). Hierarchical workplace romance: An experimental examination of team member perceptions. *Journal of Organizational Behavior, 20,* 1057–1072.

Jurkiewicz, C. L., & Giacalone, R. A. (2004). A values framework for measuring the impact of workplace spirituality on organizational performance. *Journal of Business Ethics, 49,* 129–142.

Kahn, W. A. (2001). Holding environments at work. *Journal of Applied Behavioral Science, 37,* 260–279.

Kahn, W. A., Cross, R., & Parker, A. (2003). Layers of diagnosis for planned relational change in organizations. *Journal of Applied Behavioral Science, 39,* 259–289.

Kanter, R. M. (1977). *Men and women of the corporation.* New York: Basic Books.

Katz, D., & Kahn, R. (1966). *The social psychology of organizations.* New York: John Wiley & Sons.

Katz, D., & Kahn, R. L. (1978). *The social psychology of organizations* (2nd ed.). New York: John Wiley.

Keashly, L., Trott, V., & MacLean, L. M. (1994). Abusive behavior in the workplace: A preliminary investigation. *Violence and Victims, 9,* 341–357.

Keller, T., & Dansereau, F. (1995). Leadership and empowerment: A social exchange perspective. *Human Relations, 48,* 127–145.

Kiesler, S. (1986). The hidden messages in computer networks. *Harvard Business Review, 64,* 46–53.

Kim, P. S. (1999). Globalization of human resource management: A cross-cultural perspective for the public sector. *Public Personnel Management, 28,* 227–243.

Kinicki, A. J., & Vecchio, R. P. (1994). Influences on the quality of supervisor–subordinate relations: The role of time pressure, organizational commitment, and locus of control—Summary. *Journal of Organizational Behavior, 15,* 75–83.

Kirby, E. L. (2000). Should I do as you say, or do as you do? Mixed messages about work and family. *Electronic Journal of Communication/La Revue Electronique de Communication, 10.* Retrieved March 5, 2008, from http://www.cios.org/www/ejcrec2.htm

Kirsh, B. (2000). Work, workers, and workplaces: A qualitative analysis of narratives of mental health consumers. *Journal of Rehabilitation, 66*(4), 24–30.

Koermer, C., Ford, W. S. Z., & Brant, C. (2000). Toward the development of a service provider sociality scale and its relationship to customer satisfaction and loyalty. *Communication Research Reports, 17,* 250–259.

Konovsky, M. A., & Pugh, S. D. (1994). Citizenship behavior and social exchange. *Academy of Management Journal, 37,* 656–670.

Korac-Kakabadse, N., & Kouzmin, A. (1999). Designing for cultural diversity in an IT and globalizing milieu: Some real leadership dilemmas for the new millennium. *Journal of Management Development, 18,* 291–319.

Krackhardt, D., & Stern R. N. (1998). Informal networks and organizational crises: An experimental simulation. *Social Psychology Quarterly, 51,* 123–140.

Kram, K. E., & Isabella, L. A. (1985). Mentoring alternatives: The role of peer relationships in career development. *Academy of Management Journal, 28,* 110–132.

Kruger, L. J., Bernstein, G., & Botman, H. (1995). The relationship between team friendships and burnout among residential counselors. *Journal of Social Psychology, 135,* 191.

Kunda, G. (1992). *Engineering culture: Control and commitment in a high-tech corporation*. Philadelphia, PA: Temple University Press.

Kurland, N. B., & Pelled, L. H. (2000). Passing the word: Toward a model of gossip and power in the workplace. *Academy of Management Review, 25,* 428–438.

Lamertz, K., & Aquino, K. (2004). Social power, social status and perceptual similarity of workplace victimization: A social network analysis of stratification. *Human Relations, 57,* 795–822.

LaRocco, J., House, J., & French, J. (1980). Social support, occupational stress, and health. *Journal of Health and Social Behavior, 21,* 202–218.

Larson, J. R., Jr. (1989). The dynamic interplay between employees' feedback-seeking strategies and supervisor's delivery of performance feedback. *Academy of Management Review, 14,* 408–422.

Lattman, P. (2007, October 8). Another dry cleaners lawsuit! *Wall Street Journal Law Blog.* Retrieved April 2, 2008, from http://blogs.wsj.com/law/2007/10/08/more-dry-cleaners-litigation

Lazarsfeld, P., & Merton, R. (1954). Friendship as social process: A substantive and methodological analysis. In M. Berger, T. Abel, & C. Page (Eds.), *Freedom and control in modern society* (pp. 18–66). New York: Octagon.

Ledford, G. E., Jr., & Mohrman, S. A. (1993). Self-design for high involvement: A large-scale organizational change. *Human Relations, 46,* 143–174.

Lee, J., & Jablin, F. M. (1995). Maintenance communication in superior–subordinate work relationships. *Human Communication Research, 22,* 220–257.

Lee, J. W., & Guerrero, L. K. (2001). Types of touch in cross-sex relationships between coworkers: Perceptions of relational and emotional messages, inappropriateness, and sexual harassment. *Journal of Applied Communication Research, 29,* 197–220.

Lee, R. T., & Brotheridge, C. M. (2006). When prey turns predatory: Workplace bullying as a predictor of counteraggression/bullying, coping, and well-being. *European Journal of Work and Organizational Psychology, 15,* 352–377.

Lester, S. W., & Brower, H. H. (2003). In the eyes of the beholder: The relationship between subordinates' felt trustworthiness and their work attitudes and behaviors. *Journal of Leadership & Organizational Studies, 10,* 17–33.

Leung, J., Su, S., & Morris, M. W. (2001). When is criticism not constructive? The roles of fairness perceptions and dispositional attributions in employee acceptance of critical supervisory feedback. *Human Relations, 54,* 1155–1187.

Leymann, H. (1996). The content and development of mobbing at work. *European Journal of Work and Organizational Psychology, 5,* 165–184.

Likert, R. (1961). *New patterns of management.* New York: McGraw-Hill.

Lin, C. (2006). To help or not to help: Understanding the helping intentions from a mediating perspective of social network ties. *Journal of Business Ethics, 63,* 175–182.

Lincoln, J. R., & Miller, J. (1979). Work and friendship ties in organizations: A comparative analysis of relational networks. *Administrative Science Quarterly, 24,* 181–199.

Lindgreen, A. (2001). A framework for studying relationship marketing dyads. *Qualitative Market Research, 4,* 75–87.

Litwin, A. H., & Hallstein, L. O. (2007). Shadows and silences: How women's positioning and unspoken friendship rules in organizational settings cultivate difficulties among some women at work. *Women's Studies in Communication, 30,* 111–143.

Liu, M., & Buzzanell, P. M. (2006). When workplace pregnancy highlights difference: Openings for detrimental gender and supervisory relations. In J. M. Harden Fritz

& B. L. Omdahl (Eds.), *Problematic relationships in the workplace* (pp. 47–68). New York: Peter Lang.

Lovett, S., Harrison, D., & Virick, M. (1997). Managing the boundary spanner–customer turnover connection. *Human Resource Management Review, 7*, 405–424.

Lutgen-Sandvik, P. (2006). Take this job and . . . : Quitting and other forms of resistance to workplace bullying. *Communication Monographs, 73*, 406–433.

Macaulay, S., & Cook, S. (1993). Managing and training for customer service. *Management Development Review, 6*, 19–24.

Madhavan, R., & Grover, R. (1998). From embedded knowledge to embodied knowledge: New product development as knowledge management. *Journal of Marketing, 62*, 1–13.

Mainiero, L. A. (1989). *Office romance: Love, power, and sex in the workplace.* New York: Rawson Associates.

Mano, R., & Gabriel, Y. (2006). Workplace romances in cold and hot organizational climates: The experience of Israel and Taiwan. *Human Relations, 59*, 7–35.

Mao, H. Y. (2006). The relationship between organizational level and workplace friendship. *International Journal of Human Resource Management, 17*, 1819–1833.

Markert, J. (1999). Sexual harassment and the communication conundrum. *Gender Issues, 17*, 34–52.

Markiewicz, D., Devine, I., & Kausilas, D. (2000). Friendships of women and men at work: Job satisfaction and resource implications. *Journal of Managerial Psychology, 15*, 161–184.

Marks, S. R. (1994). Intimacy in the public realm: The case of co-workers. *Social Forces, 72*, 843–858.

Martin, C. A., & Bush, A. J. (2003). The potential influence of organizational and personal variables on customer-oriented selling. *Journal of Business & Industrial Marketing, 18*, 114–130.

Maslow, A. H. (1954). *Motivation and personality.* New York: Harper & Row.

Massey, D. (1994). *Space, place, and gender.* Minneapolis: University of Minnesota Press.

Matheson, C. (1999). The sources of upward mobility within public sector organizations: A case study. *Administration & Society, 31*, 495–524.

May, S., & Mumby, D. K. (Eds.). (2005). *Engaging organizational communication and research: Multiple perspectives.* Thousand Oaks, CA: Sage.

McBride, M. (1992). Management development in the global village: Beyond culture—A microworld approach. *Journal of Management Development, 11*, 48–58.

McGivern, C. (1983). Some facets of the relationship between consultants and clients in organizations. *Journal of Management Studies, 20*, 367–387.

McGrath, C., & Krackhardt, D. (2003). Network conditions for organizational change. *Journal of Applied Behavioral Science, 39*, 324–336.

McGregor, D. (1960). *The human side of enterprise.* New York: McGraw-Hill.

McLagan, P., & Christo, N. (1995). The dawning of a new age in the workplace. *Journal for Quality and Participation, 18*, 10–15.

McPherson, M., Smith-Lovin, L., & Cook, J. M. (2001). Birds of a feather: Homophily in social networks. *Annual Review of Sociology, 27*, 415–444.

Medved, C. E. (2004). The everyday accomplishment of work and family: Exploring practical actions in daily routines. *Communication Studies, 55*, 128–45.

Mehra, A., Dixon, A. L., Brass, D. J., & Robertson, B. (2006). The social network ties of group leaders: Implications for group performance and leader reputation. *Organization Science, 17*, 64–79.

Mehra, A., Kilduff, M., & Brass, D. J. (1998). At the margins: A distinctiveness approach to the social identity and social networks of underrepresented groups. *Academy of Management Journal, 41,* 441–452.

Merriam-Webster. (2003). *Merriam-Webster's collegiate dictionary* (11th ed.). Springfield, MA: Author.

Metcalf, L. E., Frear, C. R., & Krishnan, R. (1992). Buyer–seller relationships: An application of the IMP interaction model. *European Journal of Marketing, 26,* 27–47.

Meyers, P., & Wilemon, D. (1989). Learning in new technology development teams. *Journal of Product Innovation Management, 6,* 79–88.

Michael, J. (1997). A conceptual framework for aligning managerial behaviors with cultural work values. *International Journal of Commerce & Management, 7,* 81–101.

Michael, J. H., Leschinsky, R., & Gagnon, M. A. (2006). Production employee performance at a furniture manufacturer: The importance of supportive supervisors. *Forest Products Journal, 56,* 19–24.

Michelson, G., & Mouly, S. (2000). Rumour and gossip in organisations: A conceptual study. *Management Decision, 38,* 339–346.

Miller, K. I. (2000). Common ground from the post-positivist perspective: From "straw person" argument to collaborative coexistence. In S. R. Corman & M. S. Poole (Eds.), *Perspectives on organizational communication: Finding common ground* (pp. 46–67). New York: The Guilford Press.

Miller, K. I., Ellis, B. H., Zook, E. G., & Lyles, J. S. (1990). An integrated model of communication, stress, and burnout in the workplace. *Communication Research, 17,* 300–326.

Miller, V. D., & Jablin, F. M. (1991). Information seeking during organizational entry: Influences, tactics, and a model of the process. *Academy of Management Review, 16,* 92–120.

Milliman, J., Czaplewski, A. J., & Ferguson, J. (2003). Workplace spirituality and employee work attitudes: An exploratory empirical assessment. *Journal of Organizational Change Management, 16,* 426–447.

Mills, P. K., & Moshavi, D. S. (1999). Professional concern: Managing knowledge-based service relationships. *International Journal of Service Industry Management, 10,* 48–67.

Mollica, K. A., Gray, B., & Trevino, L. K. (2003). Racial homophily and its persistence in newcomers' social networks. *Organization Science, 14,* 123–131.

Morgan, R. M., & Hunt, S. D. (1994). The commitment-trust theory of relationship marketing. *Journal of Marketing, 58,* 20–38.

Morgen, S. (1994). Personalizing personnel decisions in feminist organizational theory and practice. *Human Relations, 47,* 665.

Morrison, E. W. (1993). Longitudinal study of the effects of information seeking on newcomer socialization. *Journal of Applied Psychology, 78,* 173–183.

Mossholder, K. W., Niebuhr, R. E., & Norris, D. R. (1990). Effects of dyadic duration on the relationship between leader behavior perceptions and follower outcomes. *Journal of Organizational Behavior, 11,* 379–389.

Mueller, B. H., & Lee, J. (2002). Leader–member exchange and organizational communication satisfaction in multiple contexts. *Journal of Business Communication, 39,* 220–244.

Mumby, D. K. (1988). *Communication and power in organizations: Discourse, ideology, and domination.* Norwood, NJ: Ablex.

Mumby, D. K. (1998). Organizing men: Power, discourse, and the social construction of masculinity(s) in the workplace. *Communication Theory, 8,* 164–183.

Mumby, D. K. (2000). Common ground from the critical perspective: Overcoming binary oppositions. In S. R. Corman & M. S. Poole (Eds.), *Perspectives in organizational communication: Finding common ground* (pp. 68–86). New York: The Guilford Press.

Mumby, D. K. (2001). Power and politics. In F. M. Jablin & L. L. Putnam (Eds.), *The new handbook of organizational communication: Advances in theory, research and methods* (pp. 585–623). Thousand Oaks, CA: Sage.

Mumby, D. K., & Putnam, L. L. (1992). The politics of emotion: A feminist reading of bounded rationality. *Academy of Management Review, 17,* 465–486.

Murphy, A. G. (1998). Hidden transcripts of flight attendant resistance. *Management Communication Quarterly, 11,* 499–535.

NASA astronaut Lisa Nowak charged with attempted murder in bizarre love triangle. (2007, February 7). *FOXNews.com.* Retrieved April 9, 2008, from http://www.foxnews.com/0,3566,250415,00.html

Odden, C. M., & Sias, P. M. (1997). Peer communication relationships and psychological climate. *Communication Quarterly, 45,* 153–166.

Olk, P., & Elvira, M. (2001). Friends and strategic agents: The role of friendship and discretion in negotiating strategic alliances. *Group & Organization Management, 26,* 124–164.

Olson, M. H. (1987). Telework: Practical experience and future prospects. In R. E. Kraut (Ed.), *Technology and the transformation of white collar work.* Hillsdale, NJ: Lawrence Erlbaum.

O'Toole, T., & Donaldson, B. (2000). Managing buyer–supplier relationship archetypes. *Irish Marketing Review, 13,* 12–20.

Panda, T. K. (2002). Creating customer life time value through effective CRM in financial services industry. *Journal of Services Research, 2,* 157–171.

Park, C., & Kim, Y. (2003). A framework of dynamic CRM: Linking marketing with information strategy. *Business Process Management Journal, 9,* 652–671.

Parker, P. S. (2001). African-American women executives' leadership communication within dominant-culture organizations: (Re)conceptualizing notions of collaboration and instrumentality. *Management Communication Quarterly, 15*(1), 42–82.

Paul, R. J., & Townsend, J. B. (1998). Managing the workplace romance: Protecting employee and employer rights. *Review of Business, 19,* 25–30.

Paulin, M., Perrien, J., & Ferguson, R. (1997). Relational contract norms and the effectiveness of commercial banking relationships. *International Journal of Service Industry Management, 8,* 435–454.

Paulin, P., Perrien, J., Ferguson, R. J., Salazar, A. M. A., & Seruya, L. M. (1998). Relational norms and client retention: External effectiveness of commercial banking in Canada and Mexico. *International Journal of Bank Marketing, 16,* 24–31.

Pearce, T. (1995). *Leading out loud.* San Francisco: Jossey-Bass.

Pelled, L. H., & Xin, K. R. (2000). Relational demography and relationship quality in two cultures. *Organization Studies, 21,* 1077–1094.

Persoff, I. L., & Siegel, P. H. (1998). Tax professionals, peer relationships, & CPA firm restructuring: A grounded theory approach. *Mid-Atlantic Journal of Business, 34,* 125–140.

Pfeffer, J. (1981). *Power in organizations.* Marshfield, MA: Pitman.

Pierce, C. A, & Aguinis, H. (1997). Bridging the gap between romantic relationships and sexual harassment in organizations. *Journal of Organizational Behavior, 18,* 197–200.

Pierce, C. A., & Aguinis, H. (2003). Romantic relationships in organizations: A test of a model of formation and impact factors. *Management Research, 1,* 161–169.

Pierce, C. A., Aguinis, H., & Adams, S. K. R. (2000). Effects of a dissolved workplace romance and rater characteristics on responses to a sexual harassment accusation. *Academy of Management Journal, 43,* 869–880.

Pierce, C. A., Broberg, B. J., McClure, J. R., & Aguinis, H. (2004). Responding to sexual harassment complaints: Effects of a dissolved workplace romance on decision-making standards. *Organizational Behavior and Human Decision Processes, 95,* 66–82.

Pierce, C. A., Byrne, D., & Aguinis, H. (1996). Attraction in organizations: A model of workplace romance. *Journal of Organizational Behavior, 17,* 5–33.

Piercy, K. W. (2000). When it is more than a job: Close relationships between home health aides and older clients. *Journal of Aging and Health, 12,* 362–387.

Podolny, J. M., & Baron, J. N. (1997). Resources and relationships: Social networks and mobility in the workplace. *American Sociological Review, 62,* 673–693.

Poole, M. S., & McPhee, R. D. (2005). Structuration theory. In S. May & D. K. Mumby (Eds.), *Engaging organizational communication theory and research: Multiple perspectives* (pp. 171–196). Thousand Oaks, CA: Sage

Porter, H., Wrench, J. S., & Hoskinson, C. (2007). The influence of supervisor temperament on subordinate job satisfaction and perceptions of supervisor sociocommunicative orientation and approachability. *Communication Quarterly, 55,* 129–153.

Powell, G. (2001). Workplace romances between senior-level executives and lower-level employees: An issue of work disruption and gender. *Human Relations, 54,* 1519–1544.

Putnam, L. L., & Mumby, D. K. (1993). Organizations, emotion, and the myth of rationality. In S. Fineman (Ed.), *Emotion in organizations* (pp. 36–57). Newbury Park, CA: Sage.

Putnam, L. L., & Pacanowsky, M. E. (Eds.). (1983). *Communication and organizations: An interpretive approach.* Beverly Hills, CA: Sage.

Quinn, R. E. (1977). Coping with Cupid: The formation, impact, and management of romantic relationships in organizations. *Administrative Science Quarterly, 22,* 30–45.

Quinn, R. E., & Lees, P. L. (1984). Attraction and harassment: Dynamics of sexual politics in the workplace. *Organizational Dynamics, 13,* 35–47.

Raabe, B., & Beehr, T. A. (2003). Formal mentoring versus supervisor and coworker relationships: Differences in perceptions and impact. *Journal of Organizational Behavior, 24,* 271–293.

Rafaeli, A., & Sutton, R. I. (1987). Expression of emotion as part of the work role. *Academy of Management Review, 12,* 23–37.

Ragins, B. R., Cotton, J. L., & Miller, J. S. (2000). Marginal mentoring: The effects of type of mentor, quality of relationship, and program design on work and career attitudes. *Academy of Management Journal, 43,* 1177–1194.

Ragins, B. R., & Scandura, T. A. (1997). The way we were: Gender and the termination of mentoring relationships. *Journal of Applied Psychology, 82,* 945–953.

Ramaswami, S. N., Srinivasan, S., & Gorton, S. A. (1997). Information asymmetry between salesperson and supervisor: Postulates from agency and social exchange theories. *Journal of Personal Selling & Sales Management, 17,* 29–51.

Rawlins, W. K. (1992). *Friendship matters: Communication, dialectics, and the life course.* New York: Aldine de Gruyter.

Ray, E. B. (1993). When links become chains: Considering dysfunctions of supportive communication in the workplace. *Communication Monographs, 60,* 106–111.

Reinsch, N. L., Jr. (1997). Relationships between telecommuting workers and their managers: An exploratory study. *Journal of Business Communication, 34,* 343–369.

Robinson, R. K., Franklin, G. M., Tinney, C. H., Crow, S. M., & Hartman, S. J. (2005). Sexual harassment in the workplace: Guidelines for educating healthcare managers. *Journal of Health and Human Services Administration, 27,* 501–530.

Roehling, M. V., Cavanaugh, M. A., Moynihan, L. M., & Boswell, W. R. (2000). The nature of the new employment relationship: A content analysis of the practitioner and academic literatures. *Human Resource Management, 39,* 309–320.

Roethlisberger, F. J., & Dickson, W. J. (1939). *Management and the worker.* Cambridge, MA: Harvard University Press.

Rosenbloom, S. (2007, October 11). Boss's memo: Go ahead and date (with my blessing). *New York Times.*

Rothbard, N. P. (2001). Enriching or depleting? The dynamics of engagement in work and family roles. *Administrative Science Quarterly, 46,* 655–684.

Salancik, G. R., & Pfeffer, J. (1978). A social information processing approach to job attitudes and task design. *Administrative Science Quarterly, 23,* 224–253.

Salin, D. (2003). Ways of explaining workplace bullying: A review of enabling, motivating, and precipitating structures and processes in the work environment. *Human Relations, 56,* 1213–1232.

Sass, J. S. (2000). Characterizing organizational spirituality: An organizational communication culture approach. *Communication Studies, 51,* 195–217.

Scandura, T. A. (1998). Dysfunctional mentoring relationships and outcomes. *Journal of Management, 24,* 449–467.

Scandura, T. A, & Schriesheim, C. A. (1994). Leader–member exchange and supervisor career mentoring as complementary constructs in leadership research. *Academy of Management Journal, 37,* 1588–1603.

Schneider, S. K., & Northcraft, G. B. (1999). Three social dilemmas of workforce diversity in organizations: A social identity perspective. *Human Relations, 52,* 1445–1467.

Schultz, V. (2003). The sanitized workplace. *Yale Law Journal, 112,* 2061–2193.

Schweiger, D. M., Ivancevich, J. M., & Power, F. R. (1987). Executive actions for managing human resources before and after acquisition. *Academy of Management Executive, 1*(2), 127–138.

Seibert, S. E., Kraimer, M. L., & Liden, R. C. (2001). A social capital theory of career success. *Academy of Management Journal, 44,* 219–237.

Seigne, E., Coyne, I., Randall, P., & Parker, J. (2007). Personality traits of bullies as a contributory factor in workplace bullying: An exploratory study. *International Journal of Organization Theory and Behavior, 10,* 118–133.

Selling it. (2007, April). *Consumer Reports, 72,* p. 95.

Sergeant, S., & Frenkel, A. (1998). Managing people in China: Perceptions of expatriate managers. *Journal of World Business, 33,* 17–34.

Shah, P. P. (1998). Who are employees' social referents? Using a network perspective to determine referent others. *Academy of Management Journal, 41,* 249–268.

Shaw, R. B. (1997). *Trust in the balance.* San Francisco: Jossey-Bass.

Sheep, M. L. (2006). Nurturing the whole person: The ethics of workplace spirituality in a society of organizations. *Journal of Business Ethics, 66,* 357–375.

Sheperd, G. M., St. John, J., & Striphas, T. (Eds.). (2006). *Communication as . . . : Perspectives on theory.* Thousand Oaks, CA: Sage.

Sheppard, E. (2002). The spaces and times of globalization: Place, scale, networks, and positionality. *Economic Geography, 78,* 307–330.

Sherif, M. (1958). Superordinate goals in the reduction of intergroup conflicts. *American Journal of Sociology, 63,* 349–356.

Sheth, J. N., & Parvatiyar, A. (1995). The evolution of relationship marketing. *International Business Review, 4,* 397–418.

Sias, P. M. (1996). Constructing perceptions of differential treatment: An analysis of coworker discourse. *Communication Monographs, 63,* 171–187.

Sias, P. M. (2005). Workplace relationship quality and employee information experiences. *Communication Studies, 56,* 375–395.

Sias, P. M. (2006). Workplace friendship deterioration. In J. M. H. Fritz & B. L. Omdahl (Eds.), *Problematic relationships in the workplace* (pp. 69–87). New York: Peter Lang.

Sias, P. M. (in press). Social ostracism, cliques, and outcasts. In P. Lutgen-Sandvik & B. Davenport-Sypher (Eds.), *The destructive side of organizational communication: Causes, consequences, and corrections.* Mahwah, NJ: Lawrence Erlbaum.

Sias, P. M., & Bartoo, H. (2007). Friendship, social support and health. In L. L'Abate, D. D. Embrey, & M. S. Baggett (Eds.), *Low cost approaches to promote physical and mental health: Theory, research and practice* (pp. 455–472). New York: Springer-Verlag.

Sias, P. M., & Cahill, D. J. (1998). From coworkers to friends: The development of peer friendships in the workplace. *Western Journal of Communication, 62,* 273–299.

Sias, P. M., Heath, R. G., Perry, T., Silva, D., & Fix, B. (2004). Narratives of workplace friendship deterioration. *Journal of Social and Personal Relationships, 21,* 321–340.

Sias, P. M., & Jablin, F. M. (1995). Differential superior–subordinate relations, perceptions of fairness, and coworker communication. *Human Communication Research, 22,* 5–38.

Sias, P. M., Krone, K. J., & Jablin, F. M. (2002). An ecological systems perspective on workplace relationships. In M. L. Knapp & J. Daly (Eds.), *Handbook of interpersonal communication* (3rd ed., pp. 615–642). Newbury Park, CA: Sage.

Sias, P. M., & Odden, C. M. (1996). The next best thing to being there: A test of the joint conversation reconstruction method. *Communication Research Reports, 13,* 35–42.

Sias, P. M., & Perry, T. (2004). Disengaging from workplace relationships: A research note. *Human Communication Research, 30,* 589–602.

Sias, P. M., Smith, G., & Avdeyeva, T. (2003). Sex and sex-composition differences and similarities in peer workplace friendship development. *Communication Studies, 54,* 322–340.

Sias, P. M., & Wyers, T. D. (2001). Employee uncertainty and information-seeking in newly-formed expansion organizations. *Management Communication Quarterly, 14,* 549–573.

Sluss, D. M., & Ashforth, B. E. (2007). Relational identity and identification: Defining ourselves through work relationships. *Academy of Management Review, 32,* 9–32.

Smith, H. I. (1988). Singles in the workplace: Myths and advantages. *Personnel Administrator, 33,* 76–81.

Smith, M. A., & Canger, J. M. (2004). Effects of supervisor "Big Five" personality on subordinate attitudes. *Journal of Business and Psychology, 18,* 465–481.

Smith, R. C., & Turner, P. K. (1995). A social constructionist reconfiguration of metaphor analysis: An application of "SCMA" to organizational socialization theorizing. *Communication Monographs, 62,* 151–181.

Smither, J. W., London, M., Vasilopoulos, N. L., Reilly, R. R., Millsap, R. E., & Salvemini, N. (1995). An examination of the effects of an upward feedback program over time. *Personnel Psychology, 48,* 1–34.

So, S. L. M., & Speece, M. W. (2000). Perceptions of relationship marketing among account managers of commercial banks in a Chinese environment. *International Journal of Bank Marketing, 18,* 315.

Society for Human Resource Management (SHRM). (1988). *Workplace romance survey.* Alexandria, VA: SHRM Public Affairs Department.

Solomon, D. H., & Williams, M. L. M. (1997). Perceptions of social-sexual behavior at work as sexually harassing. *Management Communication Quarterly, 11,* 147–185.

Sparks, B. A., Bradley, G. L., & Callan, V. J. (1997). The impact of staff empowerment and communication style on customer evaluations: The special case of service failure. *Psychology & Marketing, 14,* 475–494.

Sparrowe, R. T., & Liden, R. C. (1997). Process and structure in leader–member exchange. *Academy of Management Review, 22*(2), 522–552.

Spillan, J. E., Mino, M., & Rowles, M. S. (2002). Sharing organizational messages through effective lateral communication. *Communication Quarterly, 50,* 96–104.

Stage, C. W. (1999). Negotiating organizational communication cultures in American subsidiaries doing business in Thailand. *Management Communication Quarterly, 13,* 245–28.

Steelman, L. A., & Rutkowski, K. A. (2004). Moderators of employee reactions to negative feedback. *Journal of Managerial Psychology, 19,* 6–18.

Stefanou, C. J., Sarmaniotis, C., & Stafyla, A. (2003). CRM and customer-centric knowledge management: An empirical research. *Business Process Management Journal, 9,* 617–634.

Stewart, T. A. (1998). Gray flannel suit? *Fortune, 137*(5), 76–82.

Stohl, C. (2001). Globalizing organizational communication. In F. M. Jablin & L. L. Putnam (Eds.), *The new handbook of organizational communication: Advances in theory, research, and methods* (pp. 323–378). Thousand Oaks, CA: Sage.

Stohl, C. (2005). Globalization theory. In S. May & D. K. Mumby, (Eds.), *Engaging organizational communication theory and research: Multiple perspectives* (pp. 223–262). Thousand Oaks, CA: Sage.

Streich, M., Casper, W. J., & Salvaggio, A. N. (2008). Examining couple agreement about work–family conflict. *Journal of Managerial Psychology, 23,* 252–272.

Tajfel, H. (1974). Social identity and intergroup behavior. *Social Science Information, 13,* 65–93.

Tancred-Sheriff, P. (1989). Gender, sexuality and the labour process. In J. Hearn, D. L. Sheppard, P. Tancred-Sheriff, & G. Burrell (Eds.), *The sexuality of organization* (pp. 45–55). London: Sage.

Tangri, S. S., Burt, M. R., & Johnson, L. B. (1982). Sexual harassment at work: Three explanatory models. *Journal of Social Issues, 38,* 33–54.

Teboul, J. C. B. (1994). Facing and coping with uncertainty during organizational encounters. *Management Communication Quarterly, 8,* 190–224.

Teboul, J. C. B., & Cole, T. (2005). Relationship development and workplace integration: An evolutionary perspective. *Communication Theory, 15,* 389–413.

Tepper, B. J. (2000). Consequences of abusive supervision. *Academy of Management Journal, 43,* 178–190.

Tierney, P., Farmer, S. M., & Graen, G. B. (1999). An examination of leadership and employee creativity: The relevance of traits and relationships. *Personnel Psychology, 52,* 591–620.

Timmerman, C. E., & Scott, C. R. (2006). Virtually working: Communicative and structural predictors of media use and key outcomes in virtual work teams. *Communication Monographs, 73,* 108–136.

Tompkins, P. K., & Cheney, G. (1985). Communication and unobtrusive control in contemporary organizations. In R. D. McPhee & P. K. Tompkins (Eds.), *Organizational communication: Traditional themes and new directions* (pp. 179–210). Newbury Park, CA: Sage.

Tsui, A. S., & Wu, J. B. (2005). The new employment relationship versus the mutual investment approach: Implications for human resource management. *Human Resource Management, 44,* 115–121.

Turban, D. B., Jones, A. P., & Rozelle, R. M. (1990). Influences of supervisor liking of a subordinate and the reward context on the treatment and evaluation of that subordinate. *Motivation and Emotion, 14,* 215–233.

Turner, J. C., & Oakes, P. J. (1986). The significance of the social identity concept for social psychology with reference to individualism, interactionism, and social influence. *British Journal of Social Psychology, 25,* 237–252.

Umphress, E. E., Labianca, G., Brass, D. J., Kass, E., & Scholten, L. (2003). The role of instrumental and expressive social ties in employees' perceptions of organizational justice. *Organization Science, 14,* 738–753.

Varma, A., Srinivas, E. S., & Stroh, L. K. (2005). A comparative study of the impact of leader–member exchange in U.S. and Indian samples. *Cross Cultural Management, 12,* 84–95.

Varma, A., & Stroh, L. K. (2001). The impact of same-sex LMX dyads on performance evaluations. *Human Resource Management, 40*(4), 309–320.

Vaughn, M., & Stamp, G. H. (2003). The empowerment dilemma: The dialectic of emancipation and control in staff/client interaction at shelters for battered women. *Communication Studies, 54,* 154–168.

Veale, C., & Gold, J. (1998). Smashing into the glass ceiling for women managers. *Journal of Management Development, 17,* 17–24.

Vecchio, R. P., & Gobdel, B. C. (1984). The vertical dyad linkage model of leadership: Problems and prospects. *Organizational Behavior and Human Performance, 34,* 5–20.

Vecchio, R. P., Griffeth, R. W., & Hom, P. W. (1986). The predictive utility of the vertical dyad linkage approach. *Journal of Social Psychology, 126,* 617–625.

The verdict: Little work got done as the jury spoke. (1995, October 4). *Wall Street Journal,* p. B1.

Verhoef, P. C. (2003). Understanding the effect of customer relationship management efforts on customer retention and customer share development. *Journal of Marketing, 67,* 30–15.

Waldron, V. R. (1991). Achieving communication goals in superior–subordinate relationships: The multifunctionality of upward maintenance tactics. *Communication Monographs, 58,* 289–306.

Waldron, V. R. (2000). Relational experiences and emotion at work. In S. Fineman (Ed.), *Emotion in organizations* (2nd ed., pp. 64–82). London: Sage.

Walker, A., & Smither, J. (1999). A five-year study of upward feedback: What managers do with their results matters. *Personnel Psychology, 52,* 393–423.

Warren, J. A., & Johnson, P. J. (1995). The impact of workplace support on work–family role strain. *Family Relations, 44*(2), 163–169.

Wayne, S. J., & Ferris, G. R. (1990). Influence tactics, affect, and exchange quality in supervisor–subordinate interactions: A laboratory experiment and field study. *Journal of Applied Psychology, 75,* 487–500.

Wayne, S. J., & Green, S. A. (1993). The effects of leader–member exchange on employee citizenship and impression management behavior. *Human Relations, 46,* 1431–1441.

Weber, M. (1946). *From Max Weber: Essays in sociology* (H. H. Gerth & C. W. Mills, Trans. & Eds.). New York: Free Press.

Weber, M. (1947). *The theory of social and economic organization.* New York: Free Press.

Weiss, H. M. (1977). Subordinate imitation of supervisor behavior: The role of modeling in organizational socialization. *Organizational Behavior and Human Performance, 19,* 97–113.

Werbel, J. D., & Hames, D. S. (1996). Anti-nepotism reconsidered. *Group & Organization Management, 21,* 365.

Wheatley, M. (2001). *Leadership and the new science: Discovering order in a chaotic world.* San Francisco: Jossey Bass.

Wheatley, M. J. (1994). *Leadership and the new science: Learning about organization from an orderly universe.* San Francisco: Berrett-Koehler.

Williams, M. R. (1998). The influence of salespersons' customer orientation on buyer–seller relationship development. *Journal of Business & Industrial Marketing, 13,* 271–287.

Williams, S. D. (2004). Personality, attitude, and leader influences on divergent thinking and creativity in organizations. *European Journal of Innovation Management, 7,* 187–204.

Wilson, R. J., Filosa, C., & Fennel, A. (2003). Romantic relationships at work: Does privacy trump the dating police? *Defense Counsel Journal, 70,* 78–88.

Winch, R. F., Ktsanes, T., & Ktsanes V. (1954). The theory of complementary needs in mate-selection: An analytical and descriptive study. *American Sociological Review, 19,* 241–249.

Yelvington, K. A (1996). Flirting in the factory. *Journal of the Royal Anthropological Institute, 2,* 313–324.

Yrle, A. C., Hartman, S. J., & Galle, W. P. (2003). Examining communication style and leader–member exchange: Considerations and concerns for managers. *International Journal of Management, 20,* 92–101.

Zapf, D. (1999). Organizational, work group related and personal causes of mobbing/bullying at work. *International Journal of Manpower, 20,* 70–85.

Index

About the Author

Patricia M. Sias is professor of communication in the Edward R. Murrow College of Communication at Washington State University. Her research centers on workplace relationships. She has published articles in and served on the editorial boards of a variety of academic journals, including *Communication Monographs, Human Communication Research, Management Communication Quarterly, Western Journal of Communication, Communication Quarterly,* and *Journal of Applied Communication Research.* She served as secretary and chair of the Organizational Communication Division of the National Communication Association. She has won numerous awards for her research, including the W. Charles Redding Outstanding Dissertation in Organizational Communication Award from the International Communication Association, several Top Paper awards from the National Communication Association, and the Distinguished Faculty Achievement Award from the Washington State University College of Liberal Arts.

CPSIA information can be obtained
at www.ICGtesting.com
Printed in the USA
FFHW022331070219
50454012-55682FF

9 781412 957977